MVRAN

VENICE

FROM

THE

GROUND

UP

VENICE
FROM
THE
GROUND
UP

JAMES H. S. McGREGOR

THE BELKNAP PRESS OF

HARVARD UNIVERSITY PRESS

Cambridge, Massachusetts

London, England   2006

Library of Congress Cataloging-in-Publication Data

McGregor, James H. (James Harvey), 1946–

Venice from the ground up / James H. S. McGregor

    p. cm.

Includes bibliographical references and index.

ISBN-13: 978-0-674-02333-8 (alk. paper)

ISBN-10: 0-674-02333-1 (alk. paper)

1. Venice (Italy)—Description and travel.

2. Venice (Italy)—History.

3. City planning—Italy—Venice—History.

I. Title.

DG674.2.M44   2006

945'.31—dc22   2005035501

CONTENTS

INTRODUCTION

In the sixth century, waves of barbarians devastated Italy and eventually gained control of the Western Roman Empire. Just beyond their grasp on the edge of the habitable world—some would say beyond the edge—Venice came to life in the shelter of its Lagoon. Divided from the sea and its Byzantine masters by a long barrier island, and separated from the mainland of Italy by a tract of shallow water, Venice found security in its tidal estuary. Safely out of reach of potential overlords on both sides, the Venetians crafted a way of life perfectly suited to their strange environment. Fishers, salt gatherers, and traders, they lived in widely dispersed communities throughout the Lagoon.

Two events in the ninth century galvanized Venetians along the main Lagoon channel and pushed them to form a cohesive city. The regional governor appointed by the Byzantine emperor relocated to the site of the city in 810 AD. And then in 829 the body of St. Mark was stolen from its sepulcher in Alexandria and brought to Venice. From this time onward, political and theological power were consolidated in one location. Together, these forces focused and drove the development of the city.

Founded on a spongy salt marsh surrounded by open water, Venice was well placed to capitalize on the trade that passed inland from the city toward the Italian mainland in shallow-draft boats and outward into the Adriatic in heavier and larger craft. Venice stood at a point of exchange between two different markets and the specific vessels they depended on. Along the deep channel that ran past San Marco on its way from the mainland to the sea, Venetian merchants constructed distinctive houses that combined dock, warehouse, and living space in a single structure. Land was precious, and families built cheek-by-jowl all along this serpentine commercial waterway. At a pinch point in the Grand Canal they created a marketplace, which they soon expanded into the legendary Rialto. Goods from North Africa, Russia, and India were exchanged there for the products and wealth of Europe.

Land reclamation added new territory to the city, clump by clump. In the thirteenth century, expansion at what was then the city's perimeter was spurred by new religious brotherhoods, the Franciscans and Dominicans. Granted territory on opposite margins of the city, these mendicant orders reclaimed huge tracts of marshland to support their massive churches, and in the process they opened new areas of the city to domestic and commercial development.

When the Turks took Byzantium in 1453, they destroyed the last barrier between an invading Islamic force and the Mediterranean colonies and trade routes of the Venetians. Soon after, the Portuguese circumnavigated Africa and challenged the city's centuries-old trade monopoly with the East. In that same era, as Venice began to take over territories on the Italian mainland, its colonies dragged the city headlong into the unceasing and fruitless warfare that convulsed Renaissance Italy. A new style of building gained predominance in the city, one that cancelled every link with the architecture of the basilica of St. Mark and the palace of the

Doge—the two iconic buildings that had anchored the city's identity since the ninth century.

Sometime in the sixteenth century, the city of Venice stopped growing. For the next two hundred years it remained more or less in balance, poised for collapse but in many ways still vital and appealing. Throughout this long twilight, the city was a wonderful and secure place to live, and a fabled destination for the increasing number of outsiders who came to enjoy its festivals and marvel at its palaces.

Then, in 1797, a French army under the leadership of the young Napoleon Bonaparte occupied Venice. The city's precious autonomy, which ingenuity, diplomacy, and military power had preserved for nearly a thousand years, came to a sudden and absolute end. The French bled the city of its resources before passing it on to the Austrians, who governed, with occasional lapses, until unification with Italy in 1866.

The occupying powers were mainlanders, whose ideas about the proper structure of cities had no place for island clumps linked by waterways. They worked to transform the amphibious city into something more orthodox—filling in canals, building bridges, and creating pathways that have now linked almost the entire city into one homogeneous pedestrian network. The train line from the mainland, and the much later motorway built alongside it, were the most decisive steps in this transformation. Their placement on the opposite side of the city from San Marco turned Venice on its head. Food for residents and tourists began to arrive by train and then by truck, rather than by boat. Electricity, gas, and water were piped in from the mainland. Trash was hauled away in the opposite direction.

Industrialization reached Venice in the nineteenth century and fled even more quickly in the twentieth. A significant percentage of the Venetian population followed. In the same era, mainland industries poisoned the Lagoon and made it inhospitable to marine life. Deprived of its population, divorced from its environment, the Venice we know today threatens to become a historical theme park run by government entities for the benefit of a world community of the interested and curious. But the city itself seems to shrug off its fate and carry on with beauty, energy, and purpose, despite confident predictions of its imminent demise.

This book explores the culture of Venice that is imprinted most distinctly on its urban form—the webwork of canals and the counterpoint of bridges and walkways, soaring churches and crumbling palaces, the grand ceremonial Piazza San Marco and peaceful neighborhood campi. Chapters follow both a chronological and geographical arrangement, so that readers can trace the city's evolution through the narrative and, with just a little backtracking here and there, explore it area by area on foot and by boat if they are fortunate enough to make a visit. Venice is relatively free of archaeological reconstructions that showcase a particular era, or museums where the past is repackaged for modern consumption. What a visitor sees is for the most part where it has always been. As a result, few monuments are pure examples of their type or perfect representatives of the period that gave them birth. The buildings of Venice have always been immersed in its daily life, and they have grown and changed with the city.

But urban form is not the only representation of urban culture explored in *Venice from the Ground Up*. As it follows the long arc of the city's maturation and transformation, this book looks at artifacts on every scale, from the grand layout of the city as captured in Jacopo de Barbari's imaginative aerial view of 1500 to a tiny ducat of African gold stamped with the portrait of a thirteenth-century doge. The city's ambition and its sense of itself were expressed not just in the architecture of San Marco and the Palazzo Ducale but in the majestic mosaic program of the basilica's interior and the sometimes outrageous official art commissioned to decorate the Doge's Palace. Great paintings in the mendicant churches and in the city's unique confraternities chronicled the aims and self-understanding of those organizations, while private devotional paintings in homes along the Grand Canal encouraged piety and reaffirmed the restricted roles women were allowed to play in this most patriarchal society.

Venice's far-reaching influence was grounded in entrepreneurial drive and an extraordinary ability to organize. So much restless energy found expression not just in great buildings and great art but also in public institutions dedicated to the welfare of citizens and the stability of the city's way of life. In the late Middle Ages and Renaissance, granaries along the Grand Canal stored food for public use during famine. Confraternities looked after not just the spiritual health of their members but their physical needs as well. Hospitals sheltered lepers, quarantined plague victims, and nursed foundlings. Medieval housing projects for employees of the Arsenal remain, today, among the most beautiful and livable buildings in Venice.

This imminently orderly city was also home to Carnevale. The public masquerades and licensed revelry of the pre-Lenten period gave birth to an industry of the imagination. Virtually every parish in Venice boasted a theater, whose season expanded beyond Carnival as the years passed. In campi throughout the city, groups of players staged the conventional dramas of the commedia dell'arte. Gambling was a riskier outgrowth of the carnival spirit, and widespread prostitution, with its threat of death from syphilis, was its most sordid by-product. And despite the license Carnevale encouraged, Venice was a cruel enforcer of orthodoxy, and it could be heavy-handed in its pursuit of treachery and sedition.

Not every Venetian artifact speaks of the city's self-conception. Like any ambitious metropolis, Venice took up the challenge of justifying the foundations of its broader culture. The basilica of San Marco is the most Venetian of shrines, but its mosaics record the history of the apostolic movement throughout the world. Again and again the city took upon itself the costly and difficult task of expounding the fundamental doctrines of medieval Catholicism. A painting like Titian's *Assumption of the Virgin* in the monumental church known as the Frari, or Tintoretto's *Adoration of the Shepherds* in the Scuola Grande di San Rocco, was a meditation not on Venetian themes but on theological subjects at the heart of Western Christianity. Seizing on these central truths of Christian dogma and recreating them in unique and memorable ways was the work of a city that saw itself as the embodiment of a cultural ideal. Early in its history, Venice rivaled Constantinople for commercial dominance, and in the mid-sixteenth century it took on Rome in a series of military engagements. But in its aim to sponsor and house the greatest expressions of Christian dogma, the city vied with these capitals of Christianity throughout the Middle Ages and Renaissance.

Thriving metropolis, charitable haven, city of the imagination—historical Venice maintained its multiple identities with uncommon devotion and flair. Preserved in its remarkable urban fabric, its wealth of magnificent churches, and its handful of superb museums, the city's history of enlightened living can still instruct and inspire.

Chapter One

THE LAGOON

Venice is a gingerly handclasp of two mitten-shaped land masses commonly described as fish. The larger fish swims in from the ocean, the smaller one comes offshore. When they meet, the ocean fish opens her mouth to seize the upper jaw of the freshwater fish, who clamps down on the lower jaw of her antagonist. (1) The narrow belt of water that separates the two fish, outlining their heads and open mouths, is the Grand Canal. This configuration, so familiar to us today, was not filled in completely until the late nineteenth century, and the notion that Venice is more land than water would have seemed absurd not only to the city's founders but to most generations of Venetians who lived after them.

Though the name of Venice now belongs exclusively to this island cluster, with its distinctive history and deeply threatened way of life, in the ancient world the city's ancestral name referred to a place that was nearby but very different. The Veneti were one of the many indigenous peoples whom the Romans conquered and assimilated as they tightened their grip on the Italian peninsula. These men and women, described by both the Greek geographer Strabo and the Roman historian Livy, lived along the rivers or in river towns like Padua or Ravenna and supported themselves by fishing and trade. They were not children of the Lagoon. In fact, some historians believe that

1

the geographical feature which distinguishes the Venice we know today did
not exist in the classical period. Documentary evidence convinces them that
in the age of Roman domination the
Lagoon was dry land, gridded by sur-
veyors and parceled into rectangular
fields and pastures.

Geology contradicts their view. The earth record shows that the
Lagoon has been where it is, and what it is, for some five thousand years.
It is a sheltered estuary irrigated by fresh water from inland streams and
washed with tides that are tamed by their passage through three inlets in
the Lido, its barrier island. With its mix of freshwater and saltwater habi-
tats, the Lagoon once teemed with marine life. Fish, aquatic birds, shellfish, and salt were the region's first and most sustained harvests.

The rivers that bring fresh water also bring sand and silt, which fall
out of suspension and pile up in the slack water at the edge of each current. The Lagoon acts as a delta to brake and bend the seaward thrust of
the rivers, causing them to plow sinuous channels in the Lagoon bed.
Along the edges of these currents, silt builds mud banks and flats and
ultimately islands. Each channel crafts its own banks and then breaks
through them in tiny rivulets. These fragmented mudflats and the clear
channels that spawn them became the raw material of Lagoon settlement. The soft curves of Venice's outline and the reflected S of the Grand
Canal are the accommodations centuries of builders made to the insistent if gentle thrust of these estuarine currents. In Italian, *canalc* means
both channel and canal; long before settlers arrived, the currents of the
Lagoon had Venice in mind.

Lagoons are the counterweights of mountains. Rivers get their suspended soils from the breakdown of mountain rock. They grind the rock
finer the farther they carry it, and by the time rivers reach the sea, what
began as boulders has become microscopic silt. Even when ground to
powder, however, rock remains heavy, and the steady deposit of mud
banks weighs down the Lagoon floor, countering the buildup of silt above.
The Lagoon floor subsides in proportion to the islands' growth, striking a
long-term geological balance.

For millennia, the surfaces of the islands on which Venice was built
have stood above the waterline, permanently isolated from the currents
that renew soils. Pressed down by the weight of the city's architecture
and having no natural mechanism for rebuilding, the islands of modern
Venice continue to sink, their sinking accelerated by the appetite for
groundwater among mainland industries. The Lagoon's once lethargic
geological clock is now running on accelerated human time (a truth of
our era in general), and the frequent winter flooding in Venice—the
acqua alta—shows how subsidence has outpaced deposition. Shaped by
geological processes, Venice may, unless some drastic engineering solution is found, be reabsorbed into its creator.

The territory between the Lagoon and the Alps is divided into administrative units whose names reflect Venetian control of the area imposed
five centuries ago, in the Italian Renaissance. The Veneto and Venezia
Giulia fill the fan-shaped northeast margin of Italy that touches Austria
and Slovenia. Long before the people of the Lagoon achieved political
and military dominance over this area, their way of life was tied to it.
During the Bronze Age (roughly 1500 BC), Celtic settlers opened the
Brenner Pass through the Alps, clearing the last obstacle to a trans-Euro-
pean trade route that linked the Baltic, the Black Sea, and the Mediter-

ranean. Northwest of the Alps, the great river valleys of Europe were the conduits of trade. In the short space separating the Alps from the Adriatic, the River Adige and its tributaries carried trade in both directions.

The indigenous people of the Lagoon traded salt and salt-dried fish, which was lighter and more portable, to the north. Amber gathered from the shores of the Baltic, along with tin and lead from Britain and flints from Denmark, passed southward through the Elbe, Weser, and Moldau river valleys, then through the northern Adriatic and on to Greece. The Lagoon played its part in this trade, but it was not the hub—it would take up that role many, many centuries after the Celts had been conquered and assimilated by the Romans.

The Romans preferred roads to rivers. They built highways through the Alpine passes to link their administrative center with outlying provinces, but the great trunk routes over which most of the commerce of the Roman Empire passed lay south of the Alps. In northeast Italy, the most important of these roads were the Via Postumia, which linked Milan to the Adriatic, the Via Popilia, which ran from Ravenna northward along the coast, and the Via Annia, which continued these Italian routes into the Balkans and on to Constantinople. All Roman roads led to Rome, of course, but as the structure of the empire changed, links to second-tier cities became increasingly important. Constantinople, the capital of the Eastern Empire, spread its influence over the Italian peninsula as the Western Empire faltered in the fourth century. Milan became the administrative center of Italy, while Ravenna became the headquarters of the Adriatic fleet. In the fifth century, that coastal town would become the center of Gothic government on the mainland.

Successive waves of Teutonic invaders—Alemmani, Ostrogoths, Visi-

goths, and Lombards—began in the third century first to harass, then to
devastate, and finally to dominate Rome and its empire. Most of these
invaders entered Italy through the Brenner Pass. They followed the Adige
river valley south to Verona, and from there their passage along the great
Roman roads was smooth and unstoppable. They raided and pillaged and
foraged along the way, but the Lagoon lay just far enough off the major
routes to be immune from attack.

Venetian historians of the early Middle Ages believed that their city
was populated by mainland Veneti driven eastward by these barbarian
invaders to the shelter of the inland sea. Leaving the marshes, rivers, and
black, arable lands of northeastern Italy, they brought the name of Venice
with them to the very different environment of the Lagoon. "So, in fact,
there are two Venices," Johannes Diaconus wrote in the tenth century.
"The first is the one that the historians of antiquity described as lying
between the borders of Slovenia and the River Adda with its capital in
Aquileia. In that city the blessed Evangelist Mark, illuminated by Divine
Grace, preached the Lord Jesus Christ. The second is the one we know
that is situated among the island groups in the Lagoon of the Adriatic
Sea, where among rushing waves, in an unprecedented setting, a large
population lives and thrives. Certainly that population, from all that can
be concluded from its name and documented by what is written in the
annals, had its origin in the first Venice.

"Here is the reason why this nation now inhabits the islands of the
sea. The people sometimes known as the Winili but more commonly
called Lombards left their homeland on the shores of the North Sea and
after long migration and struggle reached the Balkans. They did not dare
to go further, and so they established their kingdom in this region and

remained there for forty-two years. In the year 540 AD, these Lombards erupted into the province of Venetia, the northeasternmost province of Italy. They eradicated Vicenza and Verona and many other towns, but not Padua, Monselice, Oderzo, Mantua, or Altina. Refusing to submit to Lombard rule, the people of the province took refuge in the nearby islands and in this way the name of Venice, from which they had fled, was assigned to these same islands, and those who inhabited them came to be called Venetians . . . Having decided to settle permanently in the Lagoon, they built cities and well-stocked fortifications. They created for themselves a new Venice and an extraordinary province" (*Istoria Veneticorum* 1.1–5).

The region's name resettled on the emerging city, but Johannes' notion that mainlanders driven into exile quickly adapted to an entirely new way of life is less convincing. Some may have been absorbed into Lagoon communities already acclimated, but many no doubt returned to the security of solid ground. Still, in defiance of all that the Romans had considered normal, sixth-century Venetians—whatever their origins— flourished in their watery environment. Just how alien the Lagoon must have seemed to outsiders is reflected in an eyewitness account written by Cassiodorus, a monk and a champion of classical learning who served the Gothic administration of Italy. On a mission to requisition food supplies, he passed through the Lagoon in about 535 AD. Cassiodorus probably traveled northward from Ravenna along the coastal road, but at some point he left the Via Popilia and continued his journey by boat through the Lagoon. What he saw there astonished him. He described it as a world not only out of the ordinary but one in which the norms of Roman life were either suspended or inverted like reflections on water.

"The Venetian region, worthy and rich in nobility, stretches southwest toward Ravenna and Padua; to the East it enjoys the benefit of its own Ionian shores. Here each successive tide first covers then lays bare the face of the country. The houses are like seabirds' nests. Where first you saw land, you soon see islands, even more numerous than the Cyclades, soon you see the unchanging aspect of these places. The reflections of their widespread houses stretch far on the flat sea. Nature provides a place which the care of man enriches. With slender branches tied in bundles, they consolidate the land and have no fear of facing the sea waves with such delicate defenses, that is to say, when massive waves surge over the shallow sea and overwhelm without effort every place that is not sufficiently high.

"To the inhabitants who eat nothing but fish, a little is a great deal. The poor and the rich live together in equality; all share a single food; all find shelter in similar dwellings; no one envies another man's mansion and even the rich in such an environment find no scope for vice . . . All their exertion is in the saltworks; in place of the plow and the scythe they rake the salt which yields them its fruit, when in these things even that which you do not make you possess. Food here is coined as money. By their arts the very waves yield cash. You may scorn gold, but understandably there is no one who does not desire to find salt, which makes every food more delicious. They tie their boats to the walls of their houses like domestic animals" (Cassiodorus, *Variae* 12.23).

Everything in this watery world is topsy-turvy. Boats take the place of domestic animals. Plowing and reaping of grain are displaced by the harvesting of salt from shallow pools. Gold, the universal standard of wealth, has no value compared to salt, a "food" that turns into money; the waves themselves can be coined. Cassiodorus cannot get over the oddity of what he sees. He adapts a classical literary motif, the mythological description of a primordial universal flood, to underline his feeling of estrangement. When water overwhelms the land, the normal order of things is inverted. Anything might happen.

So while it is possible to appreciate the general contours of Cassiodorus' description—the unconquerable sense of the unfamiliar that the landscape inspires; the rigors of the environment and the efforts made to accommodate human life to it; the saltworks; the pilings made of slender branches that reinforce the soil; the boats anchored at the doors—details of the social structure of the Lagoon may not be so accurate. In his world-turned-upside-down, vice gives way to virtue and the distinction between nobles and commoners is erased. Many of Cassiodorus' readers have taken these details literally, but they seem utopian if not wholly fanciful. Cassiodorus' inversion of the commonplace made it possible for him to treat an uncongenial and fundamentally alien subject in a way that his mainland readers could understand.

Unlike the bemused traveler, the islanders were thoroughly at home in this setting. They had adapted to the realities of their environment and crafted a way of life that suited its rigors and its opportunities. They were not the Lagoon's masters or its antagonists; they had not subdued it; and they did not live as exiles within its boundaries. They lived in harmony with their habitat, and the way of life they created flourished in the economy of its natural resources.

The Lagoon comes into view more clearly at the moment when the widely scattered population Cassiodorus described began to cluster. In the seventh century, a few island groups stood out, marked by churches or monasteries. Today, these islands—Torcello, Burano, and Murano—are quite small by comparison with the city of Venice, but they represent the same process of shoring up and linking nearby islets that gave birth to the metropolis. (Map 1) The few canals that still transect these tiny islands are the remains of channels that separated the original shoals from which they were made. Burano and Torcello, in the northern part of the Lagoon, stopped growing almost a thousand years ago, and Murano would have followed the same path if glass production had not been relocated there from nearby Venice in the fourteenth century. But as these other islands came to rest in remote corners of the past, Venice continued to expand, consolidating its tight cluster of islands into a thriving city.

From prehistoric to early modern times, European cities have typically grown from a single nucleus. Rome arose from a ford in the Tiber River at a boundary between cultures where two trade paths intersected. Paris began as a fortified island. Greek and Roman colonies, armed camps, and planned towns always had a clearly articulated center where build-ings for commerce, administration, and public worship were systemati-cally grouped. From gates in the city walls, major arteries led straight to these concentration points of wealth and power. During her long matura-tion, Venice took on a shape that reflected these European norms, but this was the result of prolonged and deliberate effort. Like its neighbors in the Lagoon, the city was slowly cobbled together by joining nearby islands along a central canal; and its social structure, at first fragmented, was cemented and ordered by political and religious foundations.

Churches of a certain scale and distinctive pattern bear witness to that remote time when culture throughout the Lagoon was still widely dis-persed on small clusters of islands. The oldest surviving structure is the cathedral of Santa Maria Assunta on Torcello. Founded in 639 by order of the Byzantine rulers of Italy, the church was modified in the ninth and tenth centuries. Its simple brick façade, which rises above a porch or narthex added in a second rebuilding, outlines the three-part interior and defines the church as a basilica laid out in a pattern that originated in Rome during the fourth century. (2)

Constantine, the first Roman emperor to promote official toleration and eventual institutionalization of Christianity, sponsored buildings in which the new god could be worshipped. Both for political reasons and because of the striking differences between Roman and Christian cults, these buildings bore no resemblance to temples of Jupiter, Minerva, or Juno. Images of the old gods were sheltered in shrines and looked out on open-air public altars where sacrificial offerings were burned in their honor. Christians, by contrast, worshipped indoors, en masse. While their God hovered invisible within and around them, they performed a sublimated sacrifice of bread and wine on an indoor altar. The Roman building type that best suited Christian requirements was the basilica, a structure that the Romans had originally used for administrative rather than religious purposes. Two buildings of this kind bracketed the Roman Forum: the Basilica Julia and the Basilica Aemilia.

The basilica of Torcello is simpler and smaller than the ones Constantine sponsored, but its structure

2

reflects the pattern he established. That pattern probably reached Venice by way of Ravenna, the center of Byzantine administration in Italy from the fifth through the seventh centuries. Santa Maria Assunta is a long rectangle with three apses—curved extensions or recesses—of unequal size at its east end. The interior is subdivided into three unequal parts by two longitudinal colonnades with arcades above. The wider center section—the nave of the basilica—is higher than the flanking aisles. The steep walls of the nave support a trussed wooden roof, while exterior brackets anchor the rafters of the sloping roofs that cover the two side aisles.

The altar of the church stands in a raised area, the choir (or presbytery); it is separated from the nave by an altar screen (iconostasis). Slender columns support a long panel decorated with images of the Virgin and saints. Banks of seats in the curve of the apse were meant for the cathedral clergy; there is a central marble throne for the bishop. Paired marble panels line the apse above them. Gold mosaic tiles cover the curved section, or conch, of the apse and the arch that unites it with the nave walls. Against this shimmering ground stands an image of the Virgin Mary, who holds the infant Jesus. (3) Portraits of the twelve apostles stand beneath. In the upper left corner of the arch, an angel raises his hand to greet another image of the Virgin, who is separated from him by the upper curve of the conch. These mosaics date to the thirteenth century. The floor of the cathedral is composed of colored marble tiles arranged in a complex pattern of overlaid squares.

The back, western wall of the nave is also decorated with a magnificent mosaic that represents the end of time. This familiar theme

3

responds to the traditional orientation of Christian churches along the sun's daily path from the east—the altar—to the west, where images of death and resurrection predominate. The crowning image in this mosaic is a representation of the crucified Christ with the Virgin and St. John standing below. The narrative under the crucifixion represents the Harrowing of Hell. Depictions of this event became common after the ninth century, when the phrase "He descended into Hell" was inserted into the Apostles' Creed to account for Christ's activities between the Crucifixion on Good Friday and the Resurrection three days later, on Easter Sunday. When Christ left Hell on Easter morning, he took with him the souls of all the Old Testament figures condemned to punishment through the sin of Adam and now redeemed. (4)

These two scenes, which correspond to Byzantine models, would be omitted in a typical Western Last Judgment. That tradition centers on the image of Christ in Majesty with the Virgin and twelve apostles, which forms the next band of this narrative. Below, figures begin to rise from their graves, and the final representations in the scene show the strikingly different fates of the blessed and the damned. (5)

These magnificent mosaics, the marble columns and capitals, and the polychrome inlaid marble floor contrast sharply with the bare brick of the walls, the stark beams that span the nave, and the simple wooden roof This contrast may seem normal to a modern observer, to whom it sug-

gests the authenticity of the decoration and the antiquity of the building
itself. The contrast is anything but natural, however. Instead, it is the art-

ful product of a common style of
restoration that has only recently
begun to lose favor among Italian
archaeologists. The principle
behind this form of restoration—
called repristinization—is plain
enough: identify the original style
and character of a building, then
strip away anything that fails to

4

correspond. What is left, the theory argues, will
be the closest possible approximation to the
building in its original state.

What is left in this instance, though, is a substantial paradox. The fabric of the building shows
traces of the original seventh-century foundation
and two subsequent renovations that spanned a
period of three centuries. The earliest mosaics
were not begun for another two hundred years
after that. Rather than present a single historical
period, the repristinated building collapses five or

5

six hundred years of building history into a single entirely fictive moment
in time. The homogeneity and purity of style that this restoration manifests
is an illusion, a creature of the process rather than a historical reality.

Like the basilica at Torcello, the buildings that survive in Venice and throughout the Lagoon have had very long and circumstantial histories. Their original styles may link them to one period, but their survival has thrust them headlong through period after period. Along the way, the richest and most important of them have accumulated a mass of cultural baggage. Rather than repudiate that experience in the search for an idealized, original, and authentic moment, contemporary archaeology honors history, however circuitous or mundane. And in doing that, contemporary archaeology also takes into account the present day as a historical period in the life of buildings. It asks not only what did this building mean to those who built it (the repristinator's question) or what did it mean to those who lived and died in its shadow (the historian's question) but what reason has this building found for continued existence today and into the future? This is a pressing question for preservationists and museologists, but it is also the question that every visitor to Venice must consider. Threatened by subsidence and the acqua alta, survivor of a cataclysmic occupation in the early nineteenth century, Venice is a city whose future is not to be taken for granted.

The cathedral of Santi Maria e Donato on the island of Murano is similar in many ways to the cathedral of Torcello. It is a three-aisled basilica with a deep central apse and smaller apselike extensions of the side aisles. Its nave columns are crowned by medieval versions of Corinthian capitals. From these capitals spring elongated or stilted arches, semicircular at the top but lengthened on both sides as if the arch itself incorporated part of a pillar. These arches are hallmarks of a style called Veneto-Byzantine and were common in the twelfth and early thirteenth centuries. The jeweled floor of pieced polychrome marble is punctuated

with images of birds
and animals, a very
remote recollection of
Roman mosaic floors.
(6) The conch of the
apse is decorated by a
gold-ground mosaic of
the Virgin of about the
same date as the one in
Torcello.

6

What distinguishes the interior of the Murano cathedral from its northern neighbor is a subtle change in ground plan. From the rear of the
nave, Santi Maria e Donato looks like a three-aisled basilica, but near the
presbytery the nave arcade is interrupted and the clerestory wall turns
outward toward the north and south walls of the building. This modifica-
tion creates a transept or crossing, which had no place in the original
Constantinian basilica or in the churches at Ravenna. Its inclusion here,
and in the majority of Western churches over the millennia, reflects
changes in the structure of Old St. Peter's in Rome that were introduced
in the early seventh century by Pope St. Gregory the Great.

The most striking features of the Murano cathedral are found on its
outside walls, especially those at its eastern end. Unlike the stripped-
down brickwork on the clerestory walls at Torcello, the exterior brickwork
here is meant to be seen. The façade is pierced by windows with receding
arched frames that dramatize the thickness of the supporting walls. Blind
stilted arcades and criss-crossed friezes ornament wall surfaces without

7

openings. This systematic, overall decoration is, from the point of view of the builders, apparently both necessary and self-sufficient. The taste that required such elaboration to give a sense of finish to this plain material would certainly balk at the uninflected expanses of stripped brick in the cathedral's repristinated interior. (7)

The semicircular apse of the nave and the flat-ended aisle extensions to either side are richly ornamented by a two-story arcade. The openings on both levels are slightly more elaborate versions of the window openings, but they spring from paired marble columns. The arcades in the lower story are blind; those in the upper story open onto a small gallery, protected at the end of the apse by a balustrade. A double criss-crossed frieze with inset colored marble panels separates the two stories. The effect is like a Romanesque ambulatory set on the outside rather than the inside of the apse. It may have been intended to give the church a monumental presence when seen from the main canal of Murano, which passes along its back. The church front, facing the small campo, is unadorned.

In the seventh century, Venice was not much bigger than Murano. Over time, as the city's growth outpaced its neighbors', it was organized into six administrative districts called sestieri. These districts have grown together to form the modern city, but the nucleus of each district was once a single island or cluster of islands. Canaleclo, somewhere above

the great curve in the Grand Canal, expanded to become the modern sestiere of Cannaregio. Across the Grand Canal from Canaleclo was an area
known by the enigmatic name of Luprio, where the sestieri of San Polo
and Santa Croce took shape. Rivoalto, below the great bend of the canal,
is today the sestiere of San Marco. Its name (meaning "high bank") was
gradually condensed to Rialto and assigned to the city's legendary commercial district. Dorsoduro ("hardback"), across the Grand Canal from
San Marco, is the only zone whose primitive name designates a contemporary sestiere. Seaward from San Marco were two smaller regions, Gem-
ini—the twin islands—and Olivolo, the island of olive groves. This region
alone, among all the areas of Venice, was once fortified, a fact that is
commemorated in its modern name, Castello.

Two churches not far off the Grand Canal in the sestiere of Santa
Croce, along with the centrally located church of San Giacomo di Rialto,
are among the few surviving representatives in Venice of the earliest style
of church building in the Lagoon. San Giovanni Decollato (the Decapi-
tated St. John the Baptist), named in Venetian dialect San Zan Degolà, is
the most remote. The first church on this once out-of-the-way site dated
to the eleventh century, and like most Venetian churches it has been
modified repeatedly. While such modifications have in most cases erased
not only the earliest ornamentation but even the primitive ground plans,
San Zan Degolà retains in recognizable form both its original layout and,
more importantly, its original scale. In a city where population grew
steadily throughout the Middle Ages and Renaissance, churches tended
to expand as parishes grew, but San Zan Degolà remained small. Its
basilical form and intimate size give a sense of the isolated island community it once served.

The temptation to expand the church must have been especially strong in the late fourteenth century, when what we would certainly see as a coincidence gave the church and its patron sudden prominence. The Venetians fought many battles during their long war with Genoa for trade supremacy in the Mediterranean. In 1358, on August 29—the feast day of Salome's dance, which led to the decapitation of St. John—the Vene-

8

tian fleet defeated the Genoese off the Greek island of Negroponte. The saint was credited with the victory, and the Doge vowed an annual visit to St. John's little church. The visit continued for a few years, but very soon the commemoration was transferred to San Marco, because San Zan Degolà was too small to hold it.

The brick exterior, which dates to the seventeenth century, reflects the internal three-part division of the church. (8) Inside, peaked Gothic arches supported on marble columns divide the nave from two lower side aisles. Simple wooden roofs cover all three. A transept divides the nave and choir, which ends in a vaulted projection that lacks the curve and conch of the churches of Torcello and Murano. The smaller projections of the side aisles end in flat walls. There is no mosaic decoration, no inlaid marble flooring. The bare interior, restored some twenty years ago, may not be true to the history of the church, but it does reveal the building's form and dimensions. This modest but appealing and serviceable church, which once suited the needs of a small parish, has, unlike many churches in contemporary Venice, again found a congregation. San Zan Degolà is now home to the Russian Orthodox community.

The nearby church of San Giacomo del Orio may take its name from Luprio. Like San Zan Degolà and most other early churches in the Lagoon, it faces a canal and turns its back on the campo that surrounds it. (9) Founded in the ninth or tenth century, the church was remodeled and probably enlarged in the early thirteenth. Though there have been significant changes since that time, the thirteenth-century plan is still evident. The original design was a three-aisled basilica with a single apse. Two additional apses, plus chapels on the north and an enlargement on the south, now give the center of the church more the proportions of a five-aisled structure.

9

Columns and capitals in the Gothic taste replaced the originals, and arched openings became peaked, as the new fashion demanded. A transept breaks into the nave walls. The vaulted wooden ceiling, like an inverted ship's hull, was added in the fifteenth century.

Aside from a sixth-century column of verde antico marble—brought home from some Greek or Byzantine city and proudly put on display—San Giacomo del Orio has no important decoration from its earliest period. It is, however, like many Venetian churches, extremely rich in artworks produced between the fourteenth and the eighteenth centuries. The new sacristy to the far left of the main altar includes paintings by a number of important sixteenth-century artists and a ceiling by Veronese. The ceiling of the choir was painted by Lorenzo Lotto; the old sacristy is decorated with a cycle of scenes describing passage of the biblical community from Egypt to Israel, along with New Testament parallels.

While San Zan Degolà has found its contemporary role as a working church for a new community, San Giacomo del Orio—like the bulk of Venetian churches—must rely for survival on its portfolio of artworks rather than its tiny congregation. A visitor entering this and many other Venetian churches is urged discreetly, if unmistakably, toward a small glass-enclosed ticket booth. Worshippers are not charged admission, but tourists are, and whatever the ethical implications of inviting the money-lenders back into the temple, the economic realities are plain and urgent. A church built and maintained by rich patrons, scaled to serve the needs of a large population, now hosts a congregation that meets comfortably in one of its two sacristies. Selling off the artwork, as many churches were forced to do in the nineteenth century, is obviously not a long-term solution. Charging admission to see the artwork keeps it where it belongs and pays for maintenance and restoration.

San Giacomo del Orio is a member of the Association of Venetian Churches known as Chorus. The group publishes a widely available guidebook to member churches, standardizes the process of ticketing and providing information in each church, and offers a reduced-price ticket to all of them. In the organization's view, as expressed in their guidebook, "The churches of Venice and their art treasures are now the inestimable patrimony of mankind, and Chorus aims to make known the full splendor of history, beauty and spirituality that still survives between these ancient walls through its expansive project for their appreciation and protection."

This guide is subtitled *Museums in the City* and in this label acknowledges a shift in audience and purpose that was already well under way in the nineteenth century. The foundation of Western Catholicism is the parish, the smallest geographical and administrative unit of the Church hierarchy. In theory and to a large extent in fact, every medieval Christian belonged to a parish served by a priest whose obligation was to fulfill his or her spiritual needs, a task accomplished primarily by administering the sacraments. Worshippers often ventured outside their home parishes, of course, and were drawn to other churches by a number of more or less calculated inducements. In Venice, particular churches were visited annually by the Doge (the Venetian word for "duke") and his suite on the dates of certain festivals, and vast crowds followed. It was common throughout the Middle Ages and Renaissance for churches everywhere to encourage outsiders to attend particular services by offering indulgences—spiritual rewards for attendance on certain dates or occasions.

Relics were the strongest magnets. The possession of some significant portion of a prominent saint's body, or some wonder-working image, did more to attract the faithful than anything else. Pilgrimage to holy places like Canterbury and Santiago de Compostela, where the relics of particularly important saints were revered, or to Rome and Jerusalem, where hosts of singular relics were displayed, stood at the pinnacle of religious experience. But long-distance pilgrimage was expensive and dangerous and was often viewed with suspicion by the authorities. Medieval vagrants typically claimed to be pilgrims, and modern words for purposeless travel, like "roam" (from Rome) and "saunter" (from Sainte Terre, or Holy Land), reflect this fact. Still, despite widespread abuse, pilgrimage was an almost unimpeachable reason for leaving the parish.

The decoration of churches with sculpture and painting played a role in attracting outsiders. The beauty and richness of ornamentation, which sometimes inspired controversy, could be defended as making the place of worship appropriate to the majesty of the supreme being whose cult it served. Beauty was not the only or even the primary consideration, of course: the content of pictorial programs in churches was most important. Writing in the thirteenth century, St. Thomas Aquinas outlined two reasons for displaying images in churches. They were to remind Christians of key events in sacred history and to inspire feelings of devotion. Images were an expansion of the spiritual experience provided by the sacraments. Like sermons or music, they made the church more attractive, more informative, and more emotionally compelling. The information they provided and the feelings they inspired could be shared by visitors to the churches as well as its regular congregants.

A modern visitor looking at Palma Giovane's images in the old sacristy at San Giacomo del Orio does not see what a Renaissance parishioner saw. Generally unfamiliar with the Bible and the lives of the saints, modern visitors may be hard pressed even to identify the subject of a religious painting. Modern art has deepened this mystery by focusing on style rather than content as the most significant element in painting and sculpture. Romanticism more than any other movement lies behind this dramatic shift. As an intellectual but primarily an artistic movement, Romanticism made the artist a hero, while organized religion as the fount of spirituality was replaced with nature on the one hand and art on the

other. At first these ideas were promulgated by poets
and literary critics, but by the end of the nineteenth
century these principles were codified in guidebooks.
The spirituality of churches did not wholly disappear,
but its manifestation shifted from relics and indulgences to sculpture and pictures.

The wonder-working objects in San Giacomo del
Orio and the rest of Venice's churches are now the
Palma Giovanes, the Veroneses, the Tintorettos, and the
Titians. Recognizing the legitimacy as well as the
inevitability of this shift has enabled Venetian churches
to survive. But the price has sometimes been high.

10

While recognizing a Tintoretto or a Titian by traits of style may be difficult
and praiseworthy, and while churches and patrons often competed to hire
the best-known artists, the interpretation of a biblical subject was the
single most important criterion for commissioning and judging a work of
art before about 1750. Most Western painting prior to that time was biblical or hagiographic, and viewing it today without a sense of the text it is
representing and commenting on is a little like reading the stage directions to *Merchant of Venice* and ignoring the play. No less than in earlier
times, the modern viewer needs to know what story a painting is telling
and how that story is being interpreted in order to understand its function
and importance.

Venetians assert that San Giacomo di Rialto, or San Giacometto as it
is known, is the oldest church in their city. (10) This belief may reflect the
now-central location of this wonderful little church at the hub of the
Rialto market. Something so old and so central must certainly be the

beginning point for everything else. But in Venice, centralization was a late development, following centuries when the city population and its churches were widely scattered. The second source for the belief in the primacy of San Giacometto is its unusual design. All the other early churches in the Lagoon that survive today are basilicas, but San Giacometto is centrally planned, vaulted, and domed. This form reflects a Byzantine pattern book more than a Roman one and puts this little church in the middle of a complex debate about the origins of Venetian architecture and architectural style.

The field is divided between those who see early Venice as emerging from Italian mainland traditions and others who see Byzantine influence dominating in the earliest period. The debate is further complicated by the fact that the Italian mainland tradition most likely to influence Venice—the architecture of Ravenna—is itself strongly marked by Byzantine characteristics. In the Italian repertoire of building types, the centrally planned or radially symmetrical building with a dome is certain to have been a martyr's shrine, a baptistery, or a tomb. The Byzantine tradition makes room for a wider range of uses that included a simple parish church like San Giacometto. The Byzantine tradition also preserved the secrets of how to build a dome long after that knowledge was extinct in Italy. For all these reasons, San Giacometto is seen as Byzantine or Veneto-Byzantine, a term that is widely used in discussions of early Venetian architecture.

Architectural historians have traditionally looked for a congruence between the history of building fashions and broader cultural trends. Specialists in Venetian history see the young Republic's relationship with the Byzantine Empire as the main theme of its earliest period. They conjecture, logically enough, that this political, mercantile, and ultimately military engagement led to a substantial current of Byzantine influence on architecture. When Venice solved its Byzantine problem in the thirteenth century by annexing a portion of the weakened empire, the Republic turned its attention to other parts of the world, and a new form of architecture, the Gothic, began to take hold. Venetian Gothic was mixed with a strong sampling of Eastern motifs, however, which are seen as responses to trade with the Muslim world. In the fifteenth century, when for the first time Venice took an active part in the great blood sport of the Renaissance—mainland Italian politics—architectural influences from Lombardy, Florence, and Rome began to make their mark in the city.

The identification of period styles is most useful when there is a more or less equal balance between stylistic and historical information. When one side of the balance sheet is out of proportion to the other, the association can be misleading. This is the case in Venice in the earliest period, when documentary evidence far outweighs the surviving buildings. As a result, conjectures from the historical record have guided interpretation of the very slim architectural evidence. Since Byzantium predominates historically, it is assumed to predominate architecturally, and so a Veneto-Byzantine style comes to life. Among churches, San Giacometto is its poster child; a handful of palaces scattered throughout the city make up the rest of its representatives.

Beneath its huge fifteenth-century clock and the half-round windows that light its nave and side aisles, a small sheltering porch projects. The little church of San Nicolo dei Mendicoli at the southwestern edge of the city is the only other Venetian church to preserve this once-common feature. The interior of San Giacometto is strikingly small, warm, and intimate. The incredibly crowded market outside is literally incommensurable with its scale. Six marble columns of unequal height and varying capitals support the central vault and the springing of the small dome. Mosaics that survived into the sixteenth century are gone without a trace. Large Baroque altars crowd the ends of the vaulted aisles.

Like all the earliest churches of the Lagoon, San Giacometto was built to serve a self-sufficient isolated community. Two developments changed its fate and that of the rest of the settlements in the six primitive sestieri. The first of these was a natural outgrowth of the continuing migration from the mainland to the inland sea. In 810 the authority appointed by the Byzantine government found his way there. Such government as the region still possessed had moved repeatedly, first from its mainland center, then to Malamocco on the Lido, and finally to Rivoalto. The center at Malamocco overlooked the traffic flowing along a secondary channel in the Lagoon. Rivoalto was a pinch point on a much larger and, from a tax collector's point of view, more lucrative flow. The governor held the Latin title dux, meaning leader; in Italian the word became duce; and in Venetian dialect, doge. His relocation made the nearest island groups more important and more interdependent.

The second development, however, was quite unpredictable. About twenty years after the Doge's relocation, two merchants brought the body of the Gospel writer St. Mark to Rivoalto. They had stolen the body from its original resting place in the Egyptian city of Alexandria. These two figures, the Doge and the Apostle, were the magnets that drew the city together and gave it preeminence, first in the Lagoon, then throughout the eastern Mediterranean.

Chapter Two

ST. MARK'S BASILICA

Together with the Doge's Palace to which it was physi-
cally and symbolically attached, St. Mark's Basilica
was the force that drew the island fragments of primitive Venice into a unified city. During the three centuries required for its completion, the city evolved
from a sheltered refuge in an alien environment to a center of commerce
and power.

Ninth-century Venice had stood just beyond the menacing grasp of both
the Frankish rulers in Italy—the last in a long chain of northern invaders to
control the Western Roman Empire—and the Byzantine fleet patrolling the
Adriatic. Fourteenth-century Venice dominated the land trade shuttling north
and south through the Brenner Pass, and its massive, disciplined, fast-mov-
ing galley fleet controlled the Adriatic Sea and the Dalmatian coast. Leverag-
ing naval power with diplomacy, Venetian garrisons occupied key points
throughout the Byzantine Empire, especially in the Greek mainland and
islands. These colonial outposts channeled commerce toward the city and
served as fortresses in the long wars with Genoa for dominance in trade with
the East. During the Middle Ages, Cassiodorus' world-turned-upside-down
itself turned the Mediterranean world of political power and mercantile
wealth on its head.

In indirect but unmistakable ways, the basilica of San Marco mirrored the city's increasing self-confidence and power. Left by its architects as a spare brick building based on a Byzantine model, the basilica eventually became so completely encrusted with donations from the faithful that its original form was swallowed up and these embellishments became its defining image. As Venice gained mastery of the Mediterranean, the city represented itself in this most confessional shrine as not just autonomous but autochthonous—self-created and completely free of foreign influences or ties. The multiple narratives of St. Mark that decorate its interior document this transformation. The earliest mosaics retelling the saint's legend acknowledge his ties to the mainland city of Aquileia and Egyptian Alexandria. The last mosaics in the church recount episodes in the saint's afterlife that cancel out any past not connected with Venice.

The San Marco we see today is the much-embellished third state of a church built, according to legend, soon after the arrival of Mark's relics in 829. (11) The first structure on the site suffered a disastrous fire in 976 and was extensively repaired or rebuilt shortly thereafter. The current building was begun some fifty years later in the mid-eleventh century, and despite more than a century of archaeological soundings, the extent to which it duplicates or incorporates its ninth-century original remains a mystery.

The contemporary basilica of San Marco is a cross-shaped structure composed of four intersecting vaulted arms. (Map 2) Each arm supports a dome, and another dome springs from the junction point of the four arms. It is generally agreed that the basilica was based on the form of the sixth-century Apostoleion—or Church of the Apostles—in Constantinople, a political and religious monument that was destroyed by the

Ottoman Turks soon
after their conquest
of the city in 1453.
Though Greek
architects familiar
with the Aposto-
leion supervised
the construction of
San Marco, from
the beginning the
Venetian church
deviated from its

11

prototype. The designers created a church with roots in Eastern political
and religious symbolism that brilliantly accommodated itself to the liturgy
and sensibilities of a Western religious community.

Sources describe the church in Constantinople as having four equal
arms that met in a central domed space where the high altar stood.
Arcades along each arm supported a double tier of superimposed galleries, each enclosed by a colonnade. The arms of San Marco, by contrast, are not of equal size or height, and the domes they support are also
unequal. The westernmost arm of San Marco is the widest and highest;
the other three arms are lower and narrower. The central dome and the
dome in its western projection are equally large, while the other three
domes are smaller. (12) Arcades like those in the Apostoleion, supported
on columns, line both sides of each arm and divide each one into three
unequal spaces, but the galleries that these arcades support, with their
low balustrades, lack the monumental impact of the superimposed

12

colonnades of the parent church. A vaulted porch on the western end of the church, which protrudes beyond the sidewalls of the nave at both its ends, completes the building.

These small but significant variations between the Venetian church and its Byzantine model transformed San Marco into a hybrid that compromised its Byzantine paternity to better suit the liturgy and traditions of a European church. Like a Roman basilica, San Marco has a long nave divided unevenly into three longitudinal sections and linked through a central domed space to a deep presbytery where the main altar stands. The high altar of the Apostoleion, by contrast, stood in its center. The principal doors of San Marco are on the west façade rather than at the ends of each projecting arm. And unlike its Byzantine exemplar, San Marco has a raised presbytery that lifts the choir a few steps above the general level of the church floor and makes room for a crypt beneath. Finally, the smaller arms on the north-south axis of San Marco act like the transept of a Western church. Both the crypt under the high altar and the transept are features that Western churches adopted in imitation of Old St. Peter's in Rome.

San Marco only briefly looked the way its designers left it—a brick church sharing decorative details with Santi Maria e Donato on Murano. Columns of rare and precious marble with capitals from older buildings supported wide galleries. The first light, flooding in through its many windows, shone on walls marked by shallow niches, blind arcades, and bands of ornamental brickwork. The only exterior ornament came from a few inset columns and the decorative masonry surrounding arches, niches, windows, and doors. The bricks, many of them salvaged from mainland ruins, were laid in the Western style with narrow bands of mortar; Romanesque receding frames around openings emphasized the thickness of the walls.

The apse of the presbytery, though circular within, was polygonal on the outside. The ground plan of the original church was not exactly cruciform because the porch on its western façade extended beyond the sidewalls of the nave. These protrusions created a sheltered space between the ends of the porch and the transepts on both sides of the church. On the north side, this area was filled in by a continuation of the domed bays that make up the main porch. The pointed Gothic arches separating the bays in this wing suggest that this structure was added in the thirteenth century. On the south side, a baptistery was built in and parts of a tower incorporated from the Doge's Palace were combined with an adjacent space to create the fortified treasury. A new entryway facing south toward the Basin of San Marco was opened into the porch.

Even before these additions were completed, the bare brick interior began to be covered with gold-ground mosaics. Venetian artists worked with masters from Constantinople to complete a program of decoration that welded the entire upper half of the basilica into a single composition even more adventurous and majestic in conception than Michelangelo's Sistine ceiling. Work began in the presbytery at the east end of the basilica and spread outward. A fire in the early twelfth century damaged many of the mosaics completed by that time; from then on, repairs and new work went on simultaneously. A single concept guided the decoration. At first, that plan was carried out by artists who shared a stylistic and iconographic tradition. But for centuries after that tradition lost hold, mosaic

13

work continued. As new mosaics took their place beside old ones, San Marco became a hodgepodge of styles that even the dominating program and the uniform background of shimmering gold cannot fully harmonize.

Completion of the decoration of the vaults and apses did not end the work: the building was soon cannibalized to create more space for decoration. Windows were bricked up, and the interior, especially the areas between the colonnades and the outside walls, became exceedingly dark. The galleries above these spaces were narrowed to let more light into the aisles below. The vertiginous catwalks with low balustrades to each side that now top the colonnades are the result. A Gothic rose window in the south transept and the vast demilune in the western vault are efforts to light an interior that the medieval greed for wall space made dim. The mosaics won out, however, and the basilica remains a cavernous, murky hearth where the gilded surfaces glow like the embers of a dying fire. But with its electric lights turned on, as they are during Mass and for an hour each weekday starting at 11:30, the interior blazes into life. (13)

Raised up in the half-dome conch of the apse at the eastern end of San Marco and visible from every part of the nave, the image of Christ as Pantocrator, or universal ruler, dominates the church. This mosaic of the sixteenth century replaced a twelfth-century original. The Pantocrator image grounds the program of the mosaics and underwrites its subtheme of Venetian dominance and privilege. (14)

Two figures beneath Christ's feet, the apostle Peter and the evangelist Mark, touch him most closely. These two are flanked by figures of saints Nicholas and Hermagoras. Among his many projects, St. Nicholas looks after sailors, which made him especially important in this maritime culture. Hermagoras, appointed bishop by St. Mark, was a key figure in the battle for spiritual primacy Venice once waged with its neighbor city Aquileia. The story of Peter, Mark, and Hermagoras is filled out in the two chapels set into the smaller apses at each side of the presbytery. The one on the north is dedicated to St. Peter, the one on the south to St. Clement. St. Peter's Chapel served the clergy and made the case for primacy over Aquileia. St. Clement's Chapel, which was used by the Doge, made a broader political statement about Venice as an apostolic center. In both chapels, scenes from the life of St. Mark predominate. Unfortunately, those in the north chapel, which detail his life and martyrdom, were heavily damaged by restorers in the nineteenth century.

14

The Gospel according to Mark, widely accepted as the oldest and most occult of the Gospels, reveals nothing about its author. Scattered passages in the Acts of the Apostles and the epistles of Peter and Paul fill in the picture. Mark, who is called John Mark in Acts, may have been a Levite, a member of the Jewish priestly caste. His mother, a friend of the apostle Peter, belonged to one of the earliest Christian congregations in Jerusalem. After preaching for awhile in Asia Minor, Mark went to Rome around 60 AD and returned at the time of the martyrdom of St. Paul a few years later. Noncanonical texts later than Acts provide details of his travels and ministry. One of these sources places him in Aquileia, where, according to legend, he converted multitudes to the Christian faith and oversaw the copying and dissemination of his Gospel. A more familiar continuation of Mark's story identified him as the apostle to Egypt and the bishop of Alexandria.

Throughout the Middle Ages the church in Aquileia displayed a marble bishop's throne—now in the presbytery at San Marco—in which the evangelist is said to have "sat while he etched the words of his Gospel into wax tablets" (*Acta Sanctorum* 12.349–350). This link with the apostle was enough to give the bishop of Aquileia a claim to supreme authority in northeast Italy. Once the Venetians came into possession of the relics of St. Mark, they began to challenge his primacy. The mosaics of San Marco are one expression of their counter-claim.

St. Peter's Chapel celebrates the close connection between the apostle Peter and the evangelist Mark. Extending the link between the two described in Acts, medieval legend asserted that Mark's Gospel was dictated by the eyewitness Peter and that Peter sent Mark first to Aquileia and then to Alexandria. Those two events are suggested in the apse portraits. Peter holds a book in his left hand and makes a gesture with his right that typically represented speech in early Christian art. He looks toward Mark as if to mime the dictation of his Gospel. Hermagoras, Mark's successor in Aquileia, stands next to Peter, as if he were someone Peter placed in Mark's care. St. Peter's Chapel chronicles their stories, not just to acknowledge them but to show Venice as their ultimate goal. Founded in Christ, passed on by Peter, and brought by Mark to Aquileia and Alexandria, the apostolic appointment eventually reached Venice, the evangelist's final resting place. That assertion is endorsed in the chapel in the figures of the bishop of Grado, who petitions on behalf of the Venetians for the transference of rights of apostolic primacy, which he is shown receiving from Pope Pelagius.

In Alexandria, Mark converted many Egyptians to Christianity, but a significant number continued to worship their idols. "It happened that our most blessed feast of Easter occurred on the twenty-first day of the month of Parmut, the twenty-fourth of April. At that season the Egyptians celebrate their festival of the god Serapis. Pagan conspirators took that opportunity to lay hands upon Mark as he was celebrating Easter mass. Men seized him and placed a rope around his neck by which they began to pull him away. While he was being dragged along, his persecutors chanted to their god, but Mark prayed to our Savior, saying, 'I give thanks to you my lord Jesus Christ, that you consider me worthy to suffer in your name.' His body was thrown to the ground then, and he was stoned until he bled. At nightfall his enemies threw him in prison, to keep him under guard while they decided how best to kill him.

"About midnight when the doors were well secured and the guards outside his cell had fallen asleep, a great earthquake began. An Angel of the Lord descended from heaven, who awakened Mark and said, 'Prince and servant of God, propagator of the holy faith throughout Egypt, behold your name is written in the Book of Life; your memory will be preserved through all the ages . . . Even now your spirit is winging toward Heaven where eternal rest and unwavering light will never fail you.'

"In the morning a great multitude of people gathered; when Mark came out of the prison, they replaced the cord around his neck and began to drag him again. As he was being dragged Mark prayed, thanking God again and praising his tender mercy. Then he spoke once more and said, 'Into thy hands I commend my spirit, O Lord!' and having said this, the most blessed Mark gave up the ghost" (*Acta Sanctorum* 12.351). Deprived of their victim, the frustrated crowd decided to vent their anger by burning the martyr's body and so destroying it as a relic. But a sudden rainstorm extinguished the flames and scattered the crowd, killing many among them. The Christian community of Alexandria retrieved the saint's body and buried it where "prayers are offered to God without ceasing."

In a series of original mosaics of the eleventh century, St. Clement's Chapel continued Mark's story. Alexandria was not destined to be the evangelist's final resting place. In 641 the city fell to Arab invaders, and once again the body of the evangelist was in the power of unbelievers. Almost two centuries later, in 829, two Venetians came to the rescue. This event is recounted in a wonderfully circumstantial narrative from the *Acta Sanctorum:* "When the Saracens had occupied all of Egypt including Alexandria, Leo Armenus, emperor of Byzantium, upon his assumption of the throne decreed that no one in any part of his empire should sail to Egypt for purposes of trade. Though the order was delayed in reaching Venice, Justinian Particiato, the Doge, soon reconfirmed it. Then, as is often the case among the Venetians who are always in search of markets, a group of merchants with their ships laden set out on the high sea. Through the divine will, the winds being favorable, they did inadvertently what they would not have dared to do deliberately because of their respect for the Doge. They were more or less unwillingly blown into port at Alexandria.

"At that time, the prince of the evil race of Saracens wanted to have a palace built in the city which he called by the ancient name of Babylon. Against God's will, he ordered that everywhere in the land of Egypt that marble columns or panels could be found, whether in churches or in domestic structures, they should be brought to him to enrich the building he planned. And so it came about that through this impious decree the churches of Alexandria were being stripped of their adornments.

"Now whenever Venetians spent any length of time in Alexandria, it was their custom to offer daily prayers to the relics of the most blessed Mark, and to make offerings in thanks for his intercession. The Venetian ships that God had directed to Alexandria were ten in number with many noblemen aboard. Among these nobles were two very distinguished men, the Tribune Bonus of Malamocco and Rustico of Torcello. Because of their daily devotions to St. Mark, they became friendly with the priests who kept the shrine. Noticing one day that they were sad, the Venetians commiserated with them. The guardians of the shrine were distressed because they feared that the servants of this impious prince would do to the shrine of St. Mark what they had done to others. And then, inspired by God, Bonus and Rusticus added these words to their expressions of condolence, 'Why should you grieve alone, servants of Christ? Why should only your souls be afflicted? God has warned his faithful of innumerable persecutions to come. But if you will follow our advice, we will show you what to do so that you might live in honor again, secure against this faithless race and ruler. Take up the body of St. Mark and come aboard our ship in secret. Go with us to our country.'

"At first the two took this very badly, but soon a messenger came to Stauratius to report that a servant of the pagan prince of whom we have spoken had cruelly whipped one of the other guardians of the shrine in order to find out if there were marble columns or panels in that church of any value . . . Terrified, Stauratius and Theodorus sent for Bonus and Rusticus and told them, 'It has entered into our hearts to take up the blessed body and go with you' . . .

"When the appointed day arrived, the guardians secretly opened the tomb. Such a marvelous fragrance arose from the blessed body that not only the church but the neighborhood around it and the whole city of Alexandria were filled with it. The agitated citizens, both pagan and Christian, wondered what could be the cause. Some were puzzled; others realized the truth, that Venetians were stealing the body of St. Mark. From all parts of the city people ran to the church. Meanwhile, the Venetians took up the body, placed it in a hamper, and covered it with leaves; on top of the leaves they put pieces of raw pork. When they reached the ship, they were met by Saracens who confronted them and demanded to know what they were carrying. When they saw the pork, which is an abomination to them, they shouted 'Kanzir, Kanzir!' that is, 'Pork, Pork!' In disgust they spat on the ground and walked away. Finally, the Venetians reached the dock. They lowered the hamper with ropes into a small boat and took it to their ship, where they wrapped it in a sail . . .

"During one of the nights of their passage a storm came up which pushed the ships along even more quickly; but because of the darkness, they could not see where they were heading. The Blessed Mark appeared in a dream to one of the guardians and told him, 'Go above and tell the sailors to lower sail instantly or they will be shipwrecked, for the land is near.' The monk did as he was told, the sails were lowered, and in the morning they found themselves near an island, as the blessed Mark had promised. Then all were convinced and they began to venerate the body with greater zeal.

"When they reached the port in Olivolo, the Bishop Orso, carrying his crozier and leading all the orders of the clergy who were dressed in their priestly vestments, came to receive the body most reverently. The clergy took possession of the body and carried it to the palace of the Doge. As they climbed the steps to the reception hall, the shroud with which the body was covered rippled constantly, though there was no wind . . . And to the priests who carried the body, it seemed sometimes ponderous and immobile and other times so light they could hardly feel it.

"The Doge accepted the body and placed it in the reception hall, which can be seen next to the palace in the present day. He established chantries and a chapter to protect the body and offer praises to God. He made Stauratius the head of the chapter; with Theodore to succeed him in the following year . . . The Doge Justinian Particiato was prevented by his untimely death from building a church for the blessed relic. His brother Giovanni, who was beloved of God, succeeded him as Doge and carried out his intention. Next to the palace, he constructed a basilica of elegant form, after the pattern of the church of the Holy Sepulcher in Jerusalem, and ordered it to be decorated with many and various colors. And there with incense the venerable body was enshrined with the greatest honor" (*Acta Sanctorum* 12.356–358).

This marvelous sequence of events is represented in St. Clement's Chapel in six scenes. The picture cycle—high up in the vault and partly hidden by the pipes of the organ—begins well into the story, with the removal of the saint's body from its tomb. From a casket that evidently floats on air, the two Venetians—here labeled Rusticus and Tribunus—and the Greek priest Theodorus lift the evangelist's body, while the second guardian, Stauratius, looks on. In the next image, the two Venetians carry the body in a hamper attached by rope handles to a pole they support on their shoulders. (15) The third scene conflates several episodes in a single picture. In the left foreground is the small boat the Venetians used to ferry the body to their ship. The evangelist's body is already

being wrapped in a sail as the Saracen exclaims "Kanzir, Kanzir!" even though the body in the sail is no longer covered with pork. The Saracen appears again as an ornamental figure near a window, with the words "Kanzir, Kanzir" repeated.

15

In the following scene the vessel leaves Alexandria. In the shipwreck image, the sleeping priest is awakened by an erect and animated St. Mark, no longer a corpse but a dream-image of the living saint. Sailors, craning their necks to see in the darkness, drop the sail, which partly envelopes them. Translucent waves like windblown grass beat against the ship's hull and stream over two rocky islands topped with Dr. Seuss-like trees. In the final scene the relic arrives safely in Venice, where it is received by the Doge and the clergy.

The mosaic decoration of the apse tells its story in two different ways. In most cases the wall becomes a storyboard where scenes are placed side by side in chronological sequence. More subtle juxtapositions support an associative rather than sequential reading. The Pantocrator image is not linked to the four saints below by narrative sequence or chronology. Peter, Hermagoras, and Mark can be understood in isolation as unrelated images, but if we accept their position as a clue—they are close together because they are linked symbolically—and tie them to the Pantocrator, a reading based on association and rooted in the architectural space of San Marco comes into focus.

Christ and Peter are joined in many ways, but the connection that makes most sense here rests on Jesus' designation of Peter as the rock on which the Church is to be founded. By this statement, Christ handed over some part of his sacred authority to Peter. Peter, in turn, passed on something of that same mysterious substance to Mark, who brought it to Aquileia, where he shared it with Hermagoras, then to Alexandria, where he designated a second bishop as his successor. Peter's anointment remained with Mark, however—indeed, it remained even with his dead body and so it passed with his relics to Venice.

In Christian history and theology, the passing outward through space and onward in time of Christ's spiritual authority is the apostolic movement. Mark recounted Jesus' charge to his faithful disciples after his resurrection: "He said to them, 'Go into the whole world and preach the gospel to every creature. He who believes and is baptized shall be saved, but he who does not believe shall be condemned. And these signs shall attend those who believe: in my name they shall cast out devils; they shall speak in new tongues; they shall take up serpents; and if they drink any deadly thing, it shall not hurt them; they shall lay hands upon the sick and they shall get well'" (Mark 16.15–20).

Though St. Mark was not one of the eleven who received Christ's commission directly, he played an apostolic role through his own missions and especially through his Gospel. It is entirely appropriate that a church in the shape of the Byzantine Apostoleion should be created in his honor. It is also appropriate that the decorative program of that church should explore the broadest meaning of the apostolic movement. Like Christ, who is the source of apostolic authority, the Pantocrator image is a visual point of origin. As the eye moves from that image to those beneath, it follows the flow of spiritual power from the image through the four saints at Christ's feet and into the two chapels in the subordinate apses of the presbytery. This cluster of images arrayed in space imitates the process by which the words and actions of a once-living man were disseminated by generations of witnesses.

The church is the place where Christ is remembered, but it is also the place where his presence is miraculously invoked through the Mass. At the moment when the bread and wine become the body and blood of Christ, the priest lifts up the Eucharistic wafer and everyone in the church participates in Christ's sacrifice. Every part of the architecture of San Marco supports this act and gains meaning from it. The Pantocrator image recalls the Christ of history, but it is also a permanent memorial of his fleeting presence in the moment of transubstantiation. Its role as anchor of the mosaic cycle is strengthened by its placement near the high altar of the church. The mosaic program of St. Mark's Basilica is a vision of the apostolic process as it is codified in history but also as it comes into the present through the celebration of the Eucharist.

While the presbytery illustrations tell the history of a single apostle, Peter, and his follower, the evangelist Mark, that story is only one of many that could be told. The rest of the twelfth-century mosaic program of San Marco tells the apostolic story in universal terms. While the presbytery program springs from the image of the Pantocrator, this all-encompassing story of the apostolic movement unfolds from three figures in the apex of the three sequential domes in the presbytery, crossing, and nave. Through a visual logic that replicates that of the apse, these central figures disseminate power downward to others beneath.

The central figure in the east dome, above the main altar, is Christ Emmanuel, or Christ Incarnate. The subordinate figures at the bottom of the dome are, with one exception, Old Testament prophets who, according to Christian tradition, predicted his coming. Directly above the high altar, along the central axis of the church and visible from anywhere in the nave, stands a figure of the Virgin Mary. Each of the prophets who ring her is identified by a Latin title, and each holds a scroll in his hand with a much abbreviated excerpt from his writing. In translation, the scroll in the hand of the prophet Isaiah, who stands to the right of the Virgin Mary, reads: "Behold a Virgin shall conceive and bear a Son; and shall call his name Emmanuel" (Isaiah 7.14). Emmanuel, as the text set

.16

by Handel goes on to say, means "God with us." (16)

Christian theology asserts that God inspired these prophets to recognize and to bear witness to Christ, the messiah who was to come. Christ Emmanuel, God incarnate on earth, is the savior they foretold and described enigmatically in their writings. As they spread the word about their vision, they prefigured the apostolic mission. Mary belongs in the picture because she is the portal by which the incarnate Christ entered the world. In the pendentives of the dome are the traditional symbols of the four evangelists. Beginning above the lion, symbol of St. Mark, and continuing above each of the other three symbols are the verses of a rhyming Latin poem: "What [these prophets] said about Christ in obscure terms, is said plainly by the evangelists who knew Him." Christian theologians asserted that the words of the prophets remained enigmatic until they were manifested in the events of Christ's life and narrated in the New Testament. The evangelists appear here as the prophets' interpreters and those who carried on their task.

The center dome—the second one from the altar—stands near the midpoint of the church where the nave and transept intersect. The figure in the apex of the dome is Christ at the moment of the Ascension. Dressed in gold, he sits on a golden arc, while his feet rest on a second

smaller arc that represents the last of the planetary spheres in the Ptole-
maic universe. Behind him appear the stars of the Empyrean. The sky is
laid down in concentric bands of blue that deepen toward the center. A
ribbon of cloud at the edge of the sky bowl is supported by four angels
like the winged Victories that carried Roman emperors upward to their
seat among the gods. The angels' bent bodies draw the eye around the
sky disk and give the static symbol a sense of motion that runs through
the whole composition and is echoed in the postures of the double ranks
of figures below. In Byzantine art, windswept drapery, figures that seem
to run or dance, and standing figures in contorted poses all respond to
the divine presence.

Beyond the words of a circular inscription, broccoli-sprout trees lead
the eye downward toward the crowded rim of the dome. Like rays, the
trees diagram the spiritual energy that flows out from the central figure of
Christ. They also cut the dome into dimensionless niches that enclose
figures of twelve apostles, the Virgin Mary, and two angels. Flanked by
angels this time, Mary again stands in the most visible and spiritually
significant position toward the altar. The arched windows have less ornament than those in the dome of the presbytery, and the spaces between
them are filled with full-length personifications of sixteen virtues and
beatitudes.

Heavily restored representations of the evangelists fill the pendentives,
as they do in the east dome, but here the authors of the Gospels are represented by portraits rather than symbols. Though Mark appears among
the apostles in the dome, he is included a second time among the evangelists in the pendentives. Since the evangelists were not historically

present in the age of the prophets, they are appropriately represented in the east dome by emblems. In this central dome, however, they are present in the flesh to suggest that they, like the apostles, witnessed Christ's ascension. The evangelists are again labeled with the verses of a rhyming Latin poem which here ends above St. Mark. This exceedingly enigmatic poem tries in a few short lines to sum up the relationship between what the apostles saw and what the evangelists recount. It grants the evangelists the authority of witnesses, even though they did not see with their own eyes what the apostles observed.

The vault of the presbytery and two of the arches that support the central dome are filled with episodes from the life of Christ. His story begins with the Annunciation to Mary in the eastern vault, and continues in the south arch of the crossing with episodes from the Temptation in the Wilderness to his washing of the disciples' feet at the Last Supper.

17

The western arch contains the most sacred and significant scenes, those of the Passion and Resurrection. (17) These events immediately preceded the Ascension illustrated in the dome.

The arch between the central dome and the north transept includes stories of the miracles performed by Christ, which continue on the archways of the south transept. These narratives of Christ's life are more than a visual New Testament; they are an integral part of the story that the mosaics were designed from the first to tell. It is not just the character or person of Christ that matters. These sacred events through which Christ achieved his purpose are what the apostles witnessed and the evangelists memorialized; they are what the prophets foretold.

In the west dome, midway down the nave, the focus shifts from Christ to those he left behind on earth to continue his work after the Ascension. The composition echoes the center dome, with its elements compressed and the relationships they

18

express made clearer. But the focal figure of this dome (known as the Pentecost dome) is an empty throne—called a hetoimasia—draped with purple. (18) A closed book lies on its surface and a dove stands beside it. Uncommon in Western art, the hetoimasia is a common Byzantine symbol of the Trinity, with the throne representing God the Father and the book representing the Gospels and their subject, Christ. Both in the East and West, the dove is a familiar symbol of the Holy Spirit. The throne is surrounded by an aureole of concentric rings, deep blue at the center fading to lighter blue then to a band of cloudlike white. The four victorious angels who carry the nimbus in the center dome have slipped to the pendentives of this dome.

The stark difference between the central figures of the two domes makes it evident that after the Ascension something new takes the place of the risen Christ. What the apostles saw face to face can now be seen on earth only through a symbol. From that symbol twelve rays propagate;

each passes through an encircling inscription to end at the nimbus of a seated figure. There is a clear correspondence between these radiating spokes of light and the raylike trees of the central dome. The confluence of the spokes and the seated figures, however, makes this composition simpler and its message of apostolic succession clearer. The twelve figures seated around the base of the dome are the twelve apostles pictured in the center dome. Mary is excluded now, and the twelve include Paul and all four evangelists, who have been fully integrated with the core group of those who disseminate the Christian message.

From each apostle's head a three-dimensional porphyry cone projects. These curiously solid emanations represent small flames that appeared above the heads of the apostles. "And when the days of Pentecost were drawing to a close, they were all together in one place. And suddenly there came a sound from heaven, as of a violent wind blowing, and it filled the whole house where they were sitting. And there appeared to them parted tongues as of fire, which settled upon each of them. And they were all filled with the Holy Spirit and began to speak in foreign tongues, even as the Holy Spirit prompted them to speak. Now there were staying at Jerusalem devout Jews from every nation under heaven. And when this sound was heard, the multitude gathered and were bewildered in mind, because each heard them speaking in his own language" (Acts 2.1–6).

Below the apostles and between the windows of the Pentecost dome, pairs of standing figures represent the nations of the world. The vaults to the north and south of the dome rely on the text of Acts for narratives of the life and martyrdom of individual apostles. This complex of dome and side vaults echoes the themes of the apse and presbytery chapels, which show the mission and the fate of one of these men, the church's patron, St. Mark.

The westernmost vault of the church, above the gallery that leads to the porch, is decorated with scenes of the Last Judgment in sixteenth-century style but linked symbolically to the thirteenth-century mosaic program at Torcello. This is a traditional subject for the western end of a church, but its presence in San Marco carried to conclusion a second narrative implicit in the sequence of domes that lead from the main altar westward along the sun's path. The figures on the rim of the presbytery dome represent the age of the prophets, that troubled period in the history of Israel when visionary critics challenged the errors of the nation and the abuses of its kings. At the apex of the same dome, Christ Emmanuel represents the moment of the Incarnation. In the center dome, Christ's life comes to its triumphant end in the Ascension. The Pentecost dome represents a time that is not long after in chronological terms but is theologically distant. Christ to Come, Christ Incarnate, and the Risen Christ form a sequence that is logically completed by the west wall's representation of the Second Coming of Christ at the end of human time. The primary theme of the church, the history of apostolic dissemination, encapsulates world history.

A parallel chronology unfolds in the transept. The north dome focuses on the life of John the Baptist, the forerunner who, like the prophets, prepared the way for Christ. The center dome with its depiction of the Ascension follows chronologically. The south dome, which is the least realized of all the domes in the church, contains a mixture of saints and virtues. As the Ascension dome asserts in its lowest range of allegorical figures, the spread of virtue is also an outgrowth of the life of Christ. The south dome is a weak paraphrase of the Pentecost dome and makes almost the same point, though in an understated and uninspiring visual language.

The apostolic tradition is a very significant theme in Christianity, and the treatment of it in San Marco's mosaic program is extraordinarily ample and nuanced. A program of this magnitude, with its multiple scenes and figures tightly woven into a complex and imaginative whole, was to be found in only a few other Christian churches. The mosaic programs in Rome's Santa Maria Maggiore and in San Paolo, outside the Roman walls, and the program in the Monreale Cathedral in Sicily were among the very few that came close to achieving its ambitious scope and overall unity. In the Middle Ages, rivalries among cities were expressed, like everything else, in religious terms. Housing the largest and most complex treatment of a major Christian theme was the medieval equivalent of building the tallest skyscraper or the largest domed stadium. This monumental mosaic program earned Venice international prestige.

As a statement of civic identity, however, the part of the mosaic program that expresses the apostolic movement is of limited value. The developing sense of Venetian confidence, autonomy, and self-sufficiency is visible only in the mosaics that carry on the legend of the city's patron saint, Mark. Among the mosaics in the south transept is a sequence of great appeal and importance, because here, for the first time, the scene shifts from Saracen Alexandria to Venice, in fact to a location within the church of San Marco itself. "In that very church, enriched with gold and precious marble, it came about that over time the location of the most sacred relics was forgotten. And when, after careful inquiry, it became clear that no one knew where to find them, the whole city of Venice was

ordered to observe a three-day fast. After this penance had been faith-
fully carried out by the entire population, on the fourth day all the clergy
and people converged on the church. There they formed a procession;
litanies were sung, prayers and tears were poured out to God. They
begged that in his mercy, he would deign to show them where the body
of St. Mark lay.

"God heard their prayers and showed them the place. Suddenly a
marble column split open and a chest containing his body which had
been hidden within it burst forth for all to see. A woman possessed of
seven devils drawn involuntarily to the body of the saint was at that
moment healed in the sight of all. When the body had been reverently
placed within the church, a certain workman, who was doing some
repairs at the very summit of the campanile, suddenly lost his grip and
began to plunge toward certain death and mutilation. Despite his terror,
he remembered St. Mark and prayed for his help, vowing that if he were
spared, he would serve the saint for the rest of his life. Unexpectedly, he
fell against some timbering sticking out of the structure and was able to
hold on" (*Acta Sanctorum* 12.358).

A long list of other miracles follows, all testifying to the power of the
newly recovered relics. These accounts may be factual, but certainly the
first of them describing the woman possessed of seven devils is an
embodied biblical citation as well as a miracle. The account in Mark's
Gospel of the Ascension, that crucial event that crowns Christ's apostolic
charge to his disciples, follows a description of his appearance to Mary
Magdalene. "Now when he had risen from the dead early on the first day
of the week, he appeared first to Mary Magdalene, out of whom he had
cast seven devils" (Mark 16.9). The woman cured by Mark's relics recalls

this passage and associates this story in a subtle way with the apostolic theme of the mosaic decoration throughout the church.

The marvelous story of the rediscovered relics is summarized in two thirteenth-century mosaic panels. The first shows the clergy and citizens of Venice in prayer. The second represents the moment when the column breaks open and reveals the lost relics. (19) The bishop is first to see the miracle, but the Doge follows immediately behind him, so close that his robe overlaps that of one of the tonsured monks in the bishop's retinue. The Doge wears a conical hat, not the cusped one that will become his symbol later on. He is labeled *Dux* in the mosaic. A noticeable gap

19

behind the Doge is filled by a view of the ambo or raised pulpit of the church. The rest of the image is crowded with Venetian men and women and two mini-figures who represent children.

The view of the church itself is extraordinary. It is at once interior and exterior through a cutaway that would be literally impossible to achieve but is visually clear and informative. A building, probably the Doge's Palace, is visible on the right. It sets the church in context, but like the figure of the Doge next to the bishop, it also asserts the slightly unequal though close partnership of church and state. All five of the domes are visible; each is supported on a barrel-vaulted arcade, pierced by windows, and surmounted by a cross. These shallow domes and their half-round supports were the hallmark of the building before Gothic renovators framed steep second roofs above them and transformed the building's outline.

A slice has been carved from each dome to remind us, however paradoxically, that we are looking up from within. Below the domes, a balustrade runs almost the full width of the panel. This represents the narrow interior walkways that overlook the nave and transepts. The column containing the relic is sixth on an arcade that supports these walkways. Its location is hard to read in the mosaic because its base is on a level with the feet of the figures in the procession, even though the other columns in the arcade are behind them. What appears to be a naive mistake in perspective may be the deliberate creation of a visual riddle that accentuates the uncanny character of this miraculous column.

Above the main western door of the basilica, in a lunette, is an image of Christ Enthroned, with the Virgin to the left and St. Mark to the right. The image is a special example of a traditional Byzantine deesis, though the presence of St. Mark in that scene is unusual. Both Mark and the Virgin appear to be supplicating Christ, not for their own sake but on behalf of those who chose them as intercessors.

The porch roof immediately outside the door is now pierced by a very curious skylight, called a pozzo or well, which allows those entering the church to look up at images of the Last Judgment inside. This vision underscores the notion that entering the church is crucial to the final outcome of life. Originally, this central bay was probably capped by a dome decorated with mosaics, like every other bay of the porch. The center door is set into an apse where the earliest mosaics in the church serve as an overture to the program of the interior. Above the doorway in the conch of the apse is an image of the Pantocrator, the same figure who fills the apse of the presbytery. Beneath him, the figures of the Virgin Mary and eight apostles act as prelude to the central dome. Below the apostles and to either side of the main door stand portraits of the four evangelists, who again point toward the central dome. Not only do the mosaics of the doorway anticipate the theological program of the church inside but they also enrich the notion of entry itself. Christ said, "No man cometh unto the Father except by me." The apostles through their missions and the evangelists through their words also created passageways into the faith.

Episodes from the legend of St. Mark appear in other parts of the atrium. In the vault of the Capella Zen on the south end of the porch, much-restored mosaics narrate twelve episodes from the saint's life that partly overlap those in the presbytery. Among the new scenes here is a critical Venetian elaboration of the saint's legend that firmly links the living evangelist to his final resting place. "There is a legend of many centuries' duration handed down by the original inhabitants of the Lagoon of an incident that occurred during his travels. As he was preparing to return from Aquileia to Rome, the evangelist found the surface of the sea covered with large waves stirred up by high winds, and so he chose to travel through the marshes where the waves would be gentler. He turned his course toward Rivoalto, where he was well-received by the inhabitants. In the quiet of the night a smiling angel appeared to him and said, 'I am a happy messenger from heaven, sent to you, Mark. Do you not know where you are? For much longer than you imagine this will be your resting place.'

"Mark misunderstood the angel's words, thinking that they warned of a shipwreck, but the angel continued, 'Be of good cheer,' he said. 'You are not destined for an obscure death, but after long labors, the Prince for whose honor you struggle will award you the crown of martyrdom. This place which is now so humble and bare will one day be more welcome to you than any other. Know that one day a temple will be here where your bones, stolen away from the barbarians, will find perpetual rest. Through your intercession and your power, the piety and virtue of this nation will make it great'" (Francesco Sansovino, *Venetia, Città Nobilissima et Singolare,* p. 507).

The mosaic illustrating this scene shows a small open boat among flowing waves. The boat's rope is tied to a stick that protrudes from a low mud bank dotted with a few flowering plants. This is the artist's idea of Rivoalto, the Plymouth Rock from which Venice will grow. Mark, whose head is ringed by a nimbus, is asleep in the prow of the boat, his saintly companion in the stern. A figure without a nimbus sits awake in the middle of the boat. He may serve, as similar figures often do in medieval illustrations, as a witness to the miracle. Beneath the much-abbreviated but still very long inscription at the top of the scene, an angel appears out of a starry sky and makes a gesture that signifies speech. In the many representations of this scene throughout Venice, the words of the angel are remembered as "Pax tibi Marce evangelista meus": Peace be unto you, Mark, my evangelist.

The story this image tells is a significant departure from the legend of St. Mark narrated in the presbytery. There, the aim is to establish Mark as an apostle and outline his role in spreading the Gospel of Christ. The mosaic here assigns the saint a new role as city founder. Through his influence and power, coupled with the virtues of the people of the

Lagoon, the mud bank where he anchors will become a great nation. This transformation of the saint from apostle to city founder also redefines the community and its political leadership. When the Doge and the Venetian community are depicted in the Mark cycle of the south transept, they are second to the bishop, though close in authority, and taking part in a sacred rather than secular rite. They are congregants rather than citizens. Inside the church, the Doge's spiritual role is emphasized; outside, his political authority is primary.

The Capella Zen, where this mosaic is placed, is now separated from the rest of the church. But when these mosaics were completed, the space was different. Where the altar of the chapel now stands there was a door opening to the Piazzetta—the small plaza that leads from the Basin of St. Mark directly to the church. The Piazzetta, which runs alongside the Palazzo Ducale, was the ceremonial entrance for important visitors to the city, and the door of the Capella Zen was their entryway to the church.

The last major mosaic program in San Marco was the Genesis cycle of the porch. The interior program outlining the apostolic movement was logically complete; but, understood as a universal chronology (as the west wall suggested), the cycle lacked a beginning. Inside the church, the narrative of the prehistory of Christ starts abruptly with the prophets who predicted his coming; it excludes the creation, the story of Adam's fall, the flood, and many other events of theological importance. On the porch, scenes from Genesis, where many of these events are described, fill in these missing parts of the biblical chronology. The Genesis cycle imagined for St. Mark's was monumental. Its more than one hundred scenes span the vaults and domes of all but two bays of the original atrium on the west and two of three bays in its extension along the north wall of the nave. The cycle begins on the south end of the porch in the bay to the north of the Zen Chapel. Skipping over the entrance bay, it continues uninterrupted through the remaining five domes and vaults of the atrium and its wraparound extension.

At the time of the mosaics' creation in the thirteenth century, Genesis cycles were enjoying something of a revival. Old St. Peter's in Rome and the Constantinian basilica south of that city, dedicated to St. Paul, each had such cycles, and the example of these important churches (both now replaced by newer buildings) may have been responsible for the fashion. The presence in Venice during the thirteenth century of an extraordinary illustrated book played a part both in the origin of the cycle and in the depiction of particular scenes. The Cotton Genesis is a richly illustrated Greek text of the first book of the Bible that was probably produced in Alexandria near the end of the fifth century AD. The manuscript was in Constantinople in 1204 when Crusaders sacked the city, and the work came to Venice in its share of the spoils. In the seventeenth century the book found its way into the library of the English book collector Sir Robert Bruce Cotton. In 1700 his collection was given to the British crown to form the core of a national library. A fire in 1731 damaged all the books in the Cotton bequest, including unique manuscripts of *Beowulf, Sir Gawain and the Green Knight,* and the Genesis. The work of reconstructing texts and passages damaged in the fire of 1731 continues today.

The more than three hundred scenes illustrated in the Cotton Genesis are reduced in the atrium of San Marco to about a hundred clustered around the six cupolas of the porch. The first cupola describes the Creation; the second, the story of Abraham; the third through fifth present a very detailed retelling of the story of Joseph; the last cupola, at the eastern end of the northern extension of the porch, is dedicated to Moses and takes the atrium narrative beyond the chronological limits of Genesis.

When the Capella Zen served as a gateway to the atrium, its definition of St. Mark as city founder would have inspired a nationalistic reading of the Genesis mosaics. Such a reading emphasizes the political community rather than the congregation and gives special prominence to secular leadership. From a modern point of view, the creation of the world may seem an outrageous precedent for the founding of a city, but in the Middle Ages and Renaissance, God the Creator was seen as the supreme artificer, the original of all those who, like city founders, artists, and architects, work to bring new things into being. The shepherd Abel was the favorite of the nomadic society depicted in Genesis, while Cain, the founder of cities, was its villain; but urban Venetians found Cain worthy of respect. Noah, too, is a builder whose ark saves a portion of mankind. Abraham is the founder of a nation.

Joseph, to whom the atrium devotes nearly half its attention, is a more puzzling choice. Like the other heroes represented in the cycle, he was chosen by God to secure the survival of Israel. Joseph, Abraham, and Moses were elected—though in their cases God had the only vote—to steer their nation through periods of crisis and consolidation. They did their jobs well, even if they had personal flaws, and they founded no dynasties in the process. Joseph, the son of Rachel, possessed a

birthright superior to that of his brothers, but it carried no title of king-
ship. He was not a David or Solomon, figures that European kings frequently chose as patrons. Of all the figures represented in the porch,
Joseph is the most entrepreneurial and the most closely connected with
trade. He was probably the patriarch most familiar and comforting to the
political leaders of Venice—the elected doges—as they sought biblical
grounding for their uncommon political roles. The nation of Israel
directed by these extraordinary men symbolized the political community
of Venice.

Despite its deterioration—the result, ironically, of both neglect and
repeated restoration—the cupola of the Creation is one of the most glorious mosaics in the church. Structured like a story board, the dome
groups consecutive scenes in concentric bands around a symbol of the
cosmos. Abbreviated Latin inscriptions tie the scenes to Bible passages.
The story begins in the innermost band, with the image of a dove flying
over open water, its head circled by a nimbus. The inscription echoes the
first two verses of Genesis: "In the beginning God created the Heaven
and Earth . . . The spirit of the Lord was borne upon the waters" (Genesis 1.1–2). In the second image, God separates the light from the darkness while an angel looks on.

Further acts of creation follow, including in the second band the
remarkable creation of birds and fish. With its diverse, animated, and
richly detailed population of creatures, this panel recalls the vast mosaics
that adorned the floors of Roman houses. Through the lens of the Cotton
manuscript, the illustrator captured a wealth of detail and a style of representation that was absent from the art of his day.

Two scenes later, Adam is formed and then brought to life after God blesses the seventh day. Eve's creation takes up two scenes of the outer-

20

most ring. The rest of the scenes in the cupola narrate the Fall of Adam and the Expulsion from the Garden. (20) In the world outside, Eve begins her post-lapsarian labors by spinning thread, while Adam cultivates the earth. Majestic cherubs with folded wings behind and in front and wide-spread wings to either side occupy the pendentives. The story of Adam and Eve's sons Cain and Abel fills the lunettes of the first bay.

The vault between the Creation cupola and the main door tells the story of Noah and the flood in nine frames. (21) The panels representing the loading of the ark are especially appealing. In the first of these Noah is about to place two peacocks into the hatchlike opening of the ark. Ducks of many kinds, quails, cranes, and even several breeds of chicken

surround him and watch placidly as the loading continues. In a later scene, Noah leans out from the same hatch in the chunky and unseaworthy vessel to release a dove.

Noah's story after the flood is represented in depictions of the cultivation of the drying-out earth and the drunkenness of Noah. In this scene Noah lies asleep under an arbor with drawn curtains. His posture and nudity

21

recall Roman images of sleeping satyrs, and the modeling of his torso reflects a classical sense of volume uncommon in medieval images.

The most extraordinary image in this vault represents the building of the Tower of Babel. God and three angels look down on a crew of masons mixing mortar and setting blocks, and a hod-carrier who climbs the steps of a wooden scaffold with a shallow basket of stones or bricks on his shoulder. (22) In the foreground, an apprentice in a short sleeveless tunic and laced-up Roman sandals mixes sand with a hoe, while another collects blocks. The Roman clothes of the workmen must have looked anachronistic to the mosaicists who created the panel, just as they do to us. Still, the working methods represented had changed little since the classical period.

22

The Abraham cupola, with its many striding or riding figures arranged in a single band of scenes at its verge, looks more like a procession than a series of discrete images. A white line like the margin of a book page marks the beginning of Abraham's story. It continues in the east and west lunettes in a total of nineteen scenes. Portraits of the prophets Isaiah, Ezekial, Jeremiah, and Daniel fill the pendentives. Two panels in the west lunette complete the cycle with a representation of the birth and circumcision of Isaac, the only son of Abraham and Sarah. In medieval theology, Isaac is a forerunner of Christ; his submission to the father who is commanded to sacrifice him on an altar is a representation of Christ's crucifixion. The absence of that scene is remarkable, and it reinforces the notion that the Abraham story represented here centers on the building and strengthening of the political, rather than the spiritual, community.

The Abraham cupola is followed by a much-restored post-Renaissance mosaic depicting an allegory of Justice. The last bay on the west façade and the first two of the northern wing of the atrium tell the story of Joseph. The first Joseph cupola is similar in overall form to the Abraham cupola. An eight-pointed star with entwined rays, surrounded by a classical laurel wreath, dominates the center; a double band of inscriptions sets a limit on the picture space. As in the Abraham cupola, the file of figures below seems to move freely in a space that is not broken up by frames. Clusters of figures mark individual episodes. A thin white band marks the opening scene: the appearance to a sleeping Joseph of a vision of sheaves of wheat and a starry sky.

The beginning of the Joseph story in Genesis emphasizes Joseph's birthright and the love of his father that estranges him from his brothers. Joseph is a dreamer and an interpreter of dreams—the rival of his brothers but also their eventual leader and savior. In their anger at the message of the dream, Joseph's brothers overpower him, strip him, and place him naked in a well. (23) When they retrieve him, it is only to sell

23

him to merchants, who carry him on camelback to Egypt. The final scene in the cupola shows his father Jacob's grief as he learns of his favorite son's death.

The second Joseph cupola is crowned by an emblem that refigures the rayed star of the first cupola as an idealized rose window. The eye has difficulty navigating a narrative band where figures are more static and architectural backgrounds impede movement. The scenes here are all set in Egypt in the palace of Potiphar, to whom Joseph has been sold. Recognizing his abilities, Potiphar makes him steward of his estates. Joseph's advancement provokes the lust of his owner's wife, who eventually accuses Joseph of what he refuses to do, and he is thrown into prison. In a short while he is put in charge of the prison. Pharaoh's butler and baker, victims of their master's displeasure, soon join him. The two have dreams, which Joseph correctly interprets, an episode illustrated in the cupola's last scene.

The four pendentives, which are usually devoted to figures who comment on the themes of the cupola, continue the main narrative. In one, the butler returns from prison to serve Pharaoh again; in the next, the baker is crucified. Both events fulfill Joseph's dream interpretations. The third pendentive shows Pharaoh himself asleep and dreaming; the fourth narrates his dream: "Pharaoh dreamed and, behold, he stood by the river. And, behold, there came up out of the river seven well-favored cows and fat-fleshed; and they fed in the meadow. And, behold, seven other cows came up after them out of the river, ill-favored and lean-fleshed . . . And the ill-favored and lean-fleshed cows did eat up the seven well-favored and fat cows" (Genesis 41.1–4).

The story continues in the south lunette. Pharaoh has a second dream of seven lean sheaves of grain that eat up seven fat ones. The images of these sheaves recall those in Joseph's dream in the first scene of the cycle. Pharaoh sends for magicians, who fail to interpret the dream; the butler remembers Joseph. Originally the story was carried on in three scenes in the north apse of the bay; these were replaced in the eighteenth century by a single composition. Joseph is summoned. Joseph interprets the dream as a promise of seven years of abundance to be followed by seven years of famine. Pharaoh makes Joseph overseer of Egypt. The third Joseph cupola picks up the story, as Joseph puts into action his plan to save the excess of the seven fat years to provide against the seven years of famine.

The granaries in which the Egyptian crop is stored are the most wonderful parts of a remarkable composition. Three smooth-sided pyramids

with windows and doors stand in front of two step pyramids. (24) Whether these structures come from manuscript sources or reflect the Venetian traders' knowledge of Egypt's most typical monuments, they are perfect choices. While the Venetians did not store grain for public use in pyramids, they

24

proudly displayed their own prudence and munificence in three prominent fortresslike granaries, one on the Grand Canal, a second just off Piazza San Marco, and a third near the Arsenal.

Famine in their homeland forces Joseph's brothers to Egypt to buy grain. Joseph recognizes them but does not reveal himself. Through a series of ploys, he forces them to bring his own younger brother, Benjamin, his father's new favorite, to Egypt. Once there, he arranges for Benjamin to be falsely accused of theft. Judah, the eldest brother, agrees to be a hostage in Benjamin's place. Satisfied that his brothers have learned self-sacrifice, Joseph reveals himself and orders them to bring their father so that the entire family can live in security in Egypt. The brothers, with Benjamin, enter Joseph's house. This truncated ending sets a triumphant seal on Joseph's work that Genesis itself undermines: "So Joseph died, being an hundred and ten years old: and they embalmed him and he was put in a coffin in Egypt" (Genesis 50.26). What the atrium mosaics present as a rescue would soon become captivity, and God would eventually call Moses to lead the Israelites out of Egypt.

That story, which is told not in Genesis but in the succeeding book of Exodus, is the subject of the last mosaic cycle of the atrium. Like the stories of Joseph and Abraham, it has been foreshortened to emphasize the major theme of the atrium: the leader elected by God and the nation that he preserves or rescues. Like the last of the Joseph cupolas, the Moses cupola is crowded with scenes set against architectural backgrounds. The center medallion is similar, too, but the inscriptions that form an unbroken band in all the other mosaics are here divided from one another and worked into the fictive space of individual scenes. Despite their visual integrity, the scenes in this mosaic are condensed narratives that span a number of linked events.

The south lunette of the bay now contains a seventeenth-century mosaic of the miraculous passage through the Red Sea, based on a drawing by Pietro Vecchia. The Moses cycle ends in the apse above the north door with scenes from the desert wandering of the Israelites. The first shows manna and quails miraculously raining from the heavens to sustain the wandering nation. The second illustrates the miracle of Moses striking the rock and producing a stream of water. These scenes are common representations of the Eucharist, but they also suggest that Moses is a leader who provides for the nourishment of his people.

Like the atrium which celebrates the nation, the façade of San Marco belongs to the community as a whole. It is a collaborative work on an enormous scale that has created an unexpected harmony out of the gifts of generations of anonymous donors. In the Middle Ages and well beyond, almost any Christian shrine was likely to be enriched by gifts from believers. A street-corner image of the Madonna might receive an occasional bunch of flowers and a votive candle or two. A significant shrine was sure to receive more valuable and longer-lasting gifts. After decades or centuries of such donations, the good intentions and piety of the devout completely transform a simple image into an intricate installation. The work of a single artist or workshop gradually becomes a communal expression.

The façade of San Marco is a corner shrine on a monumental scale. (25) Instead of flowers and candles to decorate his tomb, the Venetian devotees of St. Mark brought marble panels and columns. Abandoned Roman buildings on the Italian mainland, palaces and temples throughout the Byzantine Empire—especially Greece—were looted of their architectural ornaments so that the church of San Marco could become ever more magnificent. The first spoils of this massive ecclesiastical scavenger hunt were displayed inside the church. The two ambos or pulpits in the crossing are supported on small columns of exceptionally valuable marbles, including porphyry and jasper. The screen that divides the nave from the presbytery displays more columns of the same highly precious stone. The walls of the pulpits themselves are figured marble panels.

It was not uncommon for churches within the area of the former Roman Empire to reuse classical building materials. In the city of Rome, where such found materials were exceptionally abundant, almost every church built before the Renaissance incorporated reused columns and capitals. As commonplace as the practice was, classical building materials were never used unself-consciously or anonymously. After all, these artifacts were the products of a pagan culture, and many of them had

25

been used in temples devoted to the worship of gods that Christians regarded as devils. Reusing such material involved a degree of theological risk.

The Bible provided a key for adapting these objects of pagan cult to Christian worship. As the Israelites prepare to leave Egypt under Moses' guidance, they take with them unleavened bread, which is the symbol of Passover, but they also "asked of the Egyptians vessels of silver and gold" (Exodus 12.34–36). These prizes extorted from a pagan enemy were later used in the worship of God. Following the lead of St. Augustine, Christian theologians used the precedent of "Egyptian gold" to justify the adaptation of pagan materials to Christian ends. While the practice of reusing pagan objects was sanctified by this precedent, the classical tradition also influenced the way these objects were used.

Trophies captured from an enemy played a large part in Roman public life. Virgil's epic of Roman prehistory, the *Aeneid,* pays particular attention to the proper handling of the spoils of war: an object captured from an enemy and imprudently displayed precipitates the death of Aeneas' great antagonist, Turnus, at the climax of the poem. Captured enemy shields, weapons, and insignia were on public display throughout the Roman Forum, and Roman generals returning from successful campaigns typically paraded their captives and captured prizes in ritualized parades called triumphs. The classical example transformed "Egyptian gold" into a trophy that memorialized the victory of Christianity over paganism. Every classical object, every object associated with Islam, and eventually every Byzantine object in San Marco played these dual roles. Each was a votive gift to the patron saint, sanctified by the tradition of Egyptian gold. At the same time, each was a trophy that asserted the saint's power over the enemies of Christianity. Through the accumulation of spoils, San Marco retaliated against the Egyptian pagans who martyred the saint and the Saracens who threatened his Alexandrian shrine.

A San Marco that remains relatively untouched by the barrage of gifts that will soon remake it is represented in a mosaic on the arch of the northernmost entryway on the west side. (26) This is the third mosaic representation of the church included in the multiple narrations of the St.

26

Mark legend. It is the first scene in a series that runs across the façade from north to south and the only remaining fourteenth-century mosaic on the exterior. The scene shows the body of St. Mark carried in procession along this very side of the church. A few columns are visible in the background, but the most notable differences between this representation of San Marco and those in earlier mosaics are details higher up. Above the image of Christ Pantocrator that then crowned the center door, four restless golden horses with turned heads and uplifted forelegs are framed by columns. Horses have stood in this place on San Marco's façade since the late thirteenth century, though for a brief time in the early nineteenth century they were carried off to the Louvre.

Where the horses might originally have come from is uncertain and controversial. That the Venetians found them in the Hippodrome at Constantinople is clear enough, though controversial in a different sense. In 1204 a group of fractious and heavily armed foreign crusaders descended on Venice, where they were to take ship for the Holy Land. They were wild and disorganized and, what was even more vexing to the Venetians, short of cash. They could not meet the fee for passage Venice had been promised. Despite the shortfall, the Venetians were eager to remove this virtual army of occupation from their city, so they negotiated an arrangement that turned religious zeal to Venetian political ends. These crusaders were off-loaded on the Dalmatian coast, where they sacked and subdued the Christian city of Zara. Not long after, Alexius IV, a Byzantine emperor driven from his throne, joined the crusaders and promised them the treasure of his realm if they would restore him to power. At that, the fleet promptly changed course and headed toward Byzantium.

This second swerve from their pious goal of reclaiming Jerusalem was too much for many of the knights, who finally gave up and went back home. The Pope withdrew his support at the same time. Undaunted, the remnant of the army set sail for the Byzantine capital under the leadership of the blind octogenarian Doge Enrico Dandolo, whose iron will and taste for conquest more than made up for his infirmities. The adventurers actually succeeded in placing Alexius IV back on the throne, though much of Byzantium was burned in the process. Sadly, the restored monarch proved unpopular and—worse, from the Venetian point of view—penniless.

After a counterattack by Byzantine troops in which more quarters of Constantinople went up in flames, the Westerners replaced the Byzantine ruling house with one of their own and partitioned Byzantium and its empire. Venice's share, evidently the result of hard bargaining, was "one quarter and half a quarter." From what was now arguably their own city, the Venetians began to collect valuables. The Cotton Genesis was probably part of the loot; reliquaries still in the Treasury of San Marco certainly were. Icons, plaques, columns, and capitals, marble revetments, mosaic tesserae, and perhaps workmen skilled in their placement were packed in the holds of Venetian galleys and sent back home. Much of the booty ended up in San Marco; and no part of it was more prized than these four bronze horses. The originals are preserved and displayed inside the church; those on the exterior are reproductions. (27)

The greatest change to the exterior of San Marco, as documented by the mosaic, came about in a peaceful way. By the fourteenth century, the shallow domes of the original design seemed too low. To replace them would have been impossible, but to change their profile was a relatively simple matter. Wooden armatures were built above the original domes, and lead roofs in the rising balloon shapes that have become signatures of the building were laid over them. The new domes soar above the structure, giving it a height that the sensibility of the fourteenth century admired. The steep domes with their pierced bulbous lanterns and rayed antennas seem more Eastern than Western. But if they graft an Eastern physiognomy onto this Christian structure—as the profile of many of the building's archways does as well—this is probably meant in the same spirit with which materials captured from Islamic nations were displayed elsewhere. Rather than evidence of simple syncretism or unconscious Islamic influence, the domes probably reflect what other spolia in and on the church represent, the triumphant display of "Egyptian gold."

27

The western façade of San Marco that now dominates the Piazza is considerably more elaborate than the one represented in the portal mosaic. The façade appears to be divided into two horizontal zones. The lowest and farthest forward includes the five arched entrances to the church and two narrowed arched spaces to either side. Each entryway is an apselike niche recessed into the façade; the central doorway is both wider and higher than the four surrounding ones. The outermost doors to north and south are surmounted by cusped arches in the Islamic style. The doors to either side of the center have arched windows in the Gothic style above them. Their three steep multipaned windows are heavily framed in stone. The central shafts of these frames support two heavy circular frames, each pierced by four circular openings—a motif that is quoted in Gothic structures throughout Venice, most insistently and prominently in the Palazzo Ducale next door. The central door is crowned by a series of concentric arches decorated with sculptures. Both the flat of the wall between doorways and the recesses of the doors themselves are faced with a double row of columns in a variety of precious materials from every part of the Mediterranean basin.

This first façade supports an open terrace where reproductions of the four Byzantine horses stand on plinths above the central doorway. The recessed upper façade of the church retains the five central bays of the porch. The central arch frames a multipaned demilune window. The lunettes of the bays to either side contain mosaic scenes from the life of Christ. Gothic elements at this level are more marked and, like the heightened domes of the church, increase the upward reach of the building and give it a bristling outline. The top of each arch is extended by a peaked surround, like a tiara. These surrounds support figural sculptures like bands of filigree. A saint's statue crowns each peak. Between each of the bays and on either end of the upper façade, thin open shelters with trilobite arches and steepled roofs enclose other sculpted saints. The domes tower above and behind—those of the nave higher than those to either side.

With its domes heightened and its arches enriched with Gothic filigree, San Marco reached completion. While the replacement and redesign of mosaics continued inside until the fall of the Republic in 1797, the exterior of the church remained substantially untouched after the fifteenth century. No monument anywhere in the world looked at all like it. It was an instantly recognizable symbol of the city, whose rise to power and singularity it both summarized and represented. Autonomous, replete, and world-famous, it stood for a city whose like had never been seen before.

Chapter Three

COMPANY TOWN

The autonomy that Venice claimed in San Marco shaped every aspect of the city's life. Most medieval European cities maintained some measure of independence, even if it was grudgingly conceded to them by overlords greedy for the products and revenues they produced. Feudal barons calculated their strength by comparing manpower and weapons. The notion that their power could be enlarged or limited by economic rather than military might did not occur to them. In northern Europe, feudal alliances of these lords formed networks of military power that bundled regions and nations into a loose defensive web which served as a rudimentary political organization. Cities, for whom economic life was primary, hardly counted in the grand scheme of feudal politics, and most cities struggled in the grip of a political system that disdained their way of life. Merchants, as a class, shared in this lack of esteem. To the barons' way of thinking, they were nonproductive peasants. Churchmen, many of whom combined secular and spiritual leadership, regarded the life of trade and the wealth it could produce with deep suspicion.

Italian states were often ruled in the same way as their northern counterparts, but the Italian feudal network was never very widespread or effective. As a result, Italian cities such as Florence, Milan, and Genoa were typically more powerful and autonomous than cities in the north. Venice—a republic in the age of barons—repeatedly and skillfully eluded dominance by foreign powers, which meant any ruler outside the Lagoon. The Venetians were equally astute in guarding themselves against the dynastic ambitions of their own doges. Venice not only welcomed economic activity but recognized that the city's strength and well-being rested on a foundation of trade and the profits trade produced. The extension and protection of trade summed up Venetian foreign policy. Diplomats, admirals, and colonial administrators served the state part-time but served their mercantile companies throughout life. Venice was a company town.

Full political membership in the Venetian company town, though restrictive from a modern point of view, was widespread by the standards of the European Middle Ages. An economic elite stood at the top of the social ladder and governed the state. In the year 1200, this dominant class included some four hundred men. The group was expanded and its ranks officially closed in 1297. After that time, a little over twelve hundred men served on the city's Grand Council (Maggior Consiglio) and held the rank of noble. Families with noble status were registered in a series of volumes called the *Libro d'Oro*—the Golden Book—that was kept under lock and key in a special room of the Palazzo Ducale. Additional families were ennobled in recognition of contributions made during the nearly cataclysmic war against Genoa in 1381. Costly wars in the sixteenth century again gave wealthy contributors a chance to be enrolled.

A class of men called citizens held second place in the order of power and prestige. Many of this class were wealthy, but as a group they were ineligible to vote or to hold elective office. Citizens were by no means impotent. They staffed the state bureaucracy and dominated the scuole—

powerful quasi-governmental religious societies with great power and
influence. The multitudes lower in the social order had no civil rights at
all. Skilled workmen of every sort, from mosaicists to glass blowers,
masons, and fishermen, occupied the next level down. The largest
employer in Venice was the state Arsenal, where thousands of workers
built, fitted out, and maintained the Venetian commercial and military
fleets. Below these workers were servants, apprentices, and slaves. As
was always the case in the Middle Ages, the clerical hierarchy paralleled
these secular social categories.

Company headquarters for this mercantile Republic was the Palazzo
Ducale next door to San Marco. Nearly as recognizable as the basilica,
the palace is a great block of a building—only partly visible from the
Piazza—that dominates any view of the city center from the San Marco
Basin. (28) One of its façades overlooks the harbor where the Grand Canal
and the Giudecca Canal meet Adriatic traffic passing through the Lido
gateways. In the past when visitors to the city arrived by boat, this building greeted them from a distance and loomed over them as they disem-
barked.

The palazzo com-
mands a spot that was
not just picturesque but
was well suited to the job
of building a unified city
out of a spatter of
islands. Before the Grand
Canal was an urban
waterway, it offered a

28

secure channel through the shoals of the Lagoon and linked the Italian coast with one of only three open passes through the barrier island to the Adriatic. Any spot along this channel might have become an effective center point, but San Marco had advantages that other sites lacked. It stood on a wide basin, which made it useful as a harbor and mooring for deep-water ships. It communicated with the Giudecca Canal as well as the Grand Canal. (29) And its entrance was protected by the offshore island of San Giorgio.

The first palace on the site was built soon after the relocation of the Byzantine dux from Malamocco on the Lido to Rivoalto in 810. The

palace, which accommodated the duke's family and suite, was also a fortress. Next to it stood a chapel dedicated to the Byzantine warrior St. Theodore, a favorite patron of garrison towns throughout the eastern Mediterranean. When the relics

29

of St. Mark came to Venice almost two decades later, they were first housed in a wing of the duke's stronghold. Over the years, Mark's expanding church edged out the chapel of St. Theodore. The palace evolved at the same time.

As the Venetians countered, often with violence, the ambitions of their

rulers to make the office of Doge hereditary, they came to believe that a
fortified palace was a danger to their form of government. While the
fortress secured the government against invaders, it also protected
tyrants from reprisal by injured citizens. Destroyed by fire sometime in
the tenth century, the old ducal palace was replaced in the twelfth century by an unfortified and loosely linked complex of buildings. The Doge
was given a suite of rooms inland, near the basilica. The council and its
committees met in a waterfront hall. The judicial branch of Venetian government had its offices in quarters that overlooked the Piazzetta. Through
a series of renovations that lasted into the seventeenth century, these
loosely joined structures were consolidated into a four-sided building
around a vast open courtyard.

The palazzo has two nearly identical façades. The one visible from the
harbor is the older; the wing that now overlooks the Piazzetta replaced
the earlier judicial complex in the fifteenth century.
Despite the late date, this wing was designed in a
Gothic style that mimicked the harbor side, finished a
century earlier. (30) The two lower stories of both
façades are made up of Gothic arcades. At ground
level, stubby columns with capitals of great individu-
ality support the arches. (Most of the capitals on the
exterior today are nineteenth-century copies; many
originals are displayed inside the palazzo in the
ground-floor Museo dell'Opera.) The arcade offers
shelter from the weather as well as access to the
building. Some scholars believe that a similar arcade

30

of earlier date on the waterfront may have connected directly with the Basin and served as the first arsenal for mooring the Venetian fleet.

The openings in the second-floor arcade are half the width of those below. Cusped and peaked arches spring from narrow columns that each support a rondel with a four-lobed opening. This motif appears on the façade of San Marco and in countless noble houses throughout Venice. A low balustrade runs the length of the second-story colonnade. The corner columns on each story of the arcade are decorated with sculptural groups. The Judgment of Solomon surmounted by an image of the archangel Gabriel—attributed to the sculptor Bartolomeo Bon—decorates the corner nearest San Marco; the corner between the two façades has images of Adam and Eve on the bottom story and the archangel Michael on the second. The far corner of the complex is guarded by the archangel Raphael and a scene showing the drunkenness of Noah.

The largely enclosed, nearly windowless upper stories of the palace are covered with an overall pattern worked in small stone tiles arranged in diamond-shaped groups of alternating pink and white outlines. Until the eighteenth century, when Piazza San Marco was repaved with gray volcanic stone, its pink brick pavement, divided into squares by strips of Istrian stone, must have echoed this design. Like patches on a quilt, the blocks are organized into long diagonals that sweep across the face of the building in an endless, restless pattern. The eye refuses to settle and transforms what threatens to be a heavy, static surface into an apparently thin and energetic membrane. Highly stylized crenellations crown the building—purely ornamental recollections of the arrow slits that once topped the fortified ducal palace. These crenellations were repeated on other government-owned buildings in Venice and became a semi-official symbol of state ownership.

Six great pointed windows break through the fabric of the upper stories and frame somewhat eccentrically a heavily ornamented balcony surmounted by Gothic spires and enriched with sculpture. The early fifteenth-century structure on the harbor side is original. Its balcony is flanked by small aedicules enclosing sculptures crowned by long spires that reach above the roofline. A free-floating structure between them encloses other sculptures in its arched openings and is surmounted by a figure of Justice by the Renaissance sculptor Alessandro Vittoria. This work replaced a Gothic personification of Justice that served as an image of the Venetian state.

The English critic John Ruskin praised the asymmetrical arrangement of the harborside windows. In his discussion of the Gothic in *The Stones of Venice,* their irregular placement exemplified the sharp distinction between the Gothic aesthetic, which he championed, and the Renaissance ideal that had replaced it. The location of the harborside windows reflects the shape and use of the rooms behind them. In the Renaissance, their function would have been subordinated to an overmastering taste for symmetry, and the façade, Ruskin felt, would have been regularized with little thought for the rooms inside.

The main ceremonial entrance to the palazzo was the Porta della Carta set against the south wall of San Marco at the inland end of the Piazzetta façade. The doorway was designed by the sculptors Giovanni and Bartolomeo Bon and built between 1438 and 1442. A rectangular entryway on the ground floor is crowned by a Gothic window with delicate

31

tracery and flanked by slim pinnacles inset with allegorical sculptures. (31) Above the window is a rondel with a bust of the evangelist Mark. The irregular upper frame of the structure is enriched with the same flamelike figures that crown the peaked arches of the basilica. A statue of Justice tops the work.

Immediately above the doorway, a figure in the robes and horned cap of the Doge kneels before the winged lion of St. Mark. The suppliant—Francesco Foscari, the Doge at the time of the completion of the doorway—holds a bronze standard in his hands. The lion's upraised paw rests on an open book inscribed with the words "Pax tibi Marce Evangelista meus." The original image was vandalized during the French occupation of Venice in 1797 and replaced during the nineteenth-century restoration of the palazzo. In the Middle Ages and Renaissance, many parts of the sculptural decoration of the doorway were covered with gold leaf.

The figure of the kneeling Doge is easily dismissed as political cant, but it is a surprisingly subtle and important symbol. The image represents the piety of the officeholder, of course, and the conventional obeisance of the secular state to its spiritual patron. Like much of the political iconography of Venice, the source of the image lies in the conventions of ecclesiastical art. In devotional images, living people, typically patrons, generally on their knees and frequently drawn on a smaller scale than the principal figures, express their veneration. Translated into the political realm, this liturgical commonplace becomes a symbol of the Doge's subordination not just to the evangelist but to the city he rules. The sculpture, which represents the Doge's allegiance to the Republic, is a visible image of one of the fundamental principles of the Venetian constitution. While medieval kings typically thought of the country as their own property, which they could freely dispense to subordinates in exchange for loyalty and service, Venice was independent of its ruler. Finding a common artistic formula that expressed this unusual situation was a great triumph for Venetian political art.

At the corner of the basilica nearest the Porta Della Carta is a Byzantine porphyry sculptural group of four rulers, a tetrarchy that briefly ruled the empire. (32) Made from the stone that symbolized royal birth and lineage, the images belong to the family of objects looted from Byzantium and placed on the façade of the cathedral as trophies. They also symbolize the ambition to absolute sovereignty which the Porta Della Carta so strongly but subtly counters.

32

The Porta della Carta leads through a sheltered passageway into the vast interior of the Doge's Palace. To the right is an enormous courtyard overlooked by the two tiers of open loggias and multiple windows of the palace interior. Two great well heads stand above its pavement. Directly ahead is an outside stairway that was built in the last decades of the fifteenth century and topped by massive statues of Neptune and Mars sculpted by Jacopo Sansovino a century later. The huge figures, which symbolize the naval and land-based military might of the Republic, soon earned the

33

stairway a new name, Scala dei Giganti. (33) Beneath these giant figures—and pointedly dwarfed by them—the new Doge swore to uphold the laws of the Republic and fulfill the terms of a contract called the Ducal Promise. Then the oldest councilor placed the horned hat symbolizing his office into his hands.

Both the first and second stories of the Palazzo Ducale have internal as well as external arcades that shelter long corridors. Along with the oversized courtyard, these structures must have served as gathering and waiting areas, both open and sheltered, for the nobles who assembled each week to attend meetings of the Grand Council or other deliberative bodies. (34) Minor offices were located on these subordinate floors. Sansovino designed a second internal stairway called the Scala d'Oro that leads upward to the two principal floors of the palazzo. The vaults of the stairway are covered with elaborate stucco work, much of it gilded.

The San Marco end of the first upper floor—or piano nobile—served

34

as the state apartments of the Doge. From a small anteroom at the top of the stairs, visitors entered the Sala dello Scudo, which stretches the full width of the building and overlooks both the courtyard of the palace and the canal at its back. From the center of this room, a hallway leads to six additional rooms in the ducal suite. The rooms are without furniture—furnishings were supplied by the doges and removed at their deaths. Much of the original artwork has been removed too, and pieces from other rooms in the complex take their place.

The walls of the Sala dello Scudo were decorated with a collection of world maps painted in the sixteenth century and heavily restored in the nineteenth. The Sala Grimani retains its ceiling decoration and an allegorical frieze. A number of paintings representing the lion of St. Mark are displayed in the room, among them an extraordinary image by Vittore Carpaccio painted in 1516. (35) A grinning lion with multicolored wings rests an upraised paw on an open book with the familiar inscription. From the left the shore of an island thick with fantastic weeds and dark trees recedes toward the middle ground. Framed between the foliage and the lion's head is an image of the San Marco Basin, a finely detailed drawing of the waterfront façade of the palazzo, and the domes of the basilica. The mud island probably represents the scene of Mark's prophetic dream, which is fulfilled in the background  image of contemporary Venice. Carpaccio used a trick of perspective to complete the message of his painting. The lion's front paws rest on the island; his back feet are either suspended in midair or rest on the surface of the sea. Ships in the background seem to be sheltered by his wings. In addition to showing the origins of Venice, the image represents the projection of its power over land and sea.

35

The itinerary that currently funnels visitors through the palazzo continues up the Scala d'Oro to the second piano nobile. The small atrium at
the top of the next flight of stairs (the Sala dell'Atria Quadrato) originally
held a series of paintings by Tintoretto. These have been replaced with
works from the same period. This antechamber leads to the magnificent
Sala delle Quattro Porte (Room of Four Doors). Like the Sala dello Scudo
below, which serves as the entryway to the ducal suite, this room also
runs from one side of the palace to the other. Along with many other
parts of the palazzo, this area was heavily damaged in a fire in 1574. Its
rich decoration, quickly completed after the fire, was meant to overawe
foreign dignitaries and impress them with the wealth and might of the
Republic.

The room's design is partly the work of Andrea Palladio, one of the
greatest architects of the sixteenth century. It was completed by Antonio
da Ponte, who designed the Rialto Bridge and the New Prison next to the
palace. The Roman-trained Sansovino had a hand in the design of the
ceiling, which was painted by Tintoretto. The result of this extraordinary
collaboration is a room with a unified theme and decorative scheme that
has not been dismantled or reorganized like the nearby atrium or the
rooms in the ducal suite.

The ceiling frescoes include allegories that highlight the virtues of the
Republic. This theme runs through all the art in the palace, but the
artists at work in this room expressed their ideas not through ecclesiastical references, as Carpaccio or the sculptor of the Porta della Carta did,
but in classical terms. The myths of Greece and Rome described gods
with different spheres of influence who could easily personify ideas. The

scenes on the ceiling include an image of the god Jupiter giving Venice dominion over the Adriatic Sea. A much later painting by Giambattista Tiepolo uses the same symbolic vocabulary. In this small rectangular image in gold and blue, Neptune empties a cornucopia at the feet of a reclining image of the city, who is identified by her gold crown and scepter and the figure of the lion on which she leans. The image replaced a damaged Tintoretto that had depicted Venice as the bride of Neptune and queen of the seas. Large panels on the long walls of the room show important scenes in Venetian history.

The four doors from which the room takes its name led to the meeting places of some of the most important Venetian magistracies. Benches between the doorways suggest that as impressive as the room might have been, a certain amount of tedious waiting was still unavoidable. The intimate and even more sumptuous Sala dell'Anticollegio, with its rich stuccoed ceilings and walls and its elaborate fireplace, was reserved for delegations meeting with the Collegio or signoria of Venice. Tintoretto's paintings, displaced from the room at the top of the stairs, have been repositioned here. These remarkable images include scenes representing Mercury and the Graces; Pallas Athena repulsing Mars; Bacchus and Ariadne; and the forge of Vulcan. The relationship between these wonderful paintings and the legend of the Republic is indirect, and their subjects are more complex than run-of-the-mill Venetian propaganda. Mercury typically represents eloquence; Pallas Athena, wisdom; and Vulcan, industry. Their virtues stand alone, but in the palace it is inevitable that they will be seen as attributes of the Republic.

The arc of splendor that begins in the Sala delle Quattro Porte reaches a peak in the overpowering meeting room of the Collegio. The Collegio was a composite group including the Doge, his senior counselors, judges, and the heads of key government departments. In its selected membership and broad authority it represented the state as a whole. Before the 1574 fire its meeting room had been decorated with a map of the widespread territories of the Republic. This graphic statement of political dominion was replaced in the speedy reworking of this very important room by a series of allegorical paintings that combine classical and religious imagery.

On the end wall of the room, directly above the seats of the magistrates, is Paolo Veronese's votive portrait of Doge Sebastiano Venier. Sumptuously robed in scarlet velvet, the Doge kneels on the right. His outstretched arm, cased in armor, points toward the lion of Venice. St. Catherine stretches out her hands above the lion and reaches for a chalice held by a white-robed figure on the left who represents Faith. Christ, his foot pierced by a nail hole, rests on a bank of clouds directly above the chalice. Behind and beside him, a host of saints and angels look down on the pious figures in the foreground and on the armadas engaged at the great battle of Lepanto. The painting represents the Doge's vote of thanks to Christ the Redeemer for the Republic's victory in that emblematic battle against the Turks in 1571. The remaining scenes around the walls are by Tintoretto. They include a remarkable image of a symbolic wedding between the aged Doge Francesco Donà and a youthful St. Catherine.

In one of the rectangular panels in the deeply coffered ceiling Veronese painted *Venice Enthroned with Justice and Peace*. The crowned and sceptered ermine-robed symbol of the Republic is seated under a canopy at the top of a steep stairway that calls to mind the Scala d'Oro. Justice, holding a sword and balance, climbs up from the left, while Peace, with a spray of olive in her hand, approaches from the center. Between the two figures the winged lion of St. Mark guards the stairs. The personifications hold their attributes in such a way that they blend the symbols of Justice, Peace, and Venice in one hieroglyphic emblem.

The second great doorway of the Sala delle Quattro Porte leads to the Senate chamber. Like the rooms of the Collegio, the Senate chamber is overwhelmingly sumptuous. Thick and writhing gilded stucco frames and tendrils divide the ceiling into panels, each of which is decorated with an allegorical painting. (36) Wooden benches for the senators line the walls, and paintings by Palma Giovane in gilded frames stand above them. The curious and contradictory scene on the end wall of the room by Tintoretto and his assistants represents offi

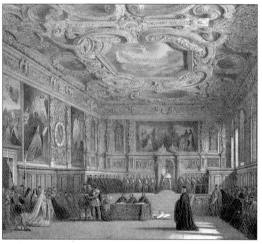

36

cial piety at its most leaden. At the center of the composition, angels on a dark cloudbank hold up the body of the dead Christ. Surrounded by a company of saints, two doges—a historical impossibility—adore the apparition. Kneeling in their gold-brocaded robes of state, draped with ermine, and staring out of the picture frame, the two symmetrical dwarfish figures refuse to accommodate themselves to the rhythm of the composition. The redeeming feature of the picture is the wonderful aerial view of the city in the background.

The third doorway leads through an L-shaped antechamber to the meeting room of the Council of Ten (Sala del Consiglio dei Dieci). A single event led the Grand Council to establish this group as a special select committee charged with the security of the Republic. "In 1310, on the eve of San Vitale, Sier Baiamonte Tiepolo, son of the late Lorenzo Tiepolo who had been Doge, and his wife the princess of Rascia, along with the majority of the Querini family and some of the Barozzi, brought together a large part of the population. Having taken an oath to seize the government of Venice and its territories, they ran through the city with their banners waving. They seized control of the Rialto and the surrounding area and began marching toward the Piazza. The Doge and many nobles along with a great number of citizens ran to the Palazzo to defend the Piazza.

"They held off the attack and during the night they had the good fortune to experience a violent rainfall and heavy winds. So that, as it pleased God and the Evangelist, the rebels could do nothing. Many of the rebels were killed or banished; others were executed or condemned to life in prison. The majority of the Querini and the Tiepolo had their houses destroyed and their property seized. The principal house of the Querini, located in the Rialto, was torn down and the property became the site of the butcher's market" (*Codex Morosini,* 70A).

The ad hoc committee that was established in the aftermath of this political emergency met for 145 years before it became a permanent magistracy. The Ten (often referred to by the Roman numeral X) were a powerful and, to most minds, sinister institution with virtually unlimited authority to punish if necessary and to preclude if possible any threat to the security of the state. Their work involved espionage and counterespionage, domestic surveillance, and provocation. The Ten invited and received secret denunciations. They had the full power of the law at their command, but they were always prepared to deal in unusual and unofficial ways with their subjects of interest. Torture was part of the normal judicial process in all Venetian courts, so its use did not distinguish the Ten. Executions were a different matter. Public mutilation and execution were the norm, but in cases where the people's sympathies were unclear, the Ten might order the condemned to be drowned silently at night.

Finding just the right images to decorate the meeting place for this mysterious and legendary committee seems a daunting task. Despite the secrecy of their methods, however, the Ten, like all Venetian magistracies, had a clear sense of the epochal importance and unimpeachable rightness of what they did. The ceiling of their meeting room reflects this self-assurance in a series of early paintings by Veronese and Battista Zelotti, who were both young men in the workshop of Giambattista Ponchino when the room was decorated in the mid-sixteenth century. The centerpiece of the ceiling was a painting of Jove striking down the vices. The original was removed by French troops in 1797 and never returned to Venice. A copy now hangs in its place. At about the same time the benches on which the Ten had sat were destroyed. Given the hatred the legendary group inspired, especially in Romantic mythologizing, it is surprising that no further damage was done.

One of the long paintings on the walls seems out of character with the rest of the room. The crowded, busy scene represents *The Adoration of the Magi.* The king who kneels before the infant Christ wears gold brocade and ermine, like the crouching doges in the Senate picture, and perhaps this is meant to be understood as a devotional image of the same kind. Given the reputation of the Ten, however, the Slaughter of the Innocents would seem more apt.

The ceremonial entrance to the meeting room of the Ten opened from the Sala delle Quattro Porte, which was reached by the Scala d'Oro. But those summoned before the magistrates, or before any of the other courts that were held in nearby rooms, entered through the more mundane Scala dei Censori. The most unlucky of them sat in the subdued though richly decorated Sala della Bussola and thought about their sins. The bussola from which the room takes its name is a protruding boothlike entryway crowned with an image of Justice in one corner of the room. Staring at its tight-seamed and windowless door, which might open at any instant or not at all, it is hard not to think of Kafka's Joseph K. Behind that doorway were the meeting rooms of the three heads of the Ten and the small chamber of the state inquisitors. The Ten shared a wing of the palace with the criminal courts, the infamous palace jail cells, and the city torture chamber. The attic cells, called piombi, and the interrogation chamber, with its nasty rope for stringing up and dropping the unforthcoming, are shown on guided tours. The New Prison and a large collection of arms and armor are part of the regular itinerary.

The Sala del Maggior Consiglio (Room of the Grand Council) is the largest meeting room in the palace. A giant space, it is surprisingly well lit by windows on three sides. Ravaged in the fire of 1574, the room was rebuilt in the same style and period as the Senate and Collegio. In the cornice are imagined portraits of the doges of Venice by Tintoretto's son Domenico. Marin Falier, who was deposed and beheaded in 1355, is represented by a black curtain and a brief statement of his fate. The vast ceiling is hatched with swirling gilt-framed panels that enclose thirty-five allegorical and historical paintings.

Veronese's oval image of *The Triumph of Venice* is a trompe l'oeil invention in which we seem to be looking through the ceiling of the room into a vast open-air architectural space beyond. Horsemen crowd the base of a balustrade where great serpentine columns lift a huge entablature toward the sky. Queen Venice, resting on a cloud and surrounded by the ancient gods, receives the crown of victory from an angelic figure hovering in the air in front and above her. (37)

In a similar though less vertiginous composition by Palma Giovane, Venice is crowned queen of her client cities. The coronation takes place under a huge canopy of red velvet imprinted with images of seraphim and a very unusual picture of the lion of St. Mark with wings outspread. Soldiers under the banner of the Republic lead captives to the foot of the throne, where they sit or sprawl half-naked, shackled, and abject. If

37

Venice appears as a smug dominatrix in this image, her self-presentation in the great painting on the end wall of the chamber is even more audacious. The enormous painting representing Paradise clearly aims to equate the nobility of Venice assembled in the Maggior Consiglio with the elect assembled on swirling bands of cloud in the Empyrean. While a comparison between the church hierarchy and the hierarchy of angels was relatively common in the Middle Ages, the pairing of laypeople and the assembly of the blessed was not.

A massive composition, *The Battle of Lepanto* by Andrea Vicentino, decorates the walls of the adjacent Sala dello Scrutinio. The canvas is so thronged with scurrying figures that the sea seems to be a pavement. The great galleys of the Venetian and Turkish fleets are hardly big enough to hold the crowds that swarm over their decks. Scrutinio, from which we get our word scrutiny, means "voting," a matter that in the vast and disorderly Grand Council was extraordinarily complicated. Yes and no votes were registered with black and white balls that were dropped into urns passed among the council members by specially chosen young noblemen. Balloting seems always to have inspired unease and concern among the nobles, and the variety of schemes created over the centuries to guard against multiple votes, displays of partisanship, and other forms of fraud reveals both the perverse ingenuity and pervasive suspicion that marked all the ministries of the Republic.

The Palazzo Ducale represents the highest degree of collaboration that the medieval nobility of Europe ever achieved. The Grand Council was unrivaled in size and power by any other body in Europe. The complex Venetian judiciary system and the executive they elected for a life term

were all distinctive, and they all worked well. Despite their success, the
Venetians were driven by fear of tyranny on the one hand and malfea-
sance on the other to concoct a maze of overlapping magistracies with
competing responsibilities and authorities. The Collegio, Senate, and
Maggior Consiglio all did more or less the same thing. The Collegio and
Senate also carried out some of the same diplomatic duties as the Doge.
The criminal courts overlapped among themselves, and the Council of
Ten passed judgments without any thought of jurisdiction. The Ten also
spied on legislators and tried to police the conduct of officeholders.
Secret denunciations were invited not only for those who threatened the
security of the state but also for those who concealed tax revenues or
conspired to understate tariffs. The walls of the Palazzo Ducale are covered with square stones whose mouth-shaped slots accepted secret
denunciations directed to virtually any magistracy.

The maze of overlapping duties and responsibilities stemmed in part
from the lack of a written constitution. It was exacerbated by the legisla-
ture's habit of enacting new laws without repealing or even consulting
those already on the books. The Republic's lawyers did their best to
organize the statutes, but they had no power to erase contradictory laws.
The tangled web of Venetian government was more than a matter of iner-
tia; it evidently responded to a deep need to forestall the chicanery of
others. The sculptures on the rooftops of the Palazzo Ducale may have
represented impersonal Justice, but human behavior as the councilors
expected to experience it corresponded more typically to the conduct of
Adam and Eve or the drunken Noah represented on the building's corners. The framers of the American Constitution took note of this under-

current of distrust and institutionalized it in a slightly skewed separation of powers. Each branch of the U.S. government is secure in its core responsibilities but in constant competition with other branches on the fringes of its authority. Competition among the branches of government, the framers hoped, would prevent their collaboration and forestall tyranny.

Outside the magistracies and the assemblies of the Republican government, cooperation among the merchant nobles was limited. Their families and companies commanded lifelong loyalty and service. In most cases the two overlapped, and traditional Venetian households evolved to accommodate both family life and trade in the same building. Original Venice, that scattering of small and undifferentiated islands, was gradually built over with houses that reflected the islands in their own self-sufficiency. Many centuries after the Lagoon was filled in and buildings crowded closer and closer together, households retained their primitive autonomy.

Venice began at the water's edge. Buildings faced the water; and boats, as they had been in Cassiodorus' day, were tied up at every house-front. Waterfront properties might extend quite deeply into an island center, and their back portions were often covered with gardens and orchards. But once the perimeter of an island was completely built up, development continued in the interior as well. Former back lots were sold at great profit, and most were soon thickly covered with buildings serving every purpose of urban life. Interior areas near churches remained open partly to accommodate burials and partly to serve as the neighborhood piazza, which Venetians call a campo. Some interior areas were served by one or more small canals; others were accessible only by a very late development in Venetian urbanism, streets. Gardens and orchards displaced by urbanization moved to the city's expanding perimeter, where in a few generations, as development caught up, they would be uprooted yet again and moved farther out.

San Marco and the Palazzo Ducale were first steps in organizing the settled archipelagoes of primitive Venice into a city. Two other centers worked to draw these island communities into coherence. The first of these was a natural feature, and the second drew life from it. The strategic sense that led the first Doge to build his fortress at St. Mark's was echoed in the decisions of hundreds of merchant families to build their houses along the inland waterway that over time became the Grand Canal. (Map 3) The abundance of heavy silt that had accumulated near the channel's edges provided a place to anchor buildings, and prudent merchants built their warehouses and homes along this meandering working harbor. Gradually, the banks evolved into an urban strip, and the waterway itself into the emerging city's principal avenue.

The second structure was an organized marketplace. Located at a steep bend in the Grand Canal, the marketplace at first supplemented the trade conducted in every merchant household, but gradually it centralized trade and brought it under government control. After San Marco, the Rialto market is today the best known of Venetian landmarks, but it was not the earliest market in Venice. The first commercial center grew up on the other side of the canal in the Campo San Bartolomeo. The church from which the campo takes its name was built in 1170 on the site of a ninth-century church dedicated to the Greek saint Demetrius.

This structure in its turn was almost completely demolished during a comprehensive remodeling that began in the eighteenth century.

The building most representative of the market and its activities stands slightly off the campo. The Fontego or Fondaco dei Tedeschi was the Venetian headquarters of the large and fluid trading community from Germany, Austria, and Eastern Europe whom the Venetians lumped together under the name Tedeschi (Teutons). With façades on both the

Grand Canal and the land side, this structure was accessible from either direction. The canal-side façade was designed for boat access. Five semicircular arches form an open arcade in the center of its ground floor. (38) Behind a shallow porch a wide double door opens on a central courtyard. The façade at

38

either side of the central arcade projects slightly and gives the building a hint of a tripartite structure that is found in many buildings of this type. The upper stories of the building are lit by double windows, arched on the second floor and square above. Part of a Renaissance rebuilding, these upper windows certainly differ from the original lighting of the structure in form and probably in placement. Heavy but purely ornamental crenellations mark the roofline. Small square towers at each corner were removed in the nineteenth century.

The interior of the building was organized around a single open courtyard the width of the external porch and supported in its ground story on five wide arches. Three superimposed arcades proportionate to the window system of the exterior reach to the roof. It is unclear what relationship these harmonious arcades bear to the medieval originals they replaced. Merchandise distributed through the central courtyard could be stored in warehouse spaces on its perimeter. Rooms opening from the upper arcades served as offices and temporary residences for northern traders. As many as two hundred people could be housed at a time. More than twenty individual shops were located on the three inland sides of the building.

With its interior courtyard glassed over, the Fondaco now serves as the central post office of Venice. Despite the many changes the building has undergone in its centuries of use, its form reflects the basic vocabulary of medieval Venetian commercial buildings. Though of very wide application, this vocabulary is quite restricted. Its main parts are a central ground-floor arcade open to the water that communicates with a central court and ground-floor storage to either side. This internal division into three areas is usually reflected in a three-part division of the building façade (left, center, and right).

There is considerable speculation about the origin of structures of this kind, of which there were many examples in Venice. Some were simple warehouses where a single product like grain or salt would be stored. Many, like the Fondaco dei Tedeschi, served a national or regional trading community. The khan or caravanserai in Muslim trading cities was a similar structure serving similar needs, and some historians have assumed that traders familiar with these structures in North Africa and the

39

Middle East brought the idea to Venice. One of the great commercial monuments of Venice, the Fondaco dei Turchi shares many of these characteristics. Unfortunately, the striking building that stands today on the Grand Canal, just across from the San Marcuola vaporetto stop, is an archaeologist's and restorer's conception of a structure that was already falling into ruin in the eighteenth century. (39) Unlike the Fondaco dei Tedeschi, this massive structure was originally designed as a home for the Pesaro family. Its grand proportions prompted the Republic to buy it and offer it as a gift to the Este dynasty of Ferrara in gratitude for their support during the War of Chioggia with Genoa in the fourteenth century. In the years following, whenever the Este family sided with the enemies of Venice, the government seized the palace; when the Estes returned to the fold, they got their palace back. This give and take went on for nearly three hundred years.

In the seventeenth century the Republic decided to use the building for another purpose entirely. Muslim merchants from the Ottoman Empire posed particular problems for a Christian state. People suspected them of intrigue, sedition, and unprincipled acts. These suspicions made them likely objects not just of prejudice but of open violence. Abuse of his subjects always made the Turkish sultan—a sullen trade partner at best—exceptionally aggressive. To protect the Turkish merchant community and to keep it under surveillance at the same time, the Republic decided to create a fondaco for them, just as it had done for the Germans.

The ground-floor colonnade of the Fondaco dei Turchi has ten open bays and enclosed spaces to either side. (40) These enclosures each have three windows whose arched tops carry the rhythm of the arcade across the whole façade. A pair of square towers spring from these enclosed areas and give the building a clear three-part structure. The second story differs radically from that in the Fondaco dei Tedeschi. Rather than a series of modest windows, the second story here is an arcade with narrower arches than those below. The towers have a third story with five openings grouped in an even tighter arcade. Both the height of the tower rooms and the window arrangement are conjectures of nineteenth-century restorers. The roof is decorated with idealized triangular crenellations designed by restorers on

40

the basis of fragments found on the site. The towers, combined with the crenellations, give the structure a sense of power and menace that is common in medieval buildings throughout Europe but unusual in Venice.

Next door to the Fondaco dei Turchi stands the Fondaco del Megio. This unadorned blocklike structure with its scattering of small square windows served as a warehouse pure and simple. Like Joseph who guarded against years of famine by storing grain, the Venetian Republic provided for the welfare of its citizens during years of shortage or famine.

An image of the lion of the Republic and the signature crenellations identify this structure as a state building. Its prominent position on the Grand Canal seems to contradict its humble function. But in fact, the state took enormous pride in the efforts it made to nourish and protect

41

its citizens, and it was not shy about advertising its prudence and munificence in this highly visible, if utilitarian, building. (41)

The architectural vocabulary of the Fondaco dei Turchi can be seen in a structure of a different, though related, kind and in a different environment on the Campo San Bartolomeo itself. The fourteenth-century Ca' Moro at San Bartolomeo, also known as the Palazzo Moro, is one of the earliest surviving structures on the campo. Ca' (short for casata or casada) signifies both house and household; traditionally Venetians referred to the palaces of the nobility by this simple name and applied the title palazzo only to the official residence of the Doge. Though Ca' Moro looks out over land rather than water and its occupants were a noble family rather than a company of traders, its form and function were similar to those of the Fondaco dei Tedeschi.

A building of this kind typically combined the operations of a household with those of a dock and warehouse. Because of this fusion, it is known as a casa fondaco, a house-warehouse. Ca' Moro shares with the Fondaco dei Tedeschi an adaptation of the ground floor to commercial use, a tripartite division of each floor in the façade, and a corresponding three-part division within. In Ca' Moro the ground floor is occupied by shops much like those on the landward sides of the Fondaco. The mezzanine windows above the square shop fronts and the arched windows directly above those suggest that this whole lower zone was redesigned in the Renaissance. But as is often the case in Venice, this change of style does not reflect a change of function.

The elegant opening on the building's third floor has no parallel in the Fondaco dei Tedeschi. Six stilted arches with cusps at their peaks are supported on two pilasters and six marble columns with classical capitals; heavily incised marble panels create a balustrade. Behind the arcade, a series of glazed windows light an elegant interior room called the portego, a Venetian dialect word for portico. Wherever they occur, these forms mark the piano nobile of the house—the main floor that was designed for use by the noble family. (42) The portego is flanked to either side with private rooms and apartments. Servants were sometimes housed in small rooms on the floor or floors above

42

the piano nobile, but more commonly they lived in rooms at the inland end of the house. On the fourth floor of Ca' Moro, square windows with uniform marble frames probably date to a much later period.

In his description of the buildings of Venice, the sixteenth-century writer Francesco Sansovino, son of the famous architect, summarized the development of the casa fondaco. "Long ago the Venetians arranged their

43

rooms in a cross or T-shape which made their buildings clumsy, but once this habit was corrected, the rooms were arranged in line from one side of the building to the other. The primary windows and the doors followed this pattern, as did the windows of rooms alongside the portego. With all the openings proportionate to their dimensions, the rooms are unobstructed and flooded with light, and the eye, turned momentarily from the view outside, can take them all in at once. It should also be noted that all the windows are glazed not with panels of waxed fabric or paper but with the clearest and finest glass panes framed in wood or lead and closed with iron hardware. This is true not just of the palaces but of every building, no matter how insignificant. This always amazes foreigners, who realize through the omnipresence of these window panes the extraordinary productivity of the glass furnaces of Murano" (*Venezia, Città Nobilissima,* p. 384).

A short distance up the Grand Canal from the Fondaco dei Tedeschi (and on the same side) stands another early casa fondaco, the Ca' da Mosto. (43) Built in the thirteenth or fourteenth century, this house was expanded by the addition of two upper stories in a much later period. The two lower floors have many of the same features found in Ca' Moro. The ground floor retains three asymmetrical arches of its original water-level arcade. The piano nobile has six elongated arches carried on four

matched marble columns and one square-cut pillar. The three-part vertical division of the façade (which is marred by the closing of the arcade
and the opening of a low arched doorway on the ground floor) is carried
on not only in the original piano nobile but in the later addition on the
third floor.

Between the Ca' da Mosto and the Fondaco dei Tedeschi, and almost
hidden from the Grand Canal, stands the Ca' Lion-Morosini. This diminu-
tive and reclusive building is one of the very few remaining examples of
what, for the Venetian casa fondaco, signals the road
not taken. The house is set back from the water's
edge on an open space that is too small to be called
a campo and is named instead the Campiello San
Remer. (44) Though the space is now public, it originally belonged to the house. At the back of this
courtyard, wide arcades open into the typical commercial space, but these arcades are not flush with
the façade. Instead, they carry a staircase that begins
at the front edge of the courtyard, then turns at right
angles to cross the front of the building. Stilted
arches with pointed summits define the piano nobile,
but the monumental entryway on this floor is unique.

44

Some architectural historians see in this house and the few others like
it a link with a European building tradition that mutated in Venice into a
distinct local style. The Romans developed a structure with a two-story
arcade on its long side; the arcade, which was reached by an outdoor
stair, looked over a courtyard. In their vocabulary of building types, this

was a palatium, a palace for housing emperors and kings. Europeans extended the range of this prestigious building type by adapting it first to political leaders at all levels and then to wealthy burghers. When this style reached Venice, it ran up against very unusual demands. Since canal access was more important than land access, frontage on the water was scarce and expensive. These twin pressures, according to some historians, prompted Venetians to place the ceremonial façade on the short side of the building and to move the courtyard and stairs to the rear, where space was abundant. For other architectural historians, however, the Venetian casa fondaco is decidedly non-Western. They trace its origins

to Byzantine or Islamic traditions. After nearly two centuries of debate, the argument remains unsettled.

Two magnificent examples of the Venetian casa fondaco of the early Middle Ages stand side by side on a length of the Grand Canal called the Riva del Carbon

45

(just across from the San Silvestro vaporetto stop). (45) Ca' Dandolo-Farsetti, on the right, was built around the year 1200. It belonged for many centuries to the extended family of Doge Andrea Dandolo, a distant relative of Doge Enrico Dandolo, who led the Fourth Crusade. Two other members of the Dandolo clan became doges before the palace passed to the Farsetti family in the seventeenth century. The first two stories correspond most closely to the original design of the house. The third story was added in the Renaissance, the fourth in the nineteenth century.

At first glance, the two lower stories read as superimposed arcades running the full width of the building. On the ground floor, pillars support arches with rounded tops and straight extensions at their sides, and on the second floor sixteen pairs of slim columns support a long arcade of arches. But the extra-wide pillars dividing the central five bays of the ground floor from the two bays to either side create the familiar three-part division. This is carried into the second floor, where smaller arcades of four bays frame seven wider central openings.

By the early nineteenth century, Ca' Dandolo-Farsetti, like the majority of buildings on the Grand Canal, had lost its purpose. Outrageously expensive to maintain and utterly unproductive, these outmoded structures slid into decay. Tourism reversed this decline, and the palace, like many others, became a hotel. In 1826 it was bought by the municipality. Extensive remodeling restored it to the dignity and grandeur it had known in the early eighteenth century. It is now home to the city government of Venice, a function it shares with the Ca' Corner-Loredan next door.

The history of ownership of Ca' Corner-Loredan is even more complex than that of its neighbor. Built for the Boccasi family in the early thirteenth century, it quickly passed to the Zane family and then the Corner. By the late fourteenth century, this family, with extensive trading partnerships throughout the Middle East, had become one of the wealthiest in Venice. In 1366 the king of Cyprus came to Venice looking for money to pay his troops. He was a guest in this house and through his host's good offices obtained the loans he needed. In exchange, his majesty granted the Corner family a fief in Cyprus and a tax-free monopoly on the island's sugar production and refining industry. The family invested heavily and worked to simplify and systematize the refining process. Other loans to princes led to similar results: royal guests in the house, grants of nobility, and lucrative trade agreements. The palazzo eventually passed to the Loredan family through marriage. By 1806 it shared its neighbor's fate and served as a hotel. It was bought by the city in 1864.

The magnificent façade on the first two floors is one of the finest examples of the pre-Gothic style in Venetian buildings. The ground floor has a central arcade of stilted arches, each surrounded by a double braid of worked stone and supported by four magnificent classical columns with Corinthian capitals. The bays to either side carry on the rhythm of the arcade in the details of their tall windows. The long arcade on the second floor is supported on a very impressive collection of matched antique columns with a variety of classical and Byzantine capitals. Double columns divide the central space of seven bays from three bays to either side. Above the arches, matched marble panels and round bosses alternate with sculpted figures and heraldic shields.

Columns, capitals, and marble panels can be found on other noble houses of the period; they reflect the wealth that could be accumulated, especially in the kind of trade and banking that the Corners specialized in. Sansovino described it well: "As for the ornaments, the ceilings and the other incredible riches of the houses of the nobles, the citizens, and the people in general, it is almost impossible to imagine them, let alone describe them. And that only stands to reason, because a thousand years have passed since the founding of the Republic, and during that time they have never been touched by the rapacious hands of an enemy. For centuries the Venetians have been engaged in trade, and continually bringing home the resources of the many cities ravaged by barbarians

and abandoned . . . Remember too that these noble households, enriched
for centuries through the possession of political offices and long-term
trade, have steadily increased their wealth. And even though the men of
the past were very parsimonious, they were open-handed in the outfitting
of splendid houses" (*Venezia, Città Nobilissima,* p. 384).

The particular ornaments displayed on the façade of Ca' Corner-
Loredan recall those on the façade of San Marco. On Ca' Corner, spolia
from the East would seem to assert a private and material conquest that
is quite distinct from the public, spiritual triumph that the same elements declare on the church front. But this bold, even hazardous declaration is overwhelmed by the stylistic parallels between the two. The decorations of the house suggest that it, like the martyr's shrine, shares in
the general work of conquest. The house and the church, in their own
different ways, carry on the same enterprise, and the visible parallels in
style are a mark of conformity, not rivalry.

The earliest Venetian houses were probably made of wood, and wood
still plays a significant if hidden role in many houses that survive. Wood
supports for floors and roofs are as common in Venice as they are elsewhere, but throughout the Lagoon wood forms the underpinning for every
kind of structure. "Because of the unstable soil which is not solid anywhere, the foundations of every building are made of extremely strong
pilings of oak which last forever underwater. These piles are driven into
the earth and then anchored with cross braces; the area between the
piles is filled in with cement and rubble. Once the cement sets up, the
foundations become so solid and stable that they can support any kind of
structure no matter how high or heavy; it will never move a hair's breadth
out of plumb.

"The bricks and the mortar are brought from the area of Padua, Treviso, or Ferrara, but those from Padua are the most prized because they are more seasoned and better fired, and also because their tiles, bricks and pavers are better proportioned than the others. One boat with two rowers at most is able to carry the material for the construction of any large building. Sand comes from the Brenta River valley or from the Lido, but the sand from freshwater is better. Wood floated down the rivers in rafts comes to the city in great abundance from the mountains of Cadore, the Friuli, and Treviso. Ironwork comes from Brescia and various other towns in Lombardy.

"But a beautiful and marvelous thing is the raw stone that is imported from the towns of Rovigno and Brionis on the Dalmatian coast. This stone is white in color and similar to marble, but so solid and strong that it is extremely durable both in sunlight and extreme cold. If it is highly polished, statues can be made from it that have the appearance of marble. Entire churches and palaces are faced with this stone, with columns as thick and long as desired because the quarries of Rovigno abound in this material, which is called Istrian stone" (*Venezia, Città Nobilissima,* pp. 382–383).

The structural principles that Sansovino described in the mid-sixteenth century were already ancient ones. As he noted, the first requirement for almost every site was secure pilings. These were first thoroughly soaked in water; then men wielding huge mallets pounded them into the loose soil. Not every wall in a structure was supported on pilings. Exterior walls in general, especially walls or foundations fronting on a canal, required support. Interior walls did not always have pilings; they rested on the consolidated cement and rubble foundations that Sansovino described. Over time these interior walls tended to sink more than those outside, and buildings found their stable equilibrium by leaning in on themselves.

What Sansovino describes as cross-bracing for the pilings is more typically a horizontal superstructure called a zatterone—a raft—that acts as a broad footing to transfer the weight of the walls to the pilings. The walls themselves were built of wide flat bricks. Exterior walls usually had a course or two of impermeable Istrian stone laid in to prevent the movement of water through capillary action from the wet foundations upward into the walls. Because it is waterproof, Istrian stone was also used on surfaces exposed to waves. The widespread ornamental use Sansovino described came later.

The ground plan of a typical casa fondaco reflected the three-part division of each floor of the façade. Two main interior walls perpendicular to the façade stretched the length of the house. Since frontage was in great demand, buildings, especially those on the Grand Canal, tended to be much deeper than they were wide. The two-story structures that may have been the norm in the earliest period were expanded upward by the addition of third and fourth stories. The façades of these additions were commonly built in styles that contrasted with those below.

Because façades were placed on the narrow end of buildings and because their foundations were more subject to erosion from the flowing waters of the canal, they were often only loosely attached to the structures behind them. Joists and rafters carried the weight of roofs and floors to the long sides and interior walls of the building. Façades did lit-

46

tle structural work; so rather than being tied into the masonry of these bearing walls, they were often loosely linked by brackets. Settling in the façade had little effect on the building behind it. Because of this structural independence, it was a relatively simple matter to change the look of a building without altering the foundations of its main bearing walls.

In many houses, façades in the Gothic style replaced the stilted arches and ornamental braidwork that distinguished the earliest Venetian houses. When the Gothic style grew old and lost its charm, the same buildings could be refaced in a Renaissance, Baroque, or Neoclassical fashion. Writing in the sixteenth century, Sebastiano Serlio, a well-known architect and theorist, advised: "If a citizen should happen to own a house that is comfortable and also sound, the façade of which is ornamented but not in that style which conforms to good architectural principles—the most common error in such situations is that the entrance is not in the middle as it should be and that the windows are irregular—now this citizen, in order not to appear inferior to his neighbors, who are building their own houses in good order or at least symmetrically, will want at the very least to replace the façade of his house and do it with the least possible inconvenience and expense" (*Architettura e Prospettiva,* p. 169).

The most beautiful Gothic palace of Venice is the celebrated Ca' d'Oro (Golden House). (46) Like many early Venetian palaces, it began life at an indefinite period and in a form that is now hard to identify. What can be seen today is work done in two very distinct campaigns. The structure first took on its present form during a prolonged if single-minded renovation that began before 1420 and continued for another fifteen years. The patron was Marino Contarini, whose father was a procurator of San Marco, one of the small group of men who managed the accumulated wealth of the basilica. Many of the building records survive, and so we know that Contarini hired sculptors, painters, gilders, and designers from Venice as well as others from Lombardy and France. These included the most famous of Gothic sculptors working in Venice at the time, Giovanni and Bartolomeo Bon.

Over the centuries, as the Contarini family multiplied and ramified, the building was parceled out among crowds of heirs, and its various floors were fractioned into increasingly tiny apartments. By the end of the eighteenth century, parts of the Ca' d'Oro were falling in, and through the first half of the nineteenth century the building was little more than a haunted house. In 1846 the property was sold to the Russian prince Alexander Troubetzkoy, who gave the house to Maria Taglioni, a prima ballerina and collector not only of royal admirers but of houses on the Grand Canal. At that time she owned four. Taglioni passed the Ca' d'Oro on to her daughter and hired an engineer to begin renovations. The engineer, Giambattista Meduna, worked with a very heavy hand. He ripped out walls and floors, removed architectural ornamentation, and sold off parts of the original decoration that did not appeal to him.

Writing in 1853, John Ruskin described the Ca' d'Oro as "a noble pile of very quaint Gothic, one superb in general effect, but now destroyed by restorations. I saw the beautiful slabs of red marble, which formed the bases of its balconies and were carved into noble spiral mouldings of strange sections, half a foot deep, dashed to pieces when I was last in Venice; its glorious interior staircase, by far the most interesting Gothic monument of the kind in Venice, had been carried away, piece by piece and sold for waste marble, two years before" (*Stones of Venice* 3.303). At the end of the nineteenth century, the palace, structurally sound but ravaged historically and aesthetically, was sold to Baron Giorgio Franchetti, a wealthy banker who dedicated the rest of his life to canceling out Meduna's work. In 1922 the house and the baron's extensive art collection were deeded to the city of Venice.

The façade on the Grand Canal combines familiar elements in an unfamiliar way. The arcade on the ground floor, with two smaller arches flanking a larger central one, echoes those in houses as ancient as Ca' da Mosto. The arcades on the two floors above are also traditional, as is the crenellation, though roof ornament of this kind is rare in a private house. What distinguishes the Ca' d'Oro from more typical Venetian houses of its period is the richness of decoration, the unity of the overall design, and the asymmetry of the façade.

Faced entirely in delicately worked Istrian stone, the façade is divided into two distinct parts. Both the symmetry and the three-part division of the typical Venetian façade cancel or at least disguise the polarity between types of interior space that this façade declares. One side is a screen of superimposed arcades that opens the house to the city. Behind it are the public and ceremonial areas of the house. The other side of the building, defined by expanses of blank wall with small square windows, seems private and enclosed. It is hard to avoid the thought that gender plays a role in this dichotomy. Women and children participated in the public ceremonies that are represented in the mosaics of San Marco, but men dominated political and commercial life in Venice, and women were confined and sequestered to a degree that was uncommon even by medieval standards.

The Ca' d'Oro is not divided equally. The actual centerline of the façade runs through the first column on the right side of the ground floor arcade and along the inner edge of the arcades on each of the upper two floors. Yet the windows to the right of this line are clearly part of the openwork façade. These windows are echoed at each edge of the enclosed façade, and this repetition helps to bind the two sides together visually. The ground-floor arcade is composed of four narrow arches that flank a wider central one. The stilted arches of the Byzantine style have been replaced here with groined Gothic arches, but the braidlike decorative stonework surrounding the arches and the pateras or bosses set above them are also found on much earlier houses and may have belonged to the previous structure on the site. The arcades on the upper floors, by contrast, have no parallel outside the vocabulary of Gothic ornament.

Springing from two pilasters and supported on five columns, a complex tracery of stone distinguishes the first story. The lowest area of the tracery is a series of trilobite arches, with frames that are steep and doubly curved and inner circumferences lightly marked with the outline of three partly overlapping circles. In the open areas between each of these adjacent arches, the stone tracery outlines four-lobed openings. The tracery comes to a point above each of these openings to form small trilobite spaces. This motif is found on the façade of San Marco and in its most magnificent form in the arcades that support the Palazzo Ducale. Its quotation here, and in other Venetian Gothic palaces, links this private building to the defining public structures of the city.

The arcaded opening on the floor above is a more compact and delicate version of the one below. Five shorter columns and two pilasters support six trilobite arches that terminate in a much simpler and more distinctly geometrical tracery above. Each column supports a kitelike frame with in-curved sides and thornlike cusps inside and out. Those on the outside define the lobes of the main arches; those on the inside create a negative space like four petals of a flower.

The more enclosed section of the house has its own three-part structure. Superimposed Gothic windows outline a center area of three stacked squares. On the ground floor, the square is defined only by the frames of the flanking windows. In the two upper stories, the squares are set off from the windows by moldings composed of an outer braiding and a recessed organic border. Inside each of the squares is a small rectangular window framed in a similar way. There is probably no more dogmatic statement of privacy and seclusion, even sequestration, to be found in any Venetian private house.

Gothic windows light each story and provide both vertical distinction and horizontal continuity for the two zones of the façade. Both corners of the building are edged by thin serpentine pilasters, and a frieze of pen-

sile arches below the roof supports a ropelike cornice. Elaborate crenellations crown the roofline.

The courtyard of the Ca' d'Oro is simpler and less adorned than the
building's magnificent façade, but it is elegant and beautiful. Its center
is an open brick terrace edged on two sides by rows of widely spaced
columns. An angled stairway by Matteo Raverti supported on arches of
increasing size leads up from the courtyard to a door on the first floor. (47)
On the same story, a portego of five arches outlined in Istrian stone and
decorated with bosses identifies the piano nobile. With the exception of a
few inset stones, the Gothic window frames, and
balcony, the interior façade is spare. Its brick surface and the asymmetrical arrangement of its
openings contrast strongly with the canal façade
and mark this space as primarily domestic. The
ensemble of courtyard, stairway, entryway, and
arcade recalls the façade of Ca' Lion-Morosini.
But in Ca' d'Oro these structures have found their
place *inside* the house rather than on its façade.
In this position, the courtyard helps to light the
interior of these typically deep, narrow Venetian
buildings.

Wide, sheltered spaces behind the colonnade
on the ground floor now house classical sculptures

47

from the Franchetti collection. While these spaces certainly descend from
ground-floor areas used for commercial storage in the traditional casa
fondaco, their elaborate mosaic tiling suggests that lighter traffic was

expected. These spaces may have sheltered eating or dining areas. The centerpiece of the courtyard is a wellhead of carved Istrian stone, the work of Bartolomeo Bon, who received the enormous sum of twenty ducats for his work. Salinity in the estuary varies with the tides, but Venice is so near the sea that its waters are always brackish. There are no freshwater streams, rivers, or perennial springs, and the ground is infiltrated with saltwater. Rainwater is the only local source of drinking water, and the so-called wells of Venice are actually cisterns connected to elaborate collecting networks.

"There are channels or gutters of carved stone at the edges of the roofs to collect the rainwater. Water collected there runs through hidden pipes into the cisterns, where it is purged of its impurities and becomes suitable for drinking . . . The water from these cisterns is healthier and more palatable than the waters of the Lagoon. The city is very well provided with these wells or cisterns, both public and private. Every piazza or campo or courtyard has its well for the most part provided by the city on one or another occasion. During the administration of Doge Foscari, for example, there was a year in which almost no rain fell between November and the following February. The Republic had thirty new wells dug, which they filled with water brought over in ships from the River Brenta" (*Venezia, Città Nobilissima,* p. 382).

As Sansovino describes, the cistern at the center of the open courtyard holds water collected from the roof of the palazzo and its courtyard. The collected water is not piped directly to the slim open chamber beneath the wellhead but is filtered through layers of fine white sand buried under the courtyard. To prevent brackish groundwater from working its way by capillary action into the well, the pit that holds the sand is lined with bricks and sealed with impermeable clay.

Palazzo Pisani-Moretta, near the San Angelo vaporetto stop, incorporates many of the same elements that distinguish the Ca' d'Oro. (48) The façade is built around two superimposed arcades, with Gothic windows and balconies to left and right. But in this case the arrangement is symmetrical and divided into three parts in the typical fashion. The decorative stone openings are set into a brick façade with stucco facing. Twin watergates with cusped arches above

48

them replace the ground-floor arcade. Like the Ca' d'Oro, Palazzo Pisani-Moretta has a monumental portego on each of its upper floors. This, coupled with the symmetrical watergates below, suggests that the house may have been built for two noble families, rather than just one.

The lower of the two arcades combines cusped arches supported on freestanding columns with four-lobed openings above, a motif shared with the Ca' d'Oro but derived from the colonnade of the Palazzo Ducale. This ensemble is repeated in a slightly different form in the portego above. There, some of the light-handed draftsmanship in stone that is displayed in the window tracery of the Ca' d'Oro is evident. The designer seems to have placed a compass on the top of each column and drawn a semicircle. The resulting figure is a series of intersecting half circles that form peaked Gothic arches between adjacent columns and Roman arches between every third column. Above this tracery sit six four-lobed roundels, lighter and less inflected versions of those below. Both the interest in figures that can be multiplied indefinitely and the geometrical fantasies that create them are persistent characteristics of the Gothic sensibility; they are given their freest expression in such forms as patterned cloth.

The most striking Gothic complex on the Grand Canal is formed by

49

the double Ca' Giustinian and the Ca' Foscari. (49) These three distinct but closely related buildings are sited at the beginning of the bend in the Grand Canal between the Rialto Bridge and the Basin of San Marco. While the façades of most buildings on the canal are seen in passing, these palaces are seen head on as one approaches from either direction.

Ca' Giustinian, which dates from the fifteenth century, is the earlier structure. Its two buildings may once have been separated by a narrow street that is now represented by a central watergate and a vertical file of windows on each story above. Whatever the original state of the site, the two structures are merged by a continuous façade and a symmetrical arrangement of windows. Each half of the building is self-sufficient; even without its partner it would appear well balanced. Each has its own central watergate, and the overall form of each half reflects the familiar three-part structure of the Venetian casa fondaco. The ground floor, with its anonymous opening on the water and its rectangular windows, is utilitarian. The upper stories have a central portego on each level; the second one, with its quadrilobate openings between Gothic arches, is the most elaborate. Balconies on the two middle floors form a continuous horizontal across both buildings. Richly ornamented Gothic windows on the piano nobile of each side draw the eye toward the center of the double structure.

Ca' Foscari next door is in line with the façades of these neighboring palaces, and its ornamentation is clearly related. Both of these factors ensure that the three structures are seen as a unit, which increases their visual impact. While relying on the weight of its neighbors to increase its own effect, Ca' Foscari also takes advantage of them to emphasize its greater size. This huge corner block, four stories tall, is built on an expanded scale that pushes its roofline and the string courses between its stories well above those of Ca' Giustinian.

An earlier structure on the site belonged to the Giustiniani, who sold it to the state in 1428. The intention was to use the site to build a palace for a mainland prince allied with the Republic, but the project was never carried out. In the 1450s the site was sold to Doge Francesco Foscari—the kneeling figure above the Porta della Carta—who had recently been forced from office after a thirty-year term. The massive structure, with its especially grand piano nobile, housed many of the highest-ranking official visitors to Venice. The three palaces, so closely united by their façades, have now been joined into a single massive block that houses the Università di Venezia a Ca' Foscari.

The harmony of the Grand Canal relies on a coordination between neighboring structures, seldom as closely linked as these houses but always active. That harmony rests on a number of common features that emerged over the course of centuries. Early buildings like the Fondaco dei Tedeschi and Fondaco dei Turchi display a dogged independence that does not blend well with other structures. Their framing towers set them off from their neighbors, but scale also isolated them. Fortunately, palaces of this size were evidently too grand even for the most ambitious families in the pre-Gothic and Gothic periods. The cost of frontage played a significant part in limiting the width of buildings as well as the spaces between them. The nearly unanimous choice of builders and patrons to reject a model like Ca' Lion-Morosini and place the façades of buildings directly on the water increased the harmony of structures along the Grand

50

Canal. (50)

The continuity of form that transcends stylistic period to a large degree also unites the buildings. Almost every building has a tripartite structure; almost every one has a piano nobile distinguished by an open portico. The earliest casate were two-story buildings. As time passed and the pressures for space increased, three- and even four-story buildings became more common. Some older buildings retained their modest scale, but the majority did not. Third and fourth stories were added to the oldest structures, which accommodated them to the increased height of the newer buildings. During the Renaissance, architects broke with these traditions: many palazzi stepped forward from the line of façades, scale increased, and blocklike masses became common. While it maintains the Gothic ornamental idiom, in its structure and shape Ca' Foscari seems to look forward to those trends.

So much of the Gothic survives in Venice that some vestige of it is likely to be seen in the line of housefronts on the tiniest canal or overlooking the campo of some remote church. The characteristic features of Gothic art are not hard to discern; they are especially distinct in the shaping of doors and windows. Gothic art had a great revival in the nineteenth century, and there are some Neo-Gothic buildings in Venice. The Palazzo Franchetti on the Grand Canal beside the Accademia Bridge is a good example. Like most Neo-Gothic structures, it outdoes its predecessors, using a profusion of Gothic decorative elements in positions and combinations that no authentic building would exhibit. Generally speaking, though, buildings that have Gothic features in Venice are genuinely Gothic.

John Ruskin, the great nineteenth-century enthusiast of Gothic, created a typology of windows and doors that includes some forty distinct examples. He believed that his typology represented more than just a catalogue of varieties; he thought it showed a logical development of Gothic styles that would allow him to date buildings accurately. This does not appear to be the case, but the catalogue is still useful. The first three examples and their subtypes are found on the earliest pre-Gothic buildings. They are either stilted arches of the kind commonly called Veneto-Byzantine or rounded and ornamented arches in a Romanesque pattern.

The bulk of the remaining examples show the Gothic preference for arches that rise to a point, have interior cusps, profiles based on double rather than single curves, and in some cases finials at their tops. The combination of arches of this kind with lobed roundels is characteristic of some of the most dramatic and prominent Gothic buildings in Venice.

Since the early nineteenth century, Venice has been transforming itself into a pedestrian city. Increasingly, its waterways are left to work-boats and gondolas whose only passengers are tourists. There are a few areas of the Grand Canal where walkways have been created, and the three bridges that cross it offer prospects onto some of its sections. But for the most part, the Grand Canal remains water-access only. The best way to explore this long avenue is from the bow or stern seats of a #1 or #82 vaporetto or through the open port of a water taxi.

Nineteenth-century visitors to Rome often commented on the multi-tudes of balconies that overlooked the city's main parade route and cere-monial street, the Via del Corso. The windows and balconies that overlook the Grand Canal were every bit as numerous and suggest that its houses were not made just to be looked at. Their linked façades formed a roman-tic stage set when seen from the water, but for those living in them or visiting them, the same houses served as theater boxes. They offered unobstructed views of the continual spectacle of commerce and the richly decorated flotillas that marked every important festival.

One of the most extraordinary things about the cityscape of Gothic Venice is something that can be sensed only by a visitor well acquainted with more typical medieval Italian towns. Fresh from San Gimignano, Flo-rence, or Milan, a medieval traveler could not fail to notice the absence of the tragic fortifications that simultaneously disfigured and defined those cities. San Gimignano, a city of towers, is the best surviving example of an urban design intended to protect neighbors from one another. Each wealthy family controlled a section of this tiny walled town; at the center of each enclave was a square windowless tower where the family could hold out against attack. The gang warfare that plagued individual towns was magnified by a widespread political schism that gave it an ideological stamp. The division between Guelfs (the party of empire) and Ghibellines (the papal party) dominated Italian politics for centuries. When the Ghibellines were driven out of Florence in the late thirteenth century, the ruling Guelf party broke into rival factions that duplicated the earlier split. Dante, a white Guelf, voted to banish his friend and fellow poet Guido Cavalcanti, a member of the blacks, who died in exile. When the blacks returned to power in 1304, they avenged themselves by banishing leading whites, Dante among them. In 1314 they reexamined his sentence of exile and converted it to death.

The medieval towers of Florence were dismantled during the Renaissance, but other artifacts of the violence of city life in the Middle Ages remain. The Florentine Palazzo della Signoria is typical of the centers of political power in medieval Italian towns. It is an immensely tall building with heavy, rusticated stone walls and a great central gateway closed by massive doors; it has crenellations where archers can shelter, and battlements that lean far out from the structure to sweep the walls with fire.

Venetians were very well aware of the violence that plagued other Italian cities, the political factions that fed on disorder, and the repressive tyranny civil warfare goaded into being. They congratulated themselves on avoiding the arming of neighbor against neighbor and the transformation of houses into fortresses. They were, if anything, even more aware of the autocratic monopoly of power that fortified government centers sustained. They were determined that fortifications of any kind would be absent from their city, and in this they were remarkably successful, too.

Looking at the domestic scene in Venice, then, requires not just an eye for the way things are but a sensitivity to the way they might have turned out if the Republic had not been so successful at averting the violence and repression common throughout the mainland.

Chapter Four

STATE OF GRACE

Many of the earliest communities in the Lagoon
formed around Benedictine abbeys. While the monks
sought little more than seclusion, the monastery's
neighbors drew substantial benefits from their presence. The abbeys were rich, and over time they grew
richer as the endowment contributed by every entering monk was supplemented by legacies and gifts. In the feudal world, a Benedictine abbey
played the part of a large landowner. Its extensive fields, flocks, and other
holdings, which might include fisheries, quarries, or mines, sustained entire
communities. Despite the monk's official pacifism, abbeys often served as
strongholds in the event of enemy attack, and a company of well-fed Benedictines could lead a vigorous if inexpert defense.

In the thirteenth century a new kind of monasticism revolutionized the
Catholic Church. The mendicant fraternal orders—Franciscans, Dominicans,
and Augustinians primarily—spurned the Benedictines' flight from the secular world and established monastic communities in cities, where they worked
to enrich the spiritual life of people of all social classes. In the thirteenth
and fourteenth centuries, these dynamic organizations grew rapidly in every
part of Western Europe. To further their goals, they founded hundreds of
churches and built monasteries that housed thousands of brothers; they

enrolled hundreds of thousands in their lay sodalities and confraternities. Organized on a large scale, and attracting huge crowds of the faithful, the mendicant orders played a major role in the revival of spirituality in the Middle Ages. They also contributed substantially to the expansion of medieval Venice.

St. Dominic and St. Francis were both exceedingly charismatic men with clear and far-ranging visions of what needed to be done to revitalize the medieval Church. Francis—who invented the crèche, married Lady Poverty, and preached an angry sermon to crows—was the less pragmatic of the two. Starkly opposed to the wealth and insularity of the Benedictines, he established and won papal approval for a religious order whose brothers would live among the people and beg for their daily bread. For a long time the Franciscans were divided over the issue of how literally to take Francis's prescriptions for the fraternal life. The Spiritual Franciscans, who were eventually declared heretical, took the founder at his word and believed that neither the friars nor the order should acquire wealth that would free them from their dependence on charity. The friars of the regular order maintained that individual brothers must renounce wealth but that the community of friars as a whole need not do so. Dominic's order was also supported by charity, but its primary interest was theology and orthodoxy; poverty was less central to the Dominicans' self-definition.

The charisma of each founder was molded by the second and third generation of his followers into a blueprint for development. The new orders—especially the Franciscans, who had almost no entry requirements—recruited enormous numbers of brothers and organized them into communities that quickly gained a foothold in every European city and town. The Franciscan recruits were often poor, and their financial contributions to the community were minimal. To expand, the Franciscans— and, to a lesser degree, the Dominicans—needed to obtain funds from donors outside the order. Each fraternal community also faced the task of establishing a base for sustenance and growth in places where the old monastic orders and the parish clergy greeted them with hostility. Francis preached in piazzas and open fields, and Franciscan brothers followed his lead. Parish churches were closed to the friars at first, and in any case these buildings were too small for the congregations that powerful preachers could draw.

Every Franciscan or Dominican community wanted a church of its own, built on a scale that could hold a multitude. This required generous donations over a long period of time; a stable monastic community with its own quarters; and tracts of land of a sufficient size to support these unprecedented structures. However grounded in spirituality, the skills that could conceive, manage, and complete such a task were essentially entrepreneurial. The mature and successful mendicant orders were expert fundraisers with a keen appreciation of the diverse abilities and susceptibilities of their audience. They were effective project managers and prudent investors of their portfolios.

There was no room in the tightly settled and long-urbanized center of Venice for a new church or monastery, and certainly not for a foundation on a scale that matched the mendicants' ambitions. With few exceptions, the fraternal orders were pushed to what were then the margins of the city. Doge Jacopo Tiepolo offered the Dominicans an expanse of mud and shallow water on what was then the city's northern rim, and a few years later, in 1236, he granted unreclaimed land on the edge of San Polo to the Franciscans. At the Franciscans' site, an abandoned monastery stood on the fringes of a partially flooded zone called Lago Badoer. The friars drained the lake, planted gardens and an orchard on part of the reclaimed land, and built a small church, which was dedicated in 1280. Fifty years later, a full century after their formation, the Franciscan friars were sufficiently wealthy and sufficiently integrated into the community to begin construction of their monumental church, Santa Maria Gloriosa dei Frari. (Map 4)

The project was enormous, and it took more than a hundred years to finish. Work began at the apse end; by 1361 this area and the transept were complete. Meanwhile, worshippers continued to crowd into the small church at the edge of the site, toward which the Gothic basilica was slowly progressing. Work sometimes went at a frenzied pace, and the site became a shantytown of scaffolding that teemed with specialists in every art. From time to time the money ran out, and the site fell silent. But in every case a donor came forward to get things moving again.

"While the present church was under construction many people, both nobles and commoners, contributed to its expense. Among others, a gentleman of the Gradeniga family financed the erection of four of its columns and the walls linking them. A member of the Giustiniani family underwrote the cost of building two more columns, and a member of the Aguie family paid for one. Paolo Savelli, Baron of Rome and Condottiere of the Army of the Republic, financed work on the vaults. The campanile was begun by one of the Viara, who contributed nearly 16,000 ducats;

not long after he had taken his vows and become a member of the order, he died unexpectedly, leaving it only half completed. The other half was financed by the Milanese confraternity and the community from Monza" (Sansovino, *Venezia, Città Nobilissima,* p. 187). The campanile, second highest in Venice, was finally completed in 1395, and in 1415 the "interim" church—now more than a century old—was demolished to make room for the last three bays of the nave. The new church was completed some thirty years later.

The exterior of the Frari is made entirely of brick, with a minimum of decorative courses and sparingly punctuated with stone ornament. Square pilasters divide the façade into three vertical zones that separate the lower shed-roofed aisles from the nave. (51) Pensile arches trace the line of the lower roofs. Heavy rounded brackets, also made of brick, hide the roofline and increase the apparent height of the side aisles and the nave. As the pilasters pass

51

through these brackets, they take on the form of slim square towers crowned with Gothic aedicula. A third aediculum marks the center of the roof. These aedicula directly recall those on the front of San Marco, and the brackets are reminiscent of the delicate stonework that softens the upper profile of its façade. A large rose window lights the nave, and two smaller circular windows illuminate the aisles. The single door has a steep Gothic tympanum and is thinly outlined with carved stonework.

The church so completely dominates its contracted site that it is impossible to get a sense of its immense scale from outside. Once inside the building, however, the massive dimensions of the Frari become over whelmingly clear. It is immediately easy to understand how even a community as wealthy as Venice would need a century-long campaign to construct it. Size also tells the story of the building's site and its place on the frontier of development in the thirteenth and fourteenth centuries. In the center of Venice, where parish churches were tiny and the palaces of the wealthiest and most powerful families stood cheek-by-jowl with their neighbors, space was precious. Only a site at the edge of habitation could have permitted an explosion of the urban scale as substantial as this building represents.

The building is a three-aisled basilica with a crossing, a deep central apse, and six smaller apse chapels. These jutting structures are lit by a double file of steep Gothic windows, some still beautifully glazed with stained glass. Secondary structures have been added to each end of the crossing and to the south wall. The most unusual feature of the church is a remarkable choir at the front of the nave with carved wooden stalls reserved for the friars. This heavy structure all but screens the altar from view by the congregation. Standard before the Counter-Reformation, this impediment was removed in most churches by the seventeenth century. Raised pulpits on either side of the choir lifted preachers over the heads of their congregation. Like all the mendicant orders, the Franciscans fostered the kind of dramatic, crowd-pleasing preaching that parish churches could not match.

Once the building was completed, the Frari's congregants still had a chance to contribute to its beauty and richness and at the same time to create memorials and monuments for their families. The privilege of decorating the six smaller apse chapels was granted to individual families and to confraternities—devotional groups of laypeople. The Milanese confraternity, which had supported the building of the campanile, also controlled the first chapel to the far left of the altar. They decorated it with paintings by Alvise Vivarini, Palma Giovane, and Tizianello. The Corner family sponsored the building of a separate chapel next to that of the Milanese, which jutted out from the end of the crossing. Paintings there included works by Vivarini and Palma Giovane. An anonymous sculptor built the tomb of Federico Corner; other unknown artists created images in stained glass of the Virgin and various saints. The tomb of Doge Niccolo Tron stands to the left of the high altar, that of Doge Francesco Foscari to the right.

On the wall at the far end of the crossing is the equestrian tomb of Paolo Savelli, the condottiere who financed construction of the vaulted ceiling. Near him are the tombs of other patrons and contributors of the Pesaro and Marcello families. These tombs cluster around the doors to the sacristy and chapter hall, which were added to the crossing even before the rest of the building was completed. The chapter hall shelters the fourteenth-century tomb of Doge Andrea Dandolo. In the painting above the tomb, St. Francis presents the kneeling Doge to the Virgin and Child. The enclosed arcade opposite looks out over one of the two great cloisters of the monastery.

The present sacristy of the church was originally the Pesaro family chapel. Above its altar is a magnificent painting by Giovanni Bellini of the Virgin and Child with saints Nicholas, Peter, Benedict, and Mark. (52) It was commissioned by Benedetto Pesaro in 1478 and delivered a decade later. The painting retains its original gilded frame, which extends the fictive architecture and summarizes it in the form that Americans

52

think of as a Palladian window. The fictive space created by this combination of illusionistic painting and solid frame is a puzzling one. Its center panel represents an apse: a brocaded cloth covers its curved recess, and a gold-ground mosaic fills its conch. The glittering mosaic is minimally figured with a symbol of the Empyrean and a Latin prayer to the Virgin: "Sure door of heaven, lead my mind and direct my life; may all I do be committed to your care." A barrel vault links the conch to the frame of the painting and makes room for an opening to either side, which communicates with two shallow flat-roofed bays. This combination of apse and flat-ended spaces is found in early Venetian churches like San Zan Degolà, but the scene here is evidently some sort of open-air loggia. Thin strips of landscape can be seen between the pillars at the outer edges of the frame.

The Virgin, with the infant Christ standing naked on her knees, sits on a dais in the open space in front of the apse. Two infant angels play musical instruments in front of the throne. Three of the saints in their separate but linked spaces bend reverently toward the center. On the right, St. Benedict in the black robes of his order turns to look directly at the viewer and invite her into the sacred space. His invitation echoes the implied inclusion of the viewer as the speaker of the prayer inscribed on the vault. The painting is a magnificent example of a Renaissance type called the sacra conversazione, or sacred conversation. Before the mid-fifteenth century, the Virgin and Child with miscellaneous saints were usually painted on different scales and divided by frames into central and subordinate figures. Bellini's frame creates separate zones for the figures in a way that evokes this traditional style, but the painted architecture transforms the compartmentalized frame into a unified structure where all the figures share a common scale and space.

Bellini died in 1516, and shortly after his death the Pesaro family commissioned his heir apparent, Tiziano Vecellio—Titian—to create two majestic paintings for the Frari. *The Assumption of the Virgin* was always intended to stand above the high altar, where it is framed by the steep Gothic apse with its soaring windows. (53) The theology on which the painting rests was formulated in the High Middle Ages but became a matter of dogma only late in the Church's history. Because Mary was without sin, medieval scholars believed that at the time of her death she was carried directly to heaven. This large canvas represents that moment.

The Virgin is dressed in crimson and wrapped in a billowing dark blue cape that is knotted in front of

53

her womb. With eyes upturned and hands upraised in a gesture of adoration, she rises to heaven on a cloud thronged with cherubs. God the Father hovers above; he reaches for a martyr's crown carried by a cherub at his side, while a green-robed angel hovers at the right. Effulgent light spreads out around and beneath him to surround the Virgin in an extended halo. At the bottom of the painting, the apostles, who have gathered to witness the Virgin's death, reach or simply gaze toward her disappearing figure. While the heavens are filled with light, the earth is marked by contrasting light and shadow. A foreground figure in a long scarlet robe facing inward on the right of the picture is echoed by another facing outward on the left. Between them are figures almost completely in darkness who give the scene a sense of chaotic energy and contradictory impulses. The viewer's attention and hope, like that of the majority of figures in the bottom of the scene, are fixed on the extraordinary figure whose mid-position between heaven and earth makes her humanity's most potent intercessor.

A few years after completing this altarpiece, which the friars at first found disturbing, Titian received another commission from the Pesaro family. The picture, delivered some seven years later, was, like its predecessor, both brilliant and shocking. The Pesaro altarpiece defies convention by placing its theological principals, the Virgin and Child, off-center at the peak of two diagonals that begin in the lower corners of the painting. The pair sit on a dais at the top of a short flight of stairs, with the façade of a massive classical building behind them. (54) A gigantic column at their back continues skyward beyond the frame of the painting. A second column rises from the shoulder of St. Peter—the rock on whom

Christ will build his church. He stands at the top
of the stairs, supporting an open book on the
edge of the dais. At his feet the family patron,
Bishop Jacopo Pesaro, kneels in prayer. Other
members of the Pesaro family look toward him
from the right margin. The youngest of this group
looks out toward the viewer. St. Francis of Assisi
stands behind them, his eyes fixed on the Christ
child, while his hands extend to take in the sup-
pliants below.

54

   The theme of the painting is intercession—
complex, hierarchical, and mediated in two different ways. The Pesaro
family members in the lower right corner seem unaware of the scene that
unfolds above them; their eyes are fixed only on the bishop of their own
family. He in turn looks directly toward the Virgin, and she bends toward
him; but even this apparently direct engagement involves two other medi-
ating figures. The great banner that unfolds behind the kneeling bishop
features the stemma of Pope Alexander VI. The papal role in bridging the
gap between man and God that this banner recalls is underscored by the
presence of St. Peter, who is identified by his trailing key. While this left-
to-right diagonal suggests mediation through the Church hierarchy, the
figure of St. Francis provides a direct link between the suppliant family
and the infant Jesus. Depicting a saint as an intercessor is thoroughly
orthodox, but pitting one form of intercession against another, as this picture appears to do, is certainly daring, however flattering it might have
been to the Franciscans.

To the right of Titian's painting stands the tomb of its principal figure, Doge Giovanni, who died in 1659. Another Pesaro, he is honored by the most extraordinary sepulcher in the church. The Gothic fabric, which is able to support multiple Renaissance installations, seems overwhelmed by Baldasarre Longhena's Baroque monument to the Doge. Built from black and white marble, with animated skeletons perched in niches and gigantic Moorish caryatids flattened against its face, this macabre tomb fails to evoke any of the emotions commonly associated with mourning or commemoration. (55) Though death remains the undiscovered country, Longhena's monument suggests that its inhabitants have not lost their

55

sense of humor. Next to it is the eighteenth-century tomb of the sculptor Antonio Canova.

Among the confraternities that centered around the Frari was a group with a special devotion to San Rocco, the patron of plague victims. After the plague of 1477, the group's power and influence increased. In 1484 two monks, following the dubious example of the two Venetian merchants who brought the body of St. Mark from Alexandria, stole the remains of St. Rocco not from Muslims but from fellow Christians and carried them to Venice. Over the next few years the confraternity built a church and a scuola—not a school but a small assembly hall—dedicated to the saint. The national threat posed by the plague, the reputation of the saint's relics, and a wonder-working painting of Christ ascribed to Giorgione catapulted the

scuola into immediate prominence. Within ten years it became one of
only six scuole grandi in the city.

In medieval European cities, workers typically belonged to organizations (guilds) based on the particular trade or art they shared. Among
Venice's more than three hundred scuole, many were organizations of
artisans that fit this common pattern, but none of the scuole grandi were.
Most Venetian scuole, large and small, were voluntary associations
focused on religious devotion; they had distinctive patron saints and participated in religious processions and ceremonies. Like the mendicant
orders, the scuole were founded on spiritual principles that gave power,
order, and definition to what were essentially social organizations, indis-
tinguishable in many ways from secular guilds or religious confraternities.

The older among the six scuole grandi were founded by flagellant
orders. The first, Santa Maria della Carità, was established in 1260, the
year that a hermit from central Italy named Raniero Fasani started a religious order called the Penitents of Christ (Disciplinati di Gesù Cristo).
This popular evangelical movement spread quickly throughout Italy and
beyond. Hooded and stripped to the waist, scourging themselves and
chanting penitential hymns, men, women, and children moved through
towns and villages in long processions. By their suffering they hoped to
atone not only for their own sins but for those of all people. The breadth
and intensity of the movement terrified bishops; and rather than offering
official sanction, the Pope outlawed the processions in 1261. In Venice,
however, the flagellant impulse found permanent expression in organizations of a very different temper.

The scuole grandi provided for the spiritual welfare of their members by easing their participation in religious ceremonies of all sorts, especially processions. Despite clerical objections, flagellation continued to be a part of these processions for many centuries, though the members of the scuole who participated in this rite were usually the poorest. The scuole were also mutual aid societies, caring for their members during illness, providing food, firewood, and housing for the indigent and aged, supplying dowries for young women, and burying the dead. Over time these economic activities became the major preoccupation of their governing bodies.

In the Middle Ages, confraternities of this kind were typically supervised by the ecclesiastical powers. In modern Venice, the surviving scuole are classified as sodalities under the direction of the patriarch. In the Venetian Republic, where nothing escaped the attention of the government and clerical power was viewed with suspicion, the scuole were regulated by the Council of Ten. This powerful executive committee maintained the distinction between scuole grandi and scuole piccole; fixed membership limits; established the general framework for government; oversaw elections to office; set accounting procedures; and closely watched public activities. While their supervision was useful for the most part, the Council of Ten could also be fussy and intrusive. In the mid-fifteenth century, for example, the Ten felt the need to define appropriate staircase design for the scuole grandi.

In a more useful intervention early in the fifteenth century, the Ten decreed that officeholding within the scuole would be off-limits to the nobility, though nobles could still be members. This prohibition had the important effect of depoliticizing these organizations. If nobles—the voting partners in the Republic—could control the scuole, they could use them as springboards for their own political careers. But it was not just their pervasive suspicion of one another that drove the nobles to regulate and oversee the confraternities; they were also conscious of the great civic value of these organizations. The social services the scuole sponsored supplemented those offered by the state, and to the extent that the scuole shared the state's burden in these areas, they were tremendously useful, both socially and economically. In times of crisis, when special taxes were assessed, the state required enormous contributions from the scuole grandi.

The government of the scuole grandi was defined by rules spelled out in each organization's mariegola. This Venetian word—a condensation of the Latin mater regulae (mother rule)—defined an organization that was theoretically democratic but in practice was governed by a small percentage of its members. Each scuola was headed by a guardian grande (a warden), who was seconded by a vicar, and by a guardian di mattin. The vicar stepped in when the warden was unavailable; the "morning warden" was in charge of processions (flagellant processions typically took place in the morning). Along with a secretary and a few other officers, these men made up the banca of the organization. Their meeting place was marked by a large judicial-style bench (banca) in a special room of the scuola called the Sala dell'Albergo. Over generations, legacies and donations from both members and nonmembers made the scuole enormously rich, and the administration of this patrimony was in the hands of the banca. The influence of these citizens on the daily life of the city rivaled that of the government or the procurators of San Marco, the city's richest institution.

By the sixteenth century, the Scuola Grande di San Rocco had more

56

than five hundred members, and in 1549 its magnificent and very costly building was completed. Venice's leading architects had all contributed: Bartolomeo Bon, Sante Lombardo, and Antonio Scarpagnino. The site created special problems. Campo San Rocco is long and narrow, and the short end is dominated by the church. The scuola sits on the long side, opposite the apse chapels of the Frari; and like many monumental buildings forced to make their way in the cramped streets of Venice, it can be seen only obliquely. (56) While it has windows and doors of extraordinary interest, the most dynamic features of the façade are its huge engaged columns and massive cornices. These columns give depth and create a sense of relative movement as the viewer walks past or looks up from the narrow campo.

The façade is divided into two parts that reflect functional divisions inside. The three bays on the left, with their massive central doorway, house the two great open halls where the members met. The two bays on the right, with their own eccentric door, house the Sala dell'Albergo, where the banca convened, along with other small rooms devoted to particular purposes. The windows on the ground floor, featuring interior frames set with small rondels, were designed by Bon in imitation of a style popularized by the northern Italian architect Mauro Codussi. These may be a stripped-down version of the quadrilobate rondels on the

Palazzo Ducale that were so influential in Venetian domestic architecture. The double windows on the second floor are framed with columns and crowned with pediments in a more strictly Neoclassical style. They are also inset with rondels.

The interior of the building is organized in a pattern that is typical of Venetian scuole. A large room downstairs is open to the full membership, while a monumental stairway leads to a more sumptuous and evidently more exclusive upper hall. In many ways the form of the scuola is an adaptation of the Venetian palazzo. Its separation of upper and lower floors corresponds to the distinction between ground floor and piano nobile. Its two-part façade, which reflects the separation of functions on the piano nobile, is similar to that of the Ca' d'Oro. Stairways of the kind typically found in the scuole became increasingly common in Venetian palaces in the sixteenth century, as ground-floor commercial spaces gave way to ceremonial reception halls, and stairways moved from open courtyards to sheltered indoor spaces.

In 1564 the directors of San Rocco announced a competition to decorate the Sala dell'Albergo. The most important artists working in Venice, including Veronese, Francesco Salviati, and Federico Zuccaro, submitted drawings. It would be wrong to say that Tintoretto won the competition; he overwhelmed it. In twenty days he painted a large *San Rocco in Glory,* which an accomplice inside the organization helped him install in the ceiling of the room. Then he offered the painting as a votive gift to the saint, which the rules of the Scuola obliged them to accept. Tintoretto worked in the scuola—of which he became not only an associate but a member of the banca—for the next twenty-five years.

The eight enormous canvases that decorate the ground floor were among the last Tintoretto completed. They represent scenes from the life of the Virgin and the infancy of Christ, popular subjects with great emotional appeal and little theological complexity. The cycle begins in the left rear of the hall with *The Annunciation*. This is followed by *The Adoration of the Magi, The Flight into Egypt,* and *The Slaughter of the Innocents.* Two unusual portraits flank the altar. Between the openings that lead to the stairway is *The Circumcision.* The final scene represents *The Assumption of the Virgin.*

Though Tintoretto's *Annunciation* includes all the elements required in

57

this very traditional scene, the painting is novel in many ways. (57) The left side is a dark chaos of boards and planks that seem at first glance to represent a world falling apart. A Roman doorway, with a mezzanine window above and the ruins of a classical column base at its side, opens into Mary's room. While the Roman ruin Tintoretto reproduces has no counterpart in Venice, the symbol of chaos he created would have been familiar to many artisans in the scuola. Joseph, the carpenter, appears in the background, and the apparent disorder is really the controlled chaos of a workman's private storage space. It is not junk but raw material.

The archangel Gabriel flies through Mary's doorway, while a mob of putti stream through her window. Between the angel's pointing finger and the first of the putti, the dove of the Holy Spirit hovers. Mary recoils from this invasion; her book drops on her lap, and her haloed head leans back into the picture toward a red canopied bed with three feather mattresses piled on top. The sumptuous bed and the gilded and coffered ceiling of the room contrast with a low chair near the door whose rush seat is coming undone. Tintoretto harmonizes extremes of the worn-out and the new, of luxury and want, to create a room with something familiar to everyone in the audience. Allegorically, these contrasts symbolize the transformation of the raw material of the old world into something wondrous and new through the incarnation of Christ.

The rhythms of daily life that animate *The Annunciation* are also felt in *The Flight into Egypt.* Here, the scene shifts from the domestic to the pastoral. A balding, white-bearded Joseph bends toward the left corner of the frame as he leads the donkey on which Mary rides, holding the infant Jesus in her lap. A sack of grain, a barrel, and a pilgrim's staff lie at the donkey's feet. The center of the picture is dominated by a confused tangle of shrubs and young trees. Forests and mountains appear in the distance behind the holy family. On the right, a river runs by a small cottage; one man probes the banks, another carries a sack of grain on his shoulder.

The same kind of landscape dominates the two small paintings nearest the altar. In both, a haloed woman sits alone by a river, reading a book. One is the Virgin Mary; the other, St. Mary of Egypt. The last rays of the sun highlight a pastoral landscape with mountains in the distance. Absorbed in their books, the women are hardly aware of the golden evening around them. The idealized women in these paintings were destined to be seen only by men; while the first flagellant processions included women and children, neither were admitted to the scuole. Perhaps they represent ideal daughters for whom the scuola would willingly supply dowries.

After *San Rocco in Glory* secured Tintoretto's commission, his first task was to complete the decoration of the Sala dell'Albergo. He filled the entire back wall of the room with an innovative and overpowering *Crucifixion*. This is typically a static scene dominated by the shape of the cross and the figure of the crucified—hieroglyphic images that transform the historical moment of the Crucifixion into a timeless symbol. By representing the moment when Christ's cross is hauled upright, Tintoretto restarts the frozen clock. The cross of the first thief is just being set into its socket, while that of the second is still being prepared. Alone, the crucified Christ dominates the scene; the other crosses, ropes, and ladders create strong diagonals, and the struggling workmen contribute contorted postures and restless movement. This transformed scene suggests that commemoration of the Passion is not a theme for passive recollection but an activity. The members of the banca, seated underneath, direct the scuola as it carries on the unfinished work of redemption.

Backed by this energetic *Crucifixion,* the banca members look toward an image above the door in the opposite wall of a scourged and bloody Christ, the supreme exemplar of the flagellant spirit. Two further scenes of the Passion surround this doorway. On the left, Christ and the two thieves carry their crosses up the slopes of Golgotha. Men with banners accompany them, and the small crowd to the extreme right of the scene includes two figures whose faces are entirely obscured by hoods. The condemned men and their attendants form a rudimentary procession like those supervised by the guardian di mattin.

The remaining scene shows *Christ before Pilate*. The Roman governor sits on a dais framed by marble columns splashed with light. A sliver of light strikes the column behind him and grazes the top of his bald head. As an attendant pours water over his hands, Pilate turns his head away from the bound and white-robed figure of Christ, who stands before him fully illuminated. The theatrical play of light and darkness tells the complex story of a Roman governor who partially understands what is at stake and yet acts against his better judgment. A second pavilion with one of its columns bathed in light fills the left background. Christ is linked visually to the column, where he will be bound and scourged. The farthest column points upward to a Roman structure that is intact and dominant in its lower story but already falling into decay above.

With the Sala dell'Albergo completed, Tintoretto's second commission was for work in the Great Hall on the upper floor. Michelangelo famously fought against the Sistine commission of Julius II in Rome, but Tintoretto not only welcomed the chance to work in the Scuola Grande di San Rocco, he often did so at his own expense. In some cases he offered his work for free; in others he asked only to be reimbursed for the cost of materials. He evidently wanted the opportunity to create and complete the cycles that this magnificent room preserves, though there is no clear evidence that he had the full program in mind when he began.

The gilded ceiling of the room forms a majestic fretwork where openings of different shapes enclose a series of Old Testament paintings grouped in three long files. Large rectilinear pictures fill the center with lozenge- and kite-shaped images to either side. The images are grouped in a symbolic rather than a chronological order that moves from the back of the hall toward the altar. The first three scenes show Adam and Eve, Moses striking the rock, and Jonah belched up by the whale. Moses raising up the brazen serpent is the central image, followed by the sacrifice of Isaac, the rain of manna, and the celebration of Passover. Taken as Old Testament illustrations, these scenes are disorganized and out of sequence. Understood allegorically, they symbolize the life of Christ, and they highlight the blessings of his sacrifice as they are commemorated in the Mass.

The Passover scene directly in front of the altar and the rain of manna represent the Eucharist both as a commemoration of deliverance and as a divine gift freely offered. Wandering for many days without water, the Israelites were rescued when Moses, at God's command, struck his staff against a rock. Water gushed out and they were saved. John's Gospel reports that after Christ's death on the cross, a soldier pierced Jesus' side with a spear, releasing blood and water. Jonah, vomited up from his temporary prison in the belly of the whale, was another common symbol of resurrection. Isaac's submission to his father's will prefigured Christ's sacrifice and promised resurrection to all believers.

The central canvas, depicting Moses lifting up the brazen serpent in the wilderness, is the first scene Tintoretto created for the room, and some have argued that it contains the germ of the entire program. During their decades of desert wandering, the Israelites repeatedly lost faith in their leader and sometimes in God himself. God responded to one of these crises by unleashing a swarm of serpents to plague the unbelievers. When the Israelites pleaded with Moses to intercede on their behalf, "the

Lord said unto him: Make a brazen serpent, and set it up for a sign. Whosoever being struck shall look on it shall live" (Numbers 21.8).

In Tintoretto's powerful image, a litter of fallen bodies contorted by suffering and threaded with serpents covers the slope of a hill. From its top, Moses gestures toward the apotropaic serpent coiled around the shaft and arms of what is unmistakably a cross. The brazen serpent as an image of Christ is authorized not only by tradition but, according to the Gospel of John, by Jesus himself. Answering a question posed by the Pharisee Nicodemus, Jesus said, "And as Moses lifted up the serpent in the desert, even so must the Son of Man be lifted up, that those who believe in him may not perish, but may have life everlasting" (John 3.14–16).

The scene belongs with the christological images of the ceiling, but Tintoretto has also linked it to his first composition for the scuola. The bodies of those poisoned by the serpent's bite might easily be taken for victims of a familiar and unmetaphorical plague. The figure of Moses recalls San Rocco as he is received into heaven.

What is prefigured in the ceiling paintings becomes explicit in scenes from the life of Christ on the walls. The stories were very well known, as were those that Tintoretto painted a decade later on the ground floor. In the upper hall of the scuola—its holy of holies—Tintoretto created scenes that are both intellectually demanding and stylistically adventurous. *The Adoration of the Shepherds* in the back left corner of the room is one of the most wonderful and one of the strangest. (58)

Tintoretto transformed this commonplace subject in an extraordinary composition that seems to reflect the structure of the scuola. Unlike the

58

adoration of the magi—the moment when the infant Christ is recognized as a sovereign and miracle-worker—the adoration of the shepherds stresses his humility. The infant Jesus is usually shown on or near the ground and surrounded by animals as the shepherds kneel before him. Tintoretto placed the holy family in a hayloft, completely separate from the shepherds and animals on the stable's lower floor. Above the hayloft, angels peer through openings between the rafters, and a golden glow lights the holy family but leaves the shepherds in partial darkness. This upper zone of the painting recalls the second floor of the scuola, with its coffered and gilded ceiling where celestial images shine through.

The brightest area in the lower half of the painting is visible to the shepherds through a square opening like a picture frame. Three animals—an ox, symbol of humility, a peacock, symbol of immortality, and a cock, symbol of the Passion—are visible within it. In the foreground, beneath the cock, is a large basket of eggs, symbolizing the abundant renewal of life. Rather than adoring the infant Christ face to face, the shepherds adore his nature, expressed through symbols completely integrated into a genre scene similar to those on the ground floor of the scuola.

The Baptism of Christ is another example of Tintoretto's ability to infuse a familiar scene with complex meaning. The dark right foreground is filled with figures who in a Neoclassical painting would be nymphs and shepherds. Relaxing in the shade, they gaze on the Baptism with curiosity but without animation. A man in sixteenth-century clothes stands at the fringe of this group. He may be a donor or he may be something more sinister, an interloper or spy. His intrusion into the scene suggests a new reading of the foreground figures. Classical images of semi-nude figures partially immersed usually represent the goddess Diana and her virgin nymphs bathing. Very often these baths are spied on by men like the sixteenth-century figure or the young shepherd who leans toward Christ. What the figures in this picture spy on is not erotic, as the Neoclassical images are, but mysterious.

The mysteries that the framing leads us to expect are abundant. John the Baptist stands in the water, but Christ kneels on its surface. Behind him, the banks of the river are crowded with men and women so faintly outlined and so heavily highlighted that they appear insubstantial. Witnesses to the scene of the Baptism, these wraithlike figures appear to represent something more. Tintoretto combined the Baptism, which takes place in the River Jordan, with the act of crossing the Jordan—which in Christian symbolism signifies the passage from death to new birth. The figures in the background are dead—it is a further mystery that we are able to see them—and waiting for the Promised Land to be opened for them. Jesus' Baptism, the beginning of his ministry, will open that final passage.

To the right of the main altar stands the image of Christ attributed to Giorgione that first made the fortune of the scuola. Before the recovery of the body of the patron saint, this image, believed to be miraculous, attracted adherents and contributions to the newly formed scuola.

59

The second oldest scuola in Venice is San Giovanni Evangelista, not far from San Rocco. Founded in 1261 (the year in which flagellant processions were outlawed), it was suppressed in the Napoleonic period and only reactivated as a confraternity in 1929. The building is closed to the public, though it hosts meetings and conferences. Its upper floor, richly decorated by Tintoretto and others, is often used as a concert hall. An extraordinary sequence of paintings by Vittore Carpaccio and others depicting the Miracles of the Holy Cross that once hung in its oratory have been reassembled in the Accademia Gallery.

The most distinctive feature of San Giovanni Evangelista today is the outdoor atrium and gateway that separate its courtyard from the small campo in front. (59) Designed by Pietro Lombardo and completed in 1485, the gateway reflects the Venetian classicizing style of the late fifteenth century. The structure is more than a wall separating two spaces, however; its architecture reaches out to enclose the campo and make it into an outdoor room. The absence of rustication, which a High Renaissance ground-level setting would require, and the delicacy and formality of the architecture make this space especially unusual. It is as if a room on the piano nobile of an early Renaissance palazzo were thrown open to the public.

The gateway, which until the school's dissolution was blocked by double doors, is framed by Corinthian pilasters that support a jutting entab-

lature and a demilune surmounted by a cross. Windows to either side of
the gateway are structured like small temple fronts, with flanking
pilasters, an entablature, and pediments. Pateras above the windows, the
marble facing, the delicate friezes, and the demilune above the doorway
recall the decorative repertoire of San Marco. While Venetian buildings in
this period reflect the trends of mainland Renaissance architecture, they
also turn to pre-Gothic elements of San Marco to ground their style. An
eagle, symbol of St. John the Evangelist, is sculpted above the door.
Angels at either end of the wall kneel and gaze at the cross. In this case
the cross is more than the common sign of a Christian building; it refers
specifically to a piece of the true cross given to the scuola in 1369 by
Filippo Masser, chancellor of Jerusalem and Cyprus. Like the body of St.
Rocco which boosted the fortunes of the scuola dedicated to him, this
relic helped transform the scuola of St. John the Evangelist into a rich
and powerful organization.

The Scuola dei Calerghi in San Polo's Campo San Tomà was an occupational association of shoemakers (calerghi), and this building combined
the role of union hall and confraternity. The simple brick façade is
adorned with two bas-reliefs. The one immediately above the door shows
St. Mark healing a turbaned man who sits before him. The scene is
Alexandria, and the turbaned figure represents St. Anianus, patron of the
shoemakers' guild and Mark's eventual successor as bishop. In 1928 an
image of the members of the confraternity adoring the Madonna della
Misericordia was set into the brick. The interior of the building, which is
now a public library, has a small downstairs hall, a stairway, and a large
upper room with remains of fifteenth-century frescoes.

The church of Santa Margherita in the nearby sestiere of Dorsoduro was built in the ninth century as a traditional three-aisled basilica and restructured without internal colonnades in the eighteenth century. Closed in the Napoleonic era, its artworks dispersed, it served briefly as a cigarette factory, a marble warehouse, an evangelical church, and a movie theater. It is now one of many properties in this area taken over by the University IUAV of Venice, which offers professional training in architecture, urban planning, art, and design. This modest church gave its name to a large campo extended at its far end by filling in a canal. Palazzi with Gothic details are interspersed with later buildings along the curving western side of the piazza. The ground floor of almost every one contains a shop, bar, or restaurant. There are benches and trees in the center of the piazza, which in decent weather is filled with residents and university students. Like many peripheral areas of Venice, this campo retains the practical comforts and unselfconscious vitality of a workaday city.

At the far end of the Campo Santa Margherita and originally isolated from it by a now-buried canal stand the Carmelite Church and monastery and the Scuola Grande del Carmine. The Carmelites were originally an order of desert hermits centered around Mount Carmel in what is now Israel. They believed themselves to be heirs of a biblical order called the Sons of the Prophets that is mentioned in Second Kings. After they were driven out of the Near East in the thirteenth century, St. Simon Stock, an Englishman, reorganized them as a mendicant order along the lines of the Dominicans and Franciscans. The Carmelites established themselves in Venice at the end of the thirteenth century. Their church, similar in structure to the Frari, was dedicated in 1348; it was remodeled in the sixteenth century.

A lay confraternity was established in the late sixteenth century that met first in the church, then in the convent, both of which it soon outgrew. The great appeal of the confraternity, which is estimated to have had more than seventy thousand adherents soon after its foundation, did not rest on a particular relic but on a peculiar talisman. Members of the confraternity were privileged to wear the scapular. A full-sized scapular is an apronlike over-garment that all members of monastic orders wear. The Carmelite scapular for laymen is a miniature version of this, consisting of two squares of cloth worn front and back connected by thin straps passing over the shoulders. On July 16, 1251, the Virgin Mary appeared to St. Simon Stock holding out the scapular and promising that whoever wore it would be under her protection in life and preserved from damnation at the moment of death. In the mid-eighteenth century, Tiepolo made this apparition the centerpiece of a group of paintings in the ceiling of the upper hall of the confraternity's scuola.

While its membership was vast, the building that housed the scuola was much smaller than San Rocco. Designed in the seventeenth century, the interior has upper and lower halls, the canonical grand stairway, and rooms for the banca and the processional banners of the confraternity. The sumptuous upper room is a faithful reflection on a reduced scale of San Rocco, with a ceiling inset with paintings and walls that are decorated with square canvases. The classicizing details here are very refined. White stucco work has replaced the dark wood of the earlier building, and gilding is less assertive than at San Rocco. Tiepolo's canvases are far less dramatic than Tintoretto's; his light is clearer and his figures less troubled. The room suggests the wealth, good taste, and serene comfort of an eighteenth-century drawing room in a patrician palace.

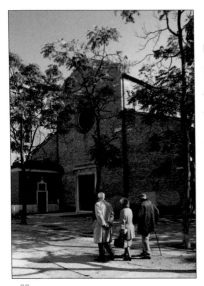

60

The ancient church of Sant'Agnese stands beside a small campo in Dorsoduro that has lost its connection with water entirely. (60) The church is a very early one built of brick. Though it was remodeled during the Middle Ages, the original walls of the nave were never destroyed or covered over. Above the roofs of the side aisles, their wonderful pre-Gothic brickwork—a repeating pattern of steep, cusped arcades in the shape of a cursive $\mathcal{M}$—is still visible. Unfortunately, the building has struggled since its closure during the French army's occupation of Venice. After decades of use as a warehouse for lumber and charcoal, the building was taken over by a private school; it has only recently reopened for weekly Mass.

The nearby Galleria dell'Accademia, in a prominent location on the lower part of the Grand Canal, occupies a complex of church, monastery, and scuola similar in many ways to the Carmine. The original church on the site was replaced in the fifteenth century with the present building in the Gothic style designed by Bon. (61) Its twelfth-century monastery was redesigned by Andrea Palladio in the sixteenth century; but by 1630, when it was partially destroyed by fire, the monastery was already in decline. The campanile of the church fell in 1744 and was never rebuilt. The oldest of the Venetian scuole relocated here from its original home at San Leonardo in Cannaregio in the mid-fourteenth century and renamed itself the Scuola Grande di Santa Maria della Carità. Despite the declin-

ing fortunes of the church and monastery, the scuola continued to flour-
ish. In the mid-eighteenth century, Giorgio Massari redesigned its façade
and created a double stairway between its two floors.

Suppressed in the Napoleonic period, the scuola, church, and
monastery complex were reconceived in the early nineteenth century as
the home of the Academy of Fine Arts. Palladio's reputation and his Neoclassicism (the dominant style at the time) ensured that the remains of
his monastery design would be respected. Appreciation for the Gothic
was at a low point, however, and Bon's church was far more brutally
treated. The soaring structure was divided into two floors, and new win-

dows were cut to light it. As for the
scuola, almost all the paintings in its
rooms were removed, to be replaced
over time by artworks collected from
other suppressed religious institutions
around the city. From an aesthetic
venture designed to give young Venetians practical instruction in the fine
arts, the Accademia quickly became
a de facto rescue operation.

In the first room—once the grand

61

hall of the scuola—almost nothing remains of the original wall decoration
except some fragments of frescoes. The fifteenth-century ceiling, with its
gilded coffers and seraph heads, survived renovation. The paintings in
the room represent the earliest period of Venetian art and include works
by Paolo Veneziano. The smaller room 2 is in some ways more notable for

what it does not contain. It was designed in 1875 to showcase Titian's *Assumption of the Virgin,* but the painting was restored to its original location in the Frari in 1919. This restoration recognized the importance of seeing works of art wherever possible in their original settings rather than in museums. It probably also acknowledged that at least some of the institutions that had been so severely damaged by the Napoleonic suppression had, after more than a century, recovered sufficiently to once again maintain their patrimonies.

This room includes a number of other large altar paintings of the second half of the fifteenth century, most notably Carpaccio's bizarre and controversial *Crucifixion and Apotheosis of the Ten Thousand Martyrs on Mount Ararat.* This Breughelesque phantasmagoria shows the earthly paradise in the background with a hovering disk representing the Empyrean above it. The left foreground and middle distance are strewn with the bodies of dead and dying martyrs who have been dispatched by the soldiers in the right foreground, vaguely Roman in armor, turbaned or otherwise exotically capped.

The magnificent room 5 includes small jewel-like paintings by Giovanni Bellini and Giorgione that were to hang in houses rather than churches. Giorgione's enigmatic *Tempest* is probably the most celebrated of these. (62) In the foreground of the famous scene are two figures. A man on the left wearing a white shirt and a short red jacket looks toward a woman sitting on a grassy bank beside a path. The woman, whose only covering is a white cloth that drapes her shoulders, looks toward the viewer as she nurses a baby. The couple are separated by a shallow stream. Behind the man are young trees, the ruins of an arcaded façade,

and two broken columns. A dense screen of
mature trees separates the woman from a
walled town in the background. A flat
wooden bridge spans the stream and enters
the arched opening of its gate. A squiggle
of lightning streaks the aqua sky.

62

The painting may have been commissioned by Gabriele Vendramin, who is its
first recorded owner. Vendramin was a
member of an early humanist circle in
Venice that shared an interest in antiquities, allegorical art, and esoteric books. The
painting was displayed along with Vendramin's collection of antiquities in
his palazzo near the church of Santa Fosca in Cannaregio. Marcantonio
Michiel, who kept notes about Venetian paintings in the early sixteenth
century, described it as "a small scene with a gypsy woman and a soldier." A later inventory from the Vendramin household recorded it as a
painting of Mercury and the goddess Isis. Perhaps the painting had a
particular meaning, the clue to which has now been lost, or it may have
been intended in the proper sense of the word as a conversation piece: a
mysterious object of great beauty that can be talked and argued about
unendingly but always with passion and pleasure.

Giorgione's portrait of an aged woman—a more transparent allegory—
also formed part of Vendramin's collection. Bleary-eyed and open-
mouthed, with thinning hair escaping from her spotless cap, the woman
looks out from a featureless black background. She may be pointing

toward herself or she may be making a gesture of penitence, the ritualized breast beating that accompanied the mea culpa of the Mass. A
scroll of paper escaping from her hand reads "col tempo," with time.
This inscription places the painting among medieval warnings against the
allures of the flesh. Like the more conventional death's head, the old
woman reminds the viewer of the inevitable decline of beauty and gra-
ciousness.

Giovanni Bellini's *Virgin and Child with St. Catherine and St. Mary
Magdalene* is in some sense the other side of the coin. Three young,
beautiful, and saintly women emerge from a dark background to surround
the infant Christ. Illuminated from the front by a suffused golden light,
the richly dressed, bejeweled figures turn their eyes away from one
another and from the viewer. This devotional rather than allegorical picture was probably meant for women and reserved for a secluded part of
the house. In contrast to the elaborate architectural framing of Bellini's
altarpieces, the domestic setting is defined by emptiness, pervasive darkness, and glowing firelight. This is the small stage commonly set for
Venetian women, and their actions on it are equally constrained. The
saints' averted eyes, expressionless faces, and hands that support a child
or fold in devotion define not just piety but feminine decorum. The picture declares not just what women must believe but how they should
behave. As is often the case in the Renaissance, the realm of morals and
the realm of manners overlap.

Painting cycles in the scuole might represent the legends of the
patron saint, like those in the Carmine, or set the work of the organization in a biblical context, like Tintoretto's series for San Rocco. The eight
enormous canvases from the oratorio of the Scuola Grande di San Gio-

vanni Evangelista, collected in room 20 of the Accademia, show the confraternity and its relic of the true cross in particular Venetian neighborhoods. Through their remarkable representations of fifteenth-century
architecture and dress, the paintings present the activity of the scuola as
a social reality with an impact that can be felt throughout the city.
Scenes take place at San Marco, on the Grand Canal near the Rialto
Bridge, and on the bridges of San Lio and San Leonardo. The details of
topography, the richly colored palazzi with their Gothic windows and
tulip-shaped chimneys, are convincing and absorbing. The day-to-day
charitable work of the scuola plays no part in the scenes. Instead, each
painting presents the scuola as custodian of a relic of the true cross and
a distributor of the grace of God that it incorporates. The wealth of physical detail in the paintings asserts that these miracles constitute the
scuola's real work in the everyday world.

There was no established tradition of representing these miracles, and
the painters who worked on the scenes relied on their own imagination
and vision. Though not a formal model, the San Marco mosaics that present the evolving legend of the city's patron served as an ideal guide.
While the earliest legends of St. Mark focused on events that happened
far from Venice, the later cycles emphasized the wonders that the relics
have worked in the church and city. A more subtle link with the updated
legend of the city's patron may underlie one of the strangest episodes in
the cycle.

Gentile Bellini's composition *Miracle of the Holy Cross on the San
Lorenzo Bridge* seems at first blush an odd if not misguided subject.
While a procession of the confraternity was crossing the bridge, the relic
slipped from the hands of the man who was carrying it and fell into the

63

waters of the canal. The painting shows a large crowd gathered on the fondamenta (walkway) along the left side of the canal, while the members of the scuola, dressed in their white robes and carrying banners and candelabra, crowd the bridge. (63)

Two men kneel to pray on the small landing at its right end. A black man, almost certainly an African slave, stripped to his underwear, stands ready to dive from a wooden platform. In the foreground, three brothers of the order, also wearing their robes, swim with their faces underwater, unaware that the guardian grande has already recovered the relic and is carrying it safely to land.

What appears to be a plank bridge fills the bottom margin of the painting. The white-veiled woman kneeling on the left is Catherine Corner, member of a prominent Venetian family and dowager queen of Cyprus. The women of her court stand along the edge of the fondamenta to her left. The figures in the right foreground are probably to be understood as ideal rather than real participants. Like donor figures in sacred scenes, they observe reverently and from a distance. Their presence helps to transform the scene from a historical representation into a sacred retelling and to suggest that the misfortune has become a miracle.

Understood from this perspective, the scene recalls the episode in the Venetian continuation of the legend of St. Mark when the saint's relics were lost for a time. After days of fasting and penance, a column in San Marco miraculously opened to reveal the relics. In both cases, a relic that was lost through human negligence is restored by a miracle. An accident becomes evidence of continuing grace.

The name of the guardian grande who rescued the relic was Andrea Vendramin. A rich merchant from Lucca who traded in grain and oil, Vendramin found a welcome in the Scuola Grande di San Giovanni Evangelista and quickly rose to prominence within it. His well-known role in this miracle as well as his contributions to the Republic during the Genoese war in 1386 led to his family's promotion to the nobility. No longer eligible for office in the scuola, Andrea's noble descendants, including the humanist and art collector Gabriele, continued to be devoted members.

Carpaccio's *Healing of the Possessed Man at the Rialto Bridge* is similarly rich in detail and recognizable in its general setting. While the board-sided drawbridge spanning the Grand Canal was long ago replaced by the familiar stone arch, the fondamenta in the foreground, though now wider and longer, is still recognizable. The round arches on the ground floor of Ca' da Mosto are just visible under the bridge in the background. The house fronts are brighter, and the gondoliers, including one African slave, are much gaudier in their Renaissance hose and doublets, but the boats are familiar. The miracle in this scene takes place in the open loggia in the left foreground. The reliquary that contains the fragment of the cross is being presented to the possessed man. Some of the men holding candelabra crowd the front of the loggia; others stand on the fondamenta below. Still others can be seen near the base of the bridge and crossing its open center. Multitudes of the nobility stand in the foreground or watch from the water.

At about the same time that these scenes were commissioned for San Giovanni Evangelista, Carpaccio was also working on a cycle for a much less significant scuola near Santi Giovanni e Paolo devoted to St. Ursula. Almost universally regarded as fanciful today, the legend of St. Ursula, like that of the ten thousand martyrs on Mount Ararat, was very popular in the Middle Ages. Ursula was a beautiful and virtuous young Christian princess, daughter of the king of Brittany, who attracted the attention of the son of England's pagan king. Ursula agreed to marry the prince but set conditions. The wedding would be postponed for three years, and the prince would convert to Christianity. During the interval, Ursula and her fiancé, along with ten virgin companions chosen by her father, would travel in Europe. So far, the conditions seem reasonable. For each of the eleven women, however, Ursula's father was to provide an additional thousand virgins.

No one is quite sure how this inflationary detail entered the story—textual misinterpretation is the common explanation—but the legend of Ursula and the eleven thousand virgins gained wide popularity. Traveling through Europe, the virgins visited Cologne, where Ursula dreamed that they would all be martyred. They went on to Rome, then returned to Cologne with an otherwise unknown Pope Cyriacus, who had abdicated in order to follow them. As predicted, the virgins and their now considerable entourage—the most popular version of the legend estimates their number at fifteen thousand—were slaughtered by the Huns.

In retelling this story, Carpaccio concentrated for the most part on ceremonial moments. Many of the scenes involve embassies passing back and forth between Ursula's father and the English court. When Ursula dictates the terms of her marriage, however, the scene shifts to her bedroom, a plausible locale for a father-daughter conversation but at the same time a telling representation of the limited sphere in which Venetian women—even those as adventurous and strong-willed as Ursula— were supposed to act.

The major appeal of the cycle is the architectural setting of the scenes, both interior and exterior, and the costumes and faces of the multitudes represented. Though the settings are fanciful, Venetian fashions in clothing and architecture predominate. In the *Return of the Ambassadors to the English Court,* the king sits in an open octagonal loggia with the cross-bracing between its columns that the unstable Venetian soil makes necessary. (64) Across a Venetian bridge, Carpaccio imagined a massive building with crenellations like those on the Ca' d'Oro and Codussi-style arched windows like those on the façade of the Scuola Grande di San Rocco. The ron-

dels of glass in the windows are typically Venetian. The building itself, however, is a free standing gateway somewhat like the Arch of Janus in Rome.

64

Like the legend itself, these buildings are wonderful fantasies rooted in the Venetian scene but distanced from it. Because of this deliberate exoticism, the program failed as myth-making, and the Scuola di Sant'Orsola remained a marginal institution without deep connections to the main currents of Venetian culture and legend.

Titian's *Presentation of the Virgin in the Temple* was commissioned by the Scuola Grande Santa Maria della Carità. Alone among the paintings in the Accademia, it has remained in its place in the original Sala dell'Albergo since Titian completed it in 1539. According to the apocryphal gospels, at the age of three the Virgin Mary was presented to the Temple in Jerusalem; she lived in the Temple precinct until her betrothal at age fourteen. This event is commemorated on November 21 in the Greek Orthodox Church, and in the aftermath of the Crusades and the occupation of Jerusalem it was added to the liturgical calendar in many Western dioceses. Venice was among the cities in which the feast became especially popular.

Set just above eye level in a relatively small room, the scene has much of the impact of Raphael's frescoes in the Vatican palace. (65) A crowd of men and women move from the towering arcade on the left into the center of the picture, where a grand stairway begins. Among the crowd are a group of four men in fifteenth-century Venetian dress who are probably members of the banca of the scuola. Scattered through the crowd are other men similarly dressed.

Despite the Venetian crowd, the Neoclassical architecture framing the scene and the mountains in the distance are decidedly non-Venetian. The mountains are those of Titian's home region, and the artist and his wife

lean out a window
in the back-
ground. Their
daughter leans on
the steps. At the
edge of a landing
halfway up the

65

stairs, a little girl with long blonde hair wearing a light blue taffeta dress
moves forward. She is surrounded by an aureole of light. The high priest
of the temple waits for her with open arms; he is wearing a crescent
headband, the fringed ephod, and the stone-studded breastplate
described in Exodus 28. A bearded and tonsured priest in Catholic liturgical vestments stands beside him, and a hooded monklike figure leans
out from the holy of holies behind.

The Scuola Grande Santa Maria della Carità is dedicated to the Virgin
as an embodiment of divine love, but Titian's precocious child is hard to
reconcile with this concept. The foreground figures of a headless classical statue, an old woman, and a basket of eggs have been seen as representations of the pagan past, before the era of the old law and the coming of Christ, who will fulfill the old law and establish the new. Mary is
poised more or less above the basket of eggs, which symbolize the
renewal of life through Christ. Her little body is framed by one of the
massive columns in the background. Titian's Pesaro altarpiece in the
Frari sets Mary against an even more massive column, and both images
probably symbolize her role in building or sustaining the Church.

The steps must have had special meaning for members of the scuola, since monumental stairways were among the architectural features mandated by the Council of Ten for these buildings. Framed by the epochs of Revelation, Mary climbs from the level of common life and common understanding to the mysterious and sacred realm at the top of the stairs. The symbolism of the picture, however, never overwhelms its literal content. Mary remains a bold, self-possessed little girl, not all that different from Titian's own daughter, who watches with interest from the bottom of the stairs.

Chapter Five

EVANGELISM ON
THE NORTHERN RIM

Located far to the north in the sestiere of Cannaregio,
the large Gothic church of Madonna dell'Orto is very
similar in style to the Frari. (Map 5) But unlike the
Frari's stark brick exterior, the façade of Madonna
dell'Orto is the most richly decorated among all of
Venice's Gothic churches. Construction, which began sometime in the fourteenth century, was sponsored by a mendicant order called the Humiliati.
Through mismanagement and scandal, the order fell into such general disre-
pute that they were replaced by a community of priests called canons in the
fifteenth century.

Madonna dell'Orto overlooks one of the rare campi in Venice that are still
paved with brick. The interior division of the church, with its high nave and
low aisles, is reflected on a façade that is divided into three bays by heavy
brick pilasters. (66) Gothic aedicules like those on the Frari and San Marco
top each one. The brick is ornamented near the rooflines with a tracery of
pensile arches. Twelve free-standing statues of the apostles are grouped
under sloping arcades along the roofline of each aisle. A large round window
with a smaller one above lights the nave. Two unusual Gothic windows
divided into multiple panels and finished with an intricate web of quadrilobate forms illuminate the aisles. The single central door is flanked by

columns and surmounted by a demilune of porphyry. A reflexed Gothic arch with elaborate floral tracery heightens the doorway and marks it as an imitation of the entry bays of San Marco. Images of Gabriel and Mary stand to either side.

The church was originally dedicated to St. Christopher, whose statue

66

tops the entryway, but the popularity of Madonna dell'Orto had nothing to do with this patron or with either of the orders that served him. It derived instead from a statue of the Virgin and Child, originally placed in a garden of the monastery or one nearby, that was found to work miracles. Like the miracle-working painting of Christ in the Scuola Grande di San Rocco, this statue, which is now in the sacristy, inspired enormous gifts that formed the endowment of the church. A branch of the celebrated Contarini family endowed a chapel, as did the Morosini and the Vendramin. Titian painted

Tobias and the Angel and Palma Giovane painted a *Crucifixion* for the Vendramin chapel. But the greatest contributor to the church was Tintoretto, who lived nearby on the Fondamenta dei Mori. (67)

Tintoretto's devotion to the Scuola Grande di San Rocco immortalized him as a painter, but it did nothing for his earthly remains. Though the scuole acted as burial societies for their members, they did not provide burial space, either inside or near their structures. Scuola members were buried in their home parishes or in the church or cemetery of a mendicant order. Tintoretto was buried in the apse of Madonna dell'Orto, along

67

with members of his family. The painter's devotion to his church was expressed in a cycle of paintings in the apse and in an additional painting that now hangs above the door to the sacristy, the *Presentation of the Virgin in the Temple.*

This magnificent work was painted in the early 1550s, some fifteen years after Titian's brilliant evocation of the scene in the Scuola Grande Santa Maria della Carità. Originally intended as a screen covering the organ, the work was Tintoretto's first commission for the church. The young artist responded aggressively to the painting of the well-established master. (68) He quoted its essential elements—the stairs, the monumental architecture, the precocious little girl seen in profile, the garments of the high priest—but recombined and transformed them. He bent Titian's heavy rectilinear stone stairway in a circle and decorated each of its risers with acanthus swirls and dots of gilding. The crowd, which stayed at the bottom of Titian's stairs, now sits along the edges of Tintoretto's, in the dark shadow of the building on the left margin. Tintoretto transformed Titian's broadside view of the stairway into a subjective view from its base. Instead of seeing someone climb, we are shown what it is to climb, as we look over the shoulder of a gesturing woman in the foreground.

The Virgin is clearly the child at the top of the stairs, but she may also be one or both of

68

the little girls at its base. However exemplary, the Virgin is one among many young women who share the prospect of this ascent. From the subjective viewpoint of the painting, Mary becomes an example for any observer, and the stairway represents a universal challenge. It is something that everyone must attempt; it is no longer a privileged passage between earth and heaven that only Mary the mediator can cross.

History, starkly divided between light and dark, also climbs Tintoretto's stairs. In Titian's painting, the high priest represents spiritual authority and stands in the light. In Tintoretto's contrasting view, he is like Pilate, touched by light but for the most part sharing the darkness with those Dantesque figures along the staircase's edge. This representation is much more in keeping with the Renaissance Venetian attitude toward the Jews, who lived in quarantine among them. The obelisk that Titian placed at the edge of his picture is, in Tintoretto's rendition, illuminated between Mary and the high priest. This Egyptian invention, which had fascinated the Roman emperors, was a favorite symbol of Renaissance artists and philosophers. Associated with the sun, it symbolized triumph over death.

Ten years after completing this commission, Tintoretto created eight major paintings for the apse of the church. These scenes include the martyrdom of St. Paul, Peter's vision of the cross, and allegories of prudence, justice, fortitude, and temperance. Facing each other at the outermost edge of the apse are his *Adoration of the Golden Calf* and *Last Judgment.* Exodus 32 describes how Aaron, in Moses' absence, created a golden image to lead the Israelites. On his return from communing with God, Moses smashed the idol, which for Christian exegetes symbolized the essence of sin, the turning away from God. The juxtaposition of this subject with the very traditional *Last Judgment* is logical but quite unusual. Painted more than twenty years after Michelangelo's *Last Judgment* in the Sistine Chapel, in its style and some of its figures Tintoretto's painting reveals its debt. The subject was traditional on the west wall of churches, but here it stands near the altar, a position it shares with Michelangelo's.

The nearby abbey of Santa Maria Valverde, which was founded in the tenth century, was once an isolated island settlement. The sestiere of Cannaregio caught up with it and engulfed it sometime in the thirteenth century. The pattern of urbanization in this area of Venice is easy to trace in the narrow islands that advance in parallel from the city center outward into the Lagoon. Just beyond the abbey, a square of open water called the Sacca della Misericordia remained unclaimed. This neat harbor with its long straight sides served as a winter shelter for boats and a storage and distribution point for great rafts of lumber that were floated down the mainland rivers and across the Lagoon.

The abbey church was remodeled several times and refaced in the seventeenth century with a Neoclassical façade by Clemente Molli, an associate of the great Roman architect Gian Lorenzo Bernini. The façade looks over a wonderful small campo divided into large sections by strings of Istrian stone blocks and paved with crumbling orange brick. Facing the campo to the left of the church is the brick façade of the Scuola Vecchia della Misericordia, which was founded in 1261. Significantly remodeled in the mid-fifteenth century, its cusped windows, undulating roofline, and aedicula at each corner are all that remain of a once rich decoration. (69)

69

For centuries a wonder-working image of the Madonna della Misericordia—the Madonna of Compassion—stood over the door; it is now in the Victoria and Albert Museum in London. This iconic image of the Virgin with cloak outspread to shelter a host of little kneeling figures remains popular in Venice, and copies of it are often seen.

By the sixteenth century, the still-powerful and popular scuola had outgrown this building. A series of architects were consulted, but nothing was done until 1530, when Jacopo Sansovino, newly arrived from Rome, took over. He projected an enormous structure on the other side of the canal that defied the modest scale of the old campo. Placing its principal façade on the inland side, away from the old building, he increased its apparent size by setting it on an elevated plinth. The small-scale buildings on the old campo were not only replaced but effectively screened from view.

Relics and ceremonial objects of the scuola were transferred to the new structure in 1589, when the old building passed to the confraternity of the weavers' guild. The stone facing and other ornaments that Sansovino intended for his building were never completed, and today the towering structure is most remarkable for its heavily articulated brickwork. After the scuola was suppressed in the nineteenth century, its artworks were dispersed and the building abandoned. For some years its upper floor served as a basketball court. Now in the hands of the city, this enormous building, officially "in restoration," is for all intents and purposes abandoned.

Like the Madonna dell'Orto, the magnificent church of Santa Maria dei Miracoli also enshrined a miraculous object. In 1408 a citizen named Francesco Amadi commissioned a painting of the Virgin and Child, which he placed on the outside of his house. The image soon gained a reputation as miraculous. Devotees bought neighboring structures in the thickly settled area and demolished them to make room for a small wooden chapel. In 1481, under the direction of Pietro Lombardo, the wooden shrine was replaced by the structure that still stands on this narrow site in Cannaregio. (70)

Like the façade of the Scuola Grande di San Marco, the exterior of Santa Maria dei Miracoli is based on the pre-Gothic vocabulary of the basilica. The building, which fits very tightly into its constricted space, is rectangular in plan. A single architectural system unites all four walls, which are divided into two zones. In the lower zone, rectangular bays are separated by Corinthian pilasters on pedestals that support a heavy entablature. The upper zone of each façade is a blind arcade, pierced in every second bay by an arched window. Paired marble panels with contrasting stripes and pateras, some of

70

them porphyry, reflect the walls of St. Mark's Basilica. The heightened rear walls of the building are marked by large arcs that frame oculi. These walls support a cupola with a drum and a lantern very similar to those on San Marco. The main façade is crowned by a massive semicircular tympanum with a large oculus and three smaller ones around it.

The interior of the church, which is as completely ornamented and as perfectly preserved as the exterior, is even more exquisite. (71) Flooded with light from its many windows, every surface from floor to ceiling gleams. The floors are paved with patterned tiles; the walls are paneled with grain-matched sheets of light-colored marble. The vaulted ceiling of

71

the nave is an amazing imitation of Roman stucco work carried out in carved wood with inset painted panels. The altar with the wonder-working image above it stands under the dome at its end, raised up on an exceptionally high presbytery with a sacristy and crypt beneath.

The towering Dominican church dedicated to Santi Giovanni e Paolo dominates the northern rim of the city, in the sestiere of Castello. In 1234 Doge Jacopo Tiepolo, who would become the benefactor of the Franciscans a few years later, gave the Dominicans a tract of marshy land beyond the northern edge of the city where they too could build a monastery. After draining and consolidating the area, the Dominicans built a small church. By the beginning of the fourteenth century they

were ready to build on a scale that rivaled
the Frari. Construction progressed in fits and
starts until the church was dedicated in
1430; even then work continued for another
twenty years.

In its upper half the façade of San Zanipolo (as the church is known to Venetians)
resembles those of the Frari and the
Madonna dell'Orto. (72) It is divided into
three bays that correspond to the inner divisions of nave and side aisles. Brick pensile
arches that spring from stone brackets and a
stone cornice above them trace the roofline
of each bay. A huge round window with a

72

tiny one far above lights the nave; smaller oculi illuminate each aisle.
Three Gothic aedicules top the center bay. The lower half of the façade,
however, has no precedent elsewhere in Venice. Steep blind arches create a series of niches along the front. Rough brickwork above them and a
majestic entryway that overlaps them suggest a dramatic shift in design
midway through construction. Each of the arches contains a marble sarcophagus where prominent sponsors of the church, including the Doge
Tiepolo, were buried.

The center door was erected in the mid-fifteenth century, and parts of
it have been attributed to Bartolomeo Bon, who was working at the same
time on the Ca' d'Oro. In Venice, a recessed doorway crowned with a
tympanum and flanked by columns necessarily recalls the entrances to

San Marco. Bon replaced his exemplar's multiple columns and double colonnade with six massive columns. Their nearly classical proportions and beautifully detailed Corinthian capitals support an entablature that steps back into the recessed doorway. The tympanum is pointed rather than semicircular, and its exaggerated moldings suggest a Gothic rather than classical sensibility. The impressive doorway illustrates the freedom with which architects combined styles that, as the Renaissance took hold, would be seen as completely incompatible.

Fear of transforming the office of Doge into a hereditary principate made the Venetians reluctant to bury their leaders in San Marco. Soon after the consecration of San Zanipolo, the church began to compete with the Frari to supply what San Marco withheld, becoming not only the typical burial place for the supreme leaders of the Republic but for others who served it in exemplary ways. In the fifteenth century the tomb of the Dominican order's first great benefactor, Doge Jacopo Tiepolo, who died in 1249, was placed on the façade.

The inner face of the west wall is dominated by tombs of the Mocenigo family, and on the far left stands the Renaissance tomb of Doge Pietro Mocenigo, who died in 1476. Designed by Pietro Lombardo, the monument combines free-standing sculptures in the blind central arcade and deep surrounding niches of what is meant to be a triumphal arch. The Romans used triumphal arches to memorialize the highly ritualized victory parades of successful generals and their armies. This tomb combines figures that commemorate the worldly triumphs of Doge Mocenigo with an image of Christ the Redeemer, who triumphed over death.

The humanist and poet Francesco Petrarca was the first to adapt the brutal routine of the Roman triumphal procession to give shape to a Christian poem. He imagined a sequence of commemorative processions celebrating the victories of Love, Time, Fame, and other personifications. His poem, called "Trionfi" (Triumphs), which was very popular in the early Renaissance, gave rise to monuments of this kind and to allegorical paintings. It also spurred the creation of the elaborate allegorical floats that became increasingly popular in public festivals.

The entire center portion of the wall, including the entryway, has been absorbed into the massive tomb of Doge Alvise Mocenigo, who died over a century later. The monument seems to turn the church inside out, transforming the inner wall into an exterior façade. While the late fifteenth-century tombs to either side use the vocabulary of classicism very freely, this rigorously Neoclassical installation only grudgingly accommodates itself to the space available and makes no concessions to the style of the church. In fact, the tapering structure, with its peaked top and heavily articulated central bay, recalls the configuration of the façade only to critique and correct its Gothic "defects." Divided into two stories by a heavy cornice supported on four pilasters, its doorway is flanked by two antefixed columns that break through the entablature and give prominence to its center, a feature that ties it to Baroque architectural trends. These same fashions are evident in the rounded lintels of the upper-story windows and the illusionistic aedicule in the top center bay.

The nearby *Polyptych of St. Vincent Ferrer,* an early work by Giovanni Bellini, comprises three nearly discrete images linked by an architectural frame that also bears some resemblance to a triumphal arch. Details of the architectural molding around the openings, however, suggest a different model. The arches are separated by pilasters that support a flat

73

entablature. (73) This combination of Roman arcade with Greek colonnade, called the Tabularium motif, is found on a handful of important early Imperial monuments in Rome, including the prominent Tabularium on the Roman Forum where Senate records were kept. Adopted by architects like Raphael and Bramante, this motif became one of the touchstones of Roman Neoclassicism in the early sixteenth century. Sansovino popularized it in Venice soon after. Its appearance here is very unusual, and its assimilation to the form of the triumphal arch is a typical example of the eclecticism that early Renaissance style shared with the Gothic.

Within this wonderful frame, Bellini's panels have a loose unity based on the gaze of his figures. St. Christopher, St. Vincent Ferrer, and St. Sebastian fill their spaces like statues in niches. St. Vincent is surrounded by seraphim, but the figures to his left and right share a common horizon line. The small-scale landscapes that frame these two saints seem intended to contrast the watery environment of St. Christopher with the arid landscape in which St. Sebastian was martyred. Christopher and Sebastian both look upward to a figure of the dead Christ supported by angels; that image is flanked by the Annunciation. Below the saints' feet, the predella panels, framed by the pedestals of the pilasters, detail the miracles of St. Vincent Ferrer.

The tomb of Marco Corner, who died at the end of the fourteenth century, highlights the dramatic difference between early Renaissance tombs and their Gothic predecessors. This monument projects from the brick wall of the church; and in typical early Renaissance fashion, the deceased is represented as a supine, inanimate figure—a *gisant*—with a pillow beneath his head and feet and a sword at his side. Figures of saints and angels stand in linked aedicula above his head.

The large twenty-four-hour clock at the northern end of the transept was built in the early sixteenth century. Directly beneath the clock is the wall tomb of Doge Andrea Venier, which features figures of the virtues instead of saints and angels. In the corner at the far left is the tomb of his wife, Agnese, their daughter, Orsola, and their daughter-in-law, Petronilla de Toco. Though Agnese's tomb is near that of her husband the Doge, it is clearly separate, and the inclusion of other women within the tomb suggests that the separation of men and women in Venetian society was meant to endure beyond the grave.

The massive Chapel of the Rosary at the north end of the apse (also called the Chapel of the Most Blessed Sacrament) was built in the early seventeenth century. In the fifteenth century, the Dominican Alan de Rupé popularized the rosary and organized confraternities around its use throughout France and Germany, all the while attributing the discovery of the rosary to St. Dominic. Like the scapular of the Carmelites, the rosary, encouraged and sponsored by the Dominicans, became an incredibly popular form of devotion. The opulent Chapel of the Rosary at San

Zanipolo is clear testimony to that popularity. The most striking decorations in this beautiful room, however, have nothing to do with the rosary or its devotees. The richly carved and gilded ceiling of the chapel, which frames a series of paintings by Veronese, is another example of the rescue of works of art from suppressed Venetian churches.

Above the nave of the chapel, three paintings represent *The Annunciation, The Adoration of the Shepherds,* and *The Assumption.* Commissioned by the Jesuits—a Counter-Reformation clerical order who came to Venice in the mid-sixteenth century—the paintings were removed from their church of Santa Maria dell'Umiltà at the time of its demolition in 1821 and transported to Vienna. They were not repatriated until the end of World War I. Like Tintoretto's nearly contemporary ceiling paintings for the Scuola Grande di San Rocco, these wonderful images take full advantage of the viewpoint from below to create the illusion of actions grounded in terrestrial architecture that soar off into heavenly space. This is a familiar and appropriate space for *The Assumption,* but it is an unusual and challenging setting for *The Annunciation.* Mary is framed within an arch in an open-roofed structure—perhaps an atrium—that is supported on massive serpentine columns. Rather than float or fly in through the door, the archangel Gabriel, who hovers in midair with the dove of the Holy Spirit beside him, has evidently come through the open roof.

The second group of paintings, now located above the altar, came from a curious little church near the Frari called St. Nicholas of the Lettuce, which was demolished in 1806. Like Madonna dell'Orto, the church of St. Nicholas commemorated a miracle-working object found in a garden. Sadly, Veronese's paintings for the church, completed some twenty years after the cycle in the nave, do not narrate this miraculous discovery. Their central image is a representation of *The Adoration of the Magi,* surrounded by four remarkable images of the evangelists.

Opening from the north wall of the nave, the sacristy of the church resembles nothing so much as the meeting hall of a confraternity. With its elaborately carved benches, rich stucco work, and inset paintings, it is an intact installation with a dominating theme. Completed in the early seventeenth century, the cycle depicts achievements of the Dominican order. The large painting in the center of the ceiling represents the dream of St. Dominic. Two others record the dream of Doge Jacopo Tiepolo and his gift of land for the building of Santi Giovanni e Paolo. These foundational stories link the sacristy program to the late mosaics in San Marco, where the saint dreams of his future home and its glory to come.

Next door to the church is one of the greatest and most appealing fifteenth-century buildings in Venice, the Scuola Grande di San Marco. (74) Founded in 1260, the year the flagellant processions swept through Europe, the scuola was first associated with a now-vanished church near the Rialto; it moved into the Dominican orbit in the early fifteenth century. After an earlier building on the site was destroyed by fire, the present structure was begun in the late 1480s. A number of architects worked on the

74

project: the scuole in general seem to have been difficult clients, hiring and firing architects at a pace that probably reflected the frequent changes in their own leadership. Pietro Lombardo designed the lower stories of the building, which Mauro Codussi completed. The decorative vocabulary from which this composite is built up is consistently based on Roman models, but the proportions of the building and its asymmetrical façade mark it as anything but Neoclassical.

This characteristic feature of early Renaissance architecture in Venice is often criticized as a misunderstanding of the Florentine Neoclassicism pioneered by men like Ghiberti, Donatello, Brunelleschi, and Alberti. Venetian classical eclecticism might better be seen as an interpretation of the rich architectural tradition of the city in a newly rediscovered vocabulary of ornament. High classicism, as the inner façade of Santi Giovanni e Paolo illustrates, is almost completely unresponsive to context. Renaissance classicism understood its site only in terms of decorum; it recognized a rural or an urban site, a formal or a pastoral one, but it saw no meaningful distinction between cities as different as Rome and Venice. Like twentieth-century Modernism, this classicism made no concessions to the particulars of history; it never evoked local styles or echoed local monuments. To judge the work of the Lombardo family or Codussi as imperfect or misconceived is to impose the grid of the High Renaissance on a movement with very different principles.

The local building that Pietro Lombardo and Codussi responded to was, of course, San Marco, whose patron saint had even greater than usual significance for this scuola dedicated to his name. The basilica these architects invoked, however, was not the San Marco that had been transformed by Gothic ornament but the underlying Byzantine structure, with its roots in Roman Imperial architecture. The Roman arch is the dominant form in every part of the scuola. Lombardo used it to define the entrance on both the scuola side and the albergo side of the building. Wonderful fictive arcades flanking the main entrance, the inner profiles of the windows, and the tympana on the scuola side are arched. Codussi's elaborate cresting, a coronal of arches, hides the building's tile roof and defines its upper profile. The pateras and the marble panels that cover the façade, many of them in porphyry, also link the building to San Marco. The winged lion above four columns at the pinnacle of the façade and the bas-relief lions in the fictive niches underscore this association.

Like so many others, the Scuola Grande di San Marco was suppressed in 1807 during Napoleon's occupation of the city. The entrance now leads to the public hospital. In the lower hall, stripped of its altar and its art, receptionists in a wooden booth route patients to their appointments. Behind the booth on the right, Codussi's stairway—destroyed in 1812 and reconstructed in 1952—leads past alcohol-scented clinics to the upper room of the scuola. The salone or chapel preserves a series of paintings by Tintoretto, Palma Giovane, and others retelling the story of St. Mark.

The bronze figure of Bartolomeo Colleoni that stands on the campo to the right of the church is the only outdoor sculpture in Venice erected before the nineteenth century. The dedicatee, whose military service to the Republic eventually outweighed his service to its enemies, secured the honor for himself by leaving the city three hundred thousand ducats in his will. The statue was designed by the Florentine sculptor Andrea

75

Verrocchio in imitation of Donatello's statue of the condottiere Gattamelata, which stands near the church of San Antonio in Padua. Both works were based on the gilded bronze statue of Marcus Aurelius that formed the centerpiece of Michelangelo's design for the Campidoglio (Capitoline Hill) in Rome. In Verrocchio's day, that prototype still stood in front of the cathedral of San Giovanni in the Lateran and was generally believed to be an image of the first Christian emperor, Constantine. By adopting this image as their model, these sculptors cast the two military leaders not just as Roman emperors—which ought to have been flattery enough—but as emperors who battled to establish Christianity, and so a kind of proto-crusader. (75)

From the Venetian point of view, Colleoni may have been a warrior for the true faith; but from the perspective of modern historians, what he served most obviously was the *Machtpolitik* of his era. The Venetian navy guarded the trade routes and island colonies in the Mediterranean. The security of overland routes between Venice and its trading partners north of the Alps was traditionally guaranteed by diplomacy. Around the year 1400, Venice began to change its approach to mainland politics. Venetian nobles, who had always been discouraged and at times forbidden to own land on terra firma, were now permitted to do so. They quickly bought up huge tracts, and much of the wealth gained through trade was reinvested in real estate. These investments sheltered the mercantile nobility from the devastating changes in Mediterranean commerce that followed the Portuguese discovery of an all-water route to the Indies. Circling Africa, the Portuguese bypassed the Mediterranean and destroyed Venice's monopoly of the spice trade. A buffer in the short term, over time the shift from commerce-based to land-based wealth encouraged the Venetian patriciate to identify with the continental nobility in a way they had never done before. This new sense of belonging to an international elite divided Venetian nobles from commoners and undermined their identification with the Republic.

With increased investment came increased political involvement. The Republic, which had always exerted its influence on the governments of its nearest neighbors, began a program of territorial expansion. Allied cities became clients; the traditional sphere of Venetian influence evolved into a web of colonies, and Venice established itself as a mainland power. In a fragmented and fractious Italy, little states carried out little wars, and big states carried out bigger wars. The major contenders for power in the northern end of the peninsula were Milan, Florence, and the Papacy. Powerful, rich, and as unscrupulous as any of the others, Venice entered the arena as a contender whose economic and territorial interests threatened big and little states alike. In 1508, not long after the Portuguese reached India, the major powers of Italy temporarily found a common purpose: they united in an alliance called the League of Cambria and attacked Venice.

During the mainland wars of the fifteenth century that led up to this debacle, the Republic frequently made use of Colleoni. His greatest success was a coup not so much of strategy as of logistics. To counter a

Milanese fleet that controlled the inland Lake Garda and threatened Venetian trade across the Alps, Colleoni transported six galleys and two galleons from the head of navigation on the River Adige overland through the foothills of the Alps to reach the lake. Despite this bold and ultimately successful maneuver, the Venetians failed to appoint Colleoni as captain general of their army. So, in a move typical of military leaders throughout the period, he joined the Milanese. More than twenty years later he was finally offered the commission to lead the Venetian army, which he continued to do until his death in 1475.

The church of Santa Maria Formosa, on a large campo in Castello directly south of San Zanipolo, was established in the seventh century on a spot which the Virgin—according to legend—revealed to St. Magnus, bishop of Oderzo. The bishop was so struck by the beauty of Mary that the church has retained the name formosa, meaning beautiful. Though almost certainly not a seventh-century church, the original structure was old enough to undergo renovation during the two great pre-Gothic building eras in Venice, the ninth and twelfth centuries. Like the much smaller San Giacomo di Rialto, Santa Maria Formosa was designed in the form of a Greek cross, square in plan with a dome at its center. Francesco Sansovino described it as being like the midportion of San Marco. Following the pattern typical of early churches, the façade was oriented toward the nearby canal.

By the late fifteenth century this ancient church was in a sufficient state of disrepair to require a complete reconstruction. Codussi extended the nave, creating a three-aisled basilica with a transept and deep choir. He separated the nave and aisles with an arcade that springs from widely separated classicizing piers. Chapels with arched openings flank the aisles and transept. As in the earlier church, a dome tops the crossing. The ceilings of the nave, transept, and choir are cross-vaulted. Shallow false domes top each bay of the aisles. The plain surfaces of the interior are cream-colored; cornices and the frames of arches are constructed in a darker neutral stone like the material Brunelleschi used in the Pazzi Chapel, San Lorenzo, and elsewhere in Florence.

The first chapel to the right of the main entrance encloses Bartolomeo Vivarini's *Misericordia Triptych*. Created in the early 1470s, it was placed here after Codussi's renovations. The three panels, painted in egg tempera, are related in color, composition, and theme, and harnessed together by a classicizing marble frame. The central panel of the three shows the popular image of the Madonna della Misericordia, who spreads open her long blue mantle to shelter the kneeling figures at her feet. The scene on the left shows the meeting of Joachim and Anna; that on the right represents the birth of the Virgin.

The first transept chapel belonged to the Scuola dei Bombardieri, or artillerymen. The Venetians began to use gunpowder in siege weapons sometime in the mid-to-late thirteenth century. Though hardly an occupational specialty in the ordinary sense, the bombardieri were united in that most typical of Venetian social groups, a scuola. Their meeting place was next to this church. In the last centuries of the Republic, this scuola was very prominent in public processions not because of any particular relic it possessed but because of the gorgeous uniforms of its members.

In the early sixteenth century the scuola commissioned Palma Vecchio to paint six panels for the altarpiece of their chapel. Installed in a classicizing architectural frame with military insignia, the panels depict the patron saint of the scuola, Santa Barbara, alongside St. John the Baptist and some others. The images, like those in the Vivarini triptych, share a frame but are independent of one another. St. Barbara stands on a small pedestal with the open mouth of a bombard in shadow at her feet. She is crowned and holds a palm frond, both symbols of martyrdom. A tower stands behind her.

According to legend, this now decanonized saint was imprisoned by her father in a tower, where she was instructed by learned pagans. Instead of embracing paganism, however, her rigorous instruction led her to question its values and to choose Christianity. Her enraged father tortured and killed her, then was killed himself by a bolt of lightning. The tower where she was kept made Barbara a plausible patron for soldiers involved in siege warfare. The fire from heaven that avenged her death made her the patron of the artillery.

Codussi died when the church was almost completed. The canal façade was added some forty years later at the expense of the Cappello family. The statue and sarcophagus above the central doorway commemorate Vincenzo Cappello, admiral of the Venetian fleet in the early sixteenth century. The façade that opens onto the campo—at the end of the transept, not the nave—was added in 1604, also at the expense of the Cappello family. Three busts commemorate other important family members. This secondary façade reflects the increasing importance of landside rather than waterside access.

Campo Santa Maria Formosa is one of the largest, most active, and most beautiful in Venice. Divided nearly in half by the church, it has two distinct personalities. The smaller open area at the rear of the church is overshadowed by linked apses that resemble grain silos and the looming Palazzo Malipiero and Palazzo Querini Stampalia—with its library and picture collection open to the public—on the opposite side of a narrow canal. Neighborhood children scream and run around on an improvised preschool playground. Beyond the apses, the campo spreads out. (76) Palazzo Vitturi, immediately across from the church, dates from the thirteenth century; the Gothic house of Sebastian Venier, victor against the

Turks in the famous battle of Lepanto, dates from the fourteenth. The linked palaces of the Donà family stretch beyond the limits of the campo. Shops and restaurants fill the ground floors of the palazzi on its long side. Children play throughout the campo, especially around its large well heads.

76

An image of the Madonna della Misericordia supported on brackets, crowned with a quadrilobate opening and framed with a steep and richly decorated Gothic molding, overlooks the entrance to the nearby Calle del Paradiso. (77) This narrow street, which is always in shadow, has ground-floor shops along both sides. Two long files of uniform wooden brackets reach into the right-of-way to support overhanging second stories designed as apartments. The buildings were remodeled and additional stories were added in the seventeenth century, but the original character

77

of the street has been preserved. The block was a real estate investment designed and built as a single unit in the early fifteenth century. The property passed from its first owner to the Foscari, then the Mocenigo family. These families owned multiple palazzi, which they rented out in whole or in part to other wealthy families, but they also invested in Venetian commercial real estate and housing for workers and artisans.

The church of San Francesco della Vigna sits on the north side of the city in Castello, not far from Santi Giovanni e Paolo. Its grant of land, originally a vineyard, came within decades of the Dominican land grant nearby and the Franciscan tract across town where the Frari would rise. The same idea—ensuring consolidation of new land at the margin of development—lay behind this grant. A three-aisled basilica on a reduced scale was constructed on the site in the fourteenth century, but urbanization around San Francesco della Vigna was slow to take hold. Revitalizing the area was part of Doge Andrea Gritti's plan when he sponsored the remodeling of the church under the direction of Sansovino in 1534.

Today, this Renaissance structure in a still-underpopulated part of town contrasts sharply in style, atmosphere, and activity with its Franciscan cousin, the Frari. A small, sterile campo littered with trash offers a prospect on only half of its façade. (78) The other half is screened by a palazzo that once housed the papal representative in Venice. Andrea Palladio, the designer who was commissioned to create this pioneering façade, had hoped to see the obscuring building razed, but his plan was frustrated. The result is a sorry compromise—typical of Palladio's hard luck in Venice—between a building meant to be seen face-on and a site that offers either a partially obstructed or an oblique view. The campo to the right of the church is no better. Surrounded by closed doors and silent apartments, this wide-open space offers an unobstructed view of the church's uninspiring flank. At its narrow end is the modest sixteenth-century building that once housed the confraternity of the Sacred Stigmata of St. Francis.

Sansovino redesigned the form of the church as a basilica with a shallow crossing, deep choir, and chapels at either side of the nave. He also intended it to have a cupola, which was never built. The unusual proportions reflect the Cabalistic number theory of one of the friars of the order, Francesco Zorzi, who published his researches in his 1525 book, *The Harmony of the Whole World*. Shortly after the building's completion, Giustiniani commissioned Veronese to create an altarpiece for the family chapel. The painting he produced is a provocative re-editing of Titian's Pesaro altarpiece in the Frari. The young painter replaced Titian's dynamic meditation on mediation

78

79

with a more static sacra conversazione. Its saturated color and
remarkable highlights make the
silks and satins more interesting than the people or the idea
they express.

The Grimani chapel, com-
pleted shortly thereafter, is
unusual not only for its form
but for the medium used. Because of Venice's perpetual dampness and
unstable subsoil, both of which are extremely damaging to fresco, most
Venetian painting is oil on canvas. This small chapel is an exception. By
its form, the barrel-vaulted space recalls many of the rooms in Nero's
Golden House in Rome, which was explored by painters and architects
beginning in the early sixteenth century. This model is most apparent in
the ceiling, which is divided into linked square and round sections outlined with stucco work and painted with simple scenes or single figures.
(79) The altarpiece done in fresco by Zuccaro shows *The Adoration of the
Magi.* Cardinal Grimani, who commissioned this chapel, also commissioned Palladio to redo the façade of the church.

The most extraordinary monument in the church is the Capella
Badoer-Giustiniani. Originally part of the earlier church, this chapel was
enlarged and reinstalled by Sansovino, a sculptor as well as an architect
who contributed works of his own and an organizing framework. The altar
of the chapel is in the form of a classical porch, with two columns, an
entablature with a narrative frieze, and pediment. These elements frame

an altarpiece very similar in form to the early Renaissance tombs in San
Zanipolo. The fictive architecture here includes illusionistic bas-reliefs
like those on the façade of the Scuola Grande di San Marco. Scenes from
the life of St. Jerome—namesake of its dedicatee—fill its niches.

The walls of the chapel are decorated with low-relief sculptures about
half life-size of twelve Old Testament prophets and the four evangelists.
(80) Each prophet holds a scroll with a brief quote from his text. Small
narrative scenes in a continuous frieze above these figures relate their
veiled words to their fulfillment in the life of Christ. These remarkably
vivid images in an extraordinary state of preservation, which can be seen
face to face in the intimate chapel, have an almost magical power and
presence. Their quality alone seems to explain and justify the ingenuity

that went into preserving and
resetting them not once but
twice. Originally part of the choir
screen of the church, they had
already been reorganized into a
decorative scheme for a chapel
before Sansovino intervened.

80

The modest Scuola di San
Giorgio degli Schiavoni—located
on the Rio di San Lorenzo at the
eastern end of Castello—was the meeting place and mutual aid society of
the Croatian community. In the early sixteenth century the scuola commissioned Vittore Carpaccio to create a cycle of paintings in the lower
hall of their small building. The paintings, which commemorated several

saints important to the community, gave special prominence to the dragon-slayer St. George and the scholar and translator of the Bible St. Jerome.

Carpaccio's cycle here shares many characteristics with his much larger paintings for the Scuola di Sant'Orsola. Both cycles retell complex stories where ceremonial scenes and miraculous or fantastic episodes alternate; and both are set among exotic versions of local architectural styles. Ursola's eleven thousand virgins and their followers, including a pope unknown to history, propel her legend into the realm of fantasy. In the St. George and St. Jerome panels, the two beasts associated with the otherwise unrelated saints are equally marvelous, but the cycle makes a coherent allegorical argument. St. George, an orthodox warrior saint, drives his lance into the open mouth of a winged dragon, which he succeeds in subduing but not killing. In a second scene, the saint leads the dragon on a leash—the lance protruding from the back of its head—into town.

The Roman St. Jerome spent part of his life in a small hermitage in the wilderness, where he practiced penitential self-discipline. Many paintings of the saint show him as an old man stripped to the waist and beating his bare chest with a rock. One day a lion with a thorn stuck in his paw wandered into the shelter of the holy man. Jerome removed the thorn, and the lion went on his way but remained—in hagiography—an emblem of the saint. Carpaccio's paintings transform the solitary monasticism of early Christianity into the communal monasticism that replaced it after the Benedictine reform. The wandering lion has become Jerome's permanent companion, but one that terrifies the rest of the brothers.

By pairing the legends of these saints and their symbolic beasts, Carpaccio created a cycle that exemplified two ways of dealing with the bestial or the irrational. St. George, embodying the warrior virtues of courage and fortitude, represents the path of conquest. St. Jerome represents the ideal of purification, cleansing the soul of those appetites that create fear and anger. In the scuola of a foreign community in Venice, irrational fear of a lion—symbol of the Republic—takes on a political cast.

The last painting in the sequence is something of a miracle in itself. St. Augustine, a near-contemporary of Jerome, once saw a vision of his fellow saint in a ray of light. In the painting, Augustine is sitting at his writing desk, pen in hand, when he suddenly becomes aware of an image in the light that streams through his window. (81) A little white dog—the bestial and irrational now thoroughly domesticated—stares up at him. The room is a combination chapel and studio, a place of devotion but

81

also a workspace for a man whose interests embrace nearly every field. There are books everywhere, in a neat row on a long bracketed shelf, on bookstands, propped haphazardly against the wall, half-opened and leaning against the dais at the saint's feet. Astrolabes, celestial spheres, and other mathematical instruments are scattered through the room and visible through an open door in an adjoining one.

Most remarkable of all are the antiquarian objects on a narrow shelf beneath the books. These include a number of Greek or Roman pots and many small classical bronzes, including some attenuated forms that look Etruscan. St. Augustine clearly represents an ideal of the learned man who is deeply religious but also avid for books and mathematical gadgets. He is a Christian who does not close his eyes either to science or the beauty of classical culture. The real St. Augustine may not have been so broad-minded, but this extraordinary painting represents him as a model for Renaisssance Venetian humanists.

Not far from the Scuola di San Giorgio degli Schiavoni and a short walk from the Piazza of San Marco, the church of San Zaccaria in Castello and its attached monastery (now suppressed) were among the most powerful institutions of the Republic. Founded in the early ninth century under the sponsorship of the first Doge and his family, the monastery was supported by the Byzantine court, which donated skilled workmen, materials, funds, and relics to it. The monastery was also endowed with land, including the eventually priceless tract in front of San Marco Basilica which, when purchased by the state in the twelfth century, became the Piazza San Marco. A Benedictine foundation like many others in the Lagoon, San Zaccaria was a convent for women from the wealthiest and most prominent of patrician families. Over the centuries of its existence, their dowries and legacies augmented the already formidable endowment of the monastery.

If the Palazzo Ducale and San Marco represented the centers of state orthodoxy and state power closely held by men of the nobility, San Zaccaria was its college of Vestal Virgins. Eight among the earliest Doges are buried in the church. In recognition of its prominence, the Doge and the other high officers of state made an annual ceremonial visit. (82) Originally this ceremony, which was celebrated for almost a thousand years, took place in early September on the anniversary of the church's foundation. It was soon transferred to Easter, the most solemn feast of the liturgical year.

The ninth-century church, a relatively modest three-aisled basilica like San Giacomo del Orio, was renovated and repaired repeatedly during the Middle Ages. In the mid-fifteenth century, with funds obtained not only from the Senate but from Pope Calixtus III, the successive renovations of the original structure were abandoned in favor of a new building. This church would stand to the left of the old structure and partially overlap it. The parts of the old church that were not incorporated into the new

82

were subdivided into a number of rooms, one of which served as a chapel, another as the sacristy. The rest of the building, which is now open to the public, is used as an exhibition space.

The new church began at ground level as a Gothic structure but acquired Renaissance characteristics as it progressed. The internal division into nave and side aisles with an ample crossing was as compatible with Gothic style as it was with its eventual Neoclassical ornamentation. The presbytery of the church, however, represents an elaboration of the Gothic found nowhere else in Venice. The apse of the church, which corresponds to the width of the nave, is surrounded by an ambulatory the width of the side aisles. A series of chapels radiate out from this ambulatory. The chapel and sacristy carved out of the old structure are also linked, making the altar end especially confusing. A tiny stairway leads down to the Romanesque crypt. Built on the Lilliputian scale of the earliest Venetian structures, its marble floor is now sunk below the water table and permanently flooded.

Antonio Gambello, who received the original commission for the new structure, died in 1481. In 1483 the task of completing the church was turned over to Codussi. He immediately modified the ornamental scheme of the church, substituting Roman arches for the Gothic ones envisioned by Gambello and, for the interior, imposing the Brunelleschian scheme of dark moldings against cream-colored walls that he used in Santa Maria Formosa. His most remarkable innovation was the front for the new church. Gambello had completed the lower two zones of the façade, basing the lowest area around an inflected surface pattern of coffered squares and the second zone on an idealized arcade of five window openings and blind arcades with scallop shells set in the curve of each arch. Both were marked by strong vertical divisions corresponding to the separation of nave and aisles. Codussi capped the lower part of the façade with a heavy entablature and preserved the three-part division, which he extended with pairs of antefixed columns. He added more window openings and broadened their proportions, disguised the aisle roofs with circular supports pierced by blind oculi, and crowned the nave with a majestic tympanum, which was completed with an oculus and a huge projecting three-dimensional cornice.

Historians looking at San Zaccaria often point to the entablature separating Gambello's façade from Codussi's as the high-water mark of the Venetian Gothic and the dividing line between one era and the next. For many, the Gothic represents the greatest era in Venetian history. Venerable, strong, and secure, with immense wealth based in trade, the Republic was still unthreatened by the fall of Byzantium, the ascendancy of the Turks, the Portuguese circumnavigation of Africa, or the mainland wars in Italy. Within a few years, these converging events would force Venice to bend politically and regroup socially. How wonderful to be able to show the telltale line on the wall and say, just so high and never higher.

But what Codussi actually built above this line in the sand shows little kinship with the architectural language of the High Renaissance. For all his familiarity with the vocabulary of arcades, pedestals, oculi, and antefixed columns, Codussi created a façade that reflects a Gothic sensibility rather than a Neoclassical one. His building is too steep and narrow to satisfy a Neoclassical sense of proportion. His subdivision of the façade into six layered zones and his creation of what appears to be a freestanding barrel-vaulted space at the top of the structure are reflections of San Marco Basilica rather than any independent classical ideal.

It is certainly true that Codussi was a Neoclassicist. But in this building he combines classical elements with a Gothic freedom of association and sense of proportion, and he invokes local models. The high classicism of the sixteenth century will represent a far more decisive break than this fissure in the façade of San Zaccaria. High classicism rejected the Venetian past in favor of an international language, at the very time when Venice herself was foraging for a new identity, a new way of being, and—most critically—a new way of being safe in a suddenly hostile world.

Chapter Six

STATE OF SIEGE

Through most of its long life, the Republic was ringed by hostile powers, but skilled diplomacy and a formidable navy kept its military perimeters far from home. Venice always traded with the enemy, and so the Turks, the Dalmatians, the Eastern Orthodox, the Jews, eventually the Protestants—all political or religious antagonists—could not be kept beyond the frontiers but lived and worked inside the city. Venice was not only unfortified but lay open to deep-water ships from the Adriatic and shallow-draft vessels from the mainland. The openness trade required brought not only the danger of heresy and sedition but the more insistent and more deadly risk of disease.

Seafarers entered the Lagoon from any one of three ports—the Venetian term for the deep channels that cut through the barrier island and gave access to the Adriatic. Warships made for the Arsenal. Mercantile vessels, closely watched by the customs police, moored in the general area of San Marco. Ships from places known to be infected with the plague were routed to the island of San Clemente. After the first case of leprosy was seen in the city in the early fourteenth century, a leper colony was established on an island now known as San Lazzaro degli Armeni. In the early sixteenth century its inmates were transferred to the hospital of San Lazzaro de' Mendicanti near Santi Giovanni e Paolo. Soon after Columbus's ships brought syphilis from the New World, hospices emerged to treat the victims of this deadly disease. Established to distribute the charity of the Republic, these institutions also served as imperfect filters to insulate and protect the population against alien infections.

Alien orthodoxies were equally troublesome. If travelers from infected regions could be confined to offshore islands, followers of different creeds could be treated the same way. In most cases confinement was benign. The Greeks settled in the neighborhood of their church of San Giorgio in Castello. The Croatian neighborhood was nearby, with the Scuola di San Giorgio degli Schiavoni as its center. German traders were confined to their fondaco and the streets around Campo San Bartolomeo. Even before the Turks were given an official residence, they were closely watched. But during the Renaissance the Jews became the most tightly confined and intensely guarded population. Forced to live in the Ghetto, their movements within the city were strictly regulated.

Yet even these strictures had some openness to them. Passage out of the Ghetto, the fondaco, or the ethnic community was always possible. Long-term residents of Venice routinely gained citizenship. For non-Catholics, the key to assimilation was conversion to Catholic Christianity. At first the work of conversion was carried out by individual families, who took in potential converts and saw them through the process. Eventually a private foundation was organized and a building set aside near the church of the Holy Apostles (Santi Apostoli) in Cannaregio. In the sixteenth century a building in Dorsoduro took its place and became popularly known as the Case de' Catecumeni. Muslim slaves or former slaves learned their catechism here, alongside young men who professed their intent to convert from Judaism.

Conversion to Christianity removed the barriers to a fuller participation in Venetian social and economic life, but it also exposed the newly minted Christian to significant risks. A convert who reverted to his original religion or even associated with his former friends was likely to attract the attention of either the Catholic Inquisition or the Venetian bureaucracy that monitored orthodoxy. While the non-Catholic was a non-person, the convert who returned to his original faith was an apostate. Being a Jew was not a crime, but reverting to Judaism after conversion was the most serious of transgressions, equal to heresy or blasphemy, for which the punishment could be death.

One uniquely Venetian form of quarantine came with no possibility of reprieve. In the fourteenth century the Venetian glass industry was transferred from locations throughout the city to the nearby island cluster of Murano. Fire protection was the main motive, but there were other important factors at play. Simply melting sand, the industry's primary raw material, at high temperatures would not produce glass that was workable and durable. Fabricating massive amounts of glass in multiple patterns required a large labor force with enormous skill and a select group of masters with trade secrets that passed from generation to generation within the tight-knit community. The consolidation of the industry gave Venice a monopoly in making glass of all sorts. After the fifteenth-century Turkish destruction of bead-making centers in the Middle East, Venice became dominant in that lucrative industry as well.

Murano grew increasingly important to the Republic's commerce, as glass-filled boats made landfall in Cannaregio or Castello en route to the mainland. To protect its economic interests, Venice forbade master glassmakers to leave the closely guarded island, and those convicted of passing the secrets of glassmaking to non-Venetians faced execution. Harsh as these policies were, they were ultimately unsuccessful. When glassmakers from Bohemia and Holland finally learned the tricks of the Venetian masters, they quickly became serious competitors.

While glassmaking was a local industry, Venice was not the producer of most of the goods it traded. It was an entrepôt where the products and wealth of one region were exchanged for the products and wealth of another. The city depended on inland commerce for wood, grain, wine, olive oil, and, in seasons of drought, fresh water. The Mediterranean fleet transported Arabian pepper and spices, plus silk and cotton from Egypt, sugar from Cyprus, and gold from Africa. The Republic needed to foster this commercial exchange—the economic expression of its openness—but it also needed to benefit from all the goods that passed through. Merchants had to profit from their services as go-betweens, and the state needed to collect taxes. Monitoring and controlling the commercial flow was essential, and the best way to do that was by slowing it down—creating buffers between ocean traffic and inland traffic.

If canals were the emblems of the city's openness to commerce, bridges were the valves that controlled the flow of goods. Land-based people think of bridges in just the opposite way—as links between places separated by water. For the water-minded Venetians, however, bridges were erected as obstacles. The Rialto Bridge, in place by the late fourteenth century, divided the Grand Canal into two parts, one of which was connected to the sea while the other was accessible from the landward side. The tall masts of ocean vessels could not pass under the arch of the bridge. Ocean cargoes had to be off-loaded on the seaward side and

transferred to smaller ships. It was no coincidence that the Rialto market
stood at this point of exchange.

The Ponte Tre Archi, which spans the Cannaregio Canal near its
Lagoon entrance, is another example of this, to our minds, curious use of
bridges. Before the bridge's construction, this major canal, which linked
mainland commerce directly to the Grand Canal, threatened Venetians'
ability to regulate commercial traffic. Similarly, at the other end of the
waterway, near the junction of the Cannaregio and Grand canals, the
Ponte delle Guglie, built in 1688, served not only as a pedestrian link
between the parallel islands of Cannaregio but also as a roadblock to
slow the flow of traffic along the canal.

The ceremonial entrance to Venice on the Piazzetta San Marco
reflects, in a symbolic way, the stricture on free passage that these
bridges imposed. The columns of St. Theodore and St. Mark are the sea
gates of Venice. Entering the city means walking between these landmarks, and the city made full use of this narrowed passage to express its
majesty. The twin columns—enormous spoils from some outpost in the
Greek islands or perhaps from Egypt—were erected in the twelfth century. On the top of the one nearer the Palazzo Ducale is an image of the
winged lion of St. Mark. A bronze sculpture of a chimera, perhaps made
in the Sassanid kingdom of Persia, it found its way to Venice at some
undetermined time. Wings were added to transform the figure into the
familiar Venetian symbol. The statue of St. Theodore was put together
from pieces of fourth-century classical sculpture. A Byzantine warrior-
saint and dragon-slayer like St. George, Theodore was the original dedicatee of the ducal chapel. (Map 6)

Walking under these columns, beneath the lion's drooping tail and the vaguely crocodilian beast at Theodore's feet, seems innocuous if not faintly comical today. Ceremonies that surrounded the arrival of distinguished visitors to the Doge's Palace would have added grandeur and dignity to the passage. But what made these monuments terrible and a true symbol of the constricting hand of the state was something else. According to legend, prisoners got a last glimpse of light from the small windows of the nearby Bridge of Sighs before being strangled in the silence and darkness of the execution chamber. But in fact, the usual practice was quite different: public executions were the norm, and these were commonly staged on a platform erected between the two columns.

At these events, Nuremberg standards of cruelty, typical of medieval and Renaissance capital punishment, were in full play. In view of the noisy crowd, the condemned were mutilated and tortured before being hanged. After death, their bodies were removed from the scaffold and hacked into pieces by the executioner. These butchered parts were dispatched to four areas of the city, where they were exposed and left to rot. Sometimes portions of the body were hung on gibbets that overlooked the inland waterways. The passage between the columns of St. Theodore and St. Mark was a place where Venice expressed itself with grandeur and majesty, or, when it chose, with sinister might.

A scant hundred feet from the twin columns, the Mint or Zecca, the first High Renaissance building in Venice, stands on the waterfront. (83) Venetians began minting coins in the ninth century. Their ascendancy in the African gold trade and in Mediterranean commerce in general was signaled by the minting of a major gold coin, the ducato (Shakespeare's

characters call it a ducat) under Doge Giovanni Dandolo in the late thirteenth century. Imitated by many
other nations, the Venetian ducat was the standard
coinage of Europe and the Mediterranean basin
throughout the Middle Ages and Renaissance. Even
after the actual coin was replaced by the zecchino,
the ducat continued to be used in accounting. Venice
expanded and remodeled its Mint many times. In
1535 the Council of Ten commissioned the recently
arrived Jacopo Sansovino to replace existing structures with a building that would be secure against
both theft and fire.

83

   Like the first mainlanders to inhabit the Lagoon,
Sansovino was fleeing from invaders who besieged
and sacked the city of Rome in 1527. Before his arrival in Venice, the
Florentine expatriate was best known as a sculptor. The tombs of Ascanio
Sforza and Giovanni Della Rovere in the choir at Santa Maria del Popolo
in Rome were his most celebrated works. Bramante, the great talent of
Renaissance architecture in Rome, designed the choir in which the
tombs were placed. Along with his collaborator, Raphael, Bramante was
at work codifying an architectural practice based on surviving Roman
buildings like the Theater of Marcellus, the Colosseum, and the Pantheon, and on the recently rediscovered text of Vitruvius' *De Architectura*.

   By the time of Raphael's death in 1520, the two had established a
consistent and authoritative style that formed the core of Renaissance
high classicism. In 1527 Sansovino brought that style to Venice. While

classicisms of various sorts had been practiced in the city for three quarters of a century by this time, Sansovino introduced an architecture based not just on a vocabulary of classicizing ornament but on a grammar of forms. His classicism demanded a rigorous adherence to antique prototypes that restricted the freedom Venetian architects had long enjoyed of combining classical ornaments willy-nilly. Unlike the practice of Pietro Lombardo or Codussi, Sansovino's architectural formalism imposed a uniformity and self-sufficiency on structures that was largely immune to local influences.

Sansovino's design for the Mint called for a two-story structure. (A third story was added after his death.) It followed the pattern that Bramante first laid out in a now-demolished Roman palazzo known as the House of Raphael. That building featured a rusticated lower story with arcaded openings for shops and a second story—intended to house a noble family—ornamented with columns and heavily articulated window frames. In Rome, the design survives in the Palazzo Vidoni-Cafarelli. Sansovino adopted this palazzo form to create his Mint. His ground floor is an arcade of nine identical arches outlined in heavy, square-cut blocks with joints that are deeply recessed. The Romans used coarse stonework of this kind, called rustication, for utilitarian projects. Rustication comes from the same Latin root as the English word "rural"; it was not originally an urban style. But Renaissance architects considered rustication a suitable style for city architecture at street level, both because it resisted wear—and occasional attack—and also because its lowly uses in the classical world seemed compatible with the workaday activities of Renaissance shops.

Sansovino's second story preserves the columns, large windows, and articulated frames that Bramante used to define the piano nobile of the House of Raphael in Rome. But he kept the utilitarian character of the building intact by carrying the rustication into that story as well. In swerving from Bramante's example, Sansovino turned back to an important Roman monument, the Porta Maggiore, a combined aqueduct support and city gate built under the emperor Claudius in the mid-first century AD. Its heavily rusticated outer wall is ornamented by columns with drums made up of alternating smooth and rough sections like stacks of coins of unequal denominations. Sansovino used these columns on the second story of the Mint, and they were later imitated on the third story, above an entablature with a frieze of triglyphs and an overhanging cornice supported on deep brackets.

As Sansovino designed it, the Mint was a squat utilitarian building with roots both in Roman antiquity and in adaptations of antique models by Roman architects of the Renaissance. The art historian and biographer Giorgio Vasari presented this architectural style as a triumph of Vitruvian classicism. But beyond the common heritage of Roman buildings with inner courtyards and façades made up of superimposed arcades, the building has no Venetian roots or links. While the Mint is not an aggressive structure, it is fully defended against a world where "thieves break in and steal, and moth and rust doth corrupt." It is the first public Venetian building that defies the Republican rhetoric of equality and communal civility. However subtly, it introduces a fortresslike building into a dogmatically unfortified city.

Compared with the courtyard of the Scuola Grande di San Giovanni Evangelista, this difference in tonality is very clear. The anonymous builder of the Neoclassical outdoor salon at San Giovanni welcomed any passerby into a space characterized as noble by its ornament but communal by its free access. While this is an anomalous space in Venice in many ways, the spirit of equality and accessibility that it expresses is not. Admittedly, a mint is not a place where public access can be encouraged, but the expression of exclusivity that enters the Venetian architectural vocabulary with the Mint was not limited to that structure. With the introduction of Sansovino's high classicism, Venice found an architectural expression of restriction and privilege that the nobility was not slow to put to private purposes.

Sansovino's second building at San Marco, begun at almost the same time as the Mint, is a treasure house of a different kind. In 1464 Cardinal Johannes Bessarion, one of the most remarkable men of the early Renaissance, donated his collection of some eight hundred Greek and Latin manuscripts to the Republic. Bessarion was born sometime near the close of the fourteenth century in the Black Sea port of Trebizond. He entered the Greek Orthodox priesthood and was appointed bishop of Nicea in 1436. Two years later he accompanied the Byzantine emperor to a council of Orthodox and Catholic bishops which, for a brief period, united the two confessions. Bessarion entered the Catholic hierarchy and remained in it after the reconciliation failed. He was soon raised to the rank of cardinal and twice came close to election as Pope. Throughout his life he worked for the accommodation of the two faiths he served, for the revival of classical learning, especially Greek learning, and for the harmonizing of the philosophies of Plato and Aristotle. His manuscript collections were part of his focused intellectual, cultural, and spiritual effort.

Bessarion was not the first classical scholar to endow Venice with books. A century before Bessarion's collection passed to the Republic, the early humanist, poet, and manuscript collector Francesco Petrarca willed his library to the city, but Petrarch's legacy never found its way to Venice. Bessarion's gift was neglected for decades, too; his books were at first kept in the Palazzo Ducale and afterward in the church of San Marco. They were not well looked after, and some of them were lost; others were defaced or stolen, because of the negligence of their custodians. Eventually the Senate recognized the need for a great public building opposite the Palazzo Ducale and decided that it should be a library. Sansovino was chosen as architect.

The library would become a public resource, where scholars conducted research and where readers in the pay of the Republic taught young men Greek and Latin. These were not the only civic goals that the building would realize, however. Sansovino saw it as a first step toward a redesign of the entire Piazza that would replace the inns and shops crowding the area with dignified structures in a uniform style. The political and ideological symbolism of a library was even more appealing to the Venetians. Constantinople had fallen in 1453; Rome had been sacked in 1527. By the mid-1530s it must have seemed entirely plausible to Venetians that their Republic—though battered by mainland wars—could be the successor to both capitals of the Roman Empire. A library that housed the learning of the Greeks and Latins would certainly symbolize that lineage.

Petrarch and Bessarion had something more specific in mind when they offered their intellectual property to a pragmatic city with a meager literary legacy. By bringing the relics of St. Mark from Alexandria, Venice had established a link between the two cities that could be understood as a transfer not only of faith but of classical learning. For many centuries Alexandria outshone even Athens as a center of Greek literature and philosophy. It symbolized and institutionalized this role through the creation of a great, indeed legendary, library. Establishing a library in Venice, especially one rich in Greek manuscripts, gave Venice a claim to be the modern repository of the Alexandrian heritage.

In the half century between Bessarion's death and the building of Sansovino's library, the art of making books had been revolutionized. In 1453, the year that Constantinople fell to the Turks, Johann Gutenberg created the first book using movable type. Before that date, every book was a hand-written copy of some other text. In the early Middle Ages in Europe, books

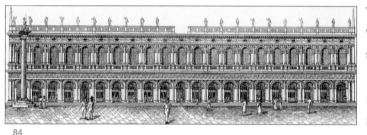

84

were invariably copied on parchment—specially cured and prepared animal skins that were extremely durable but difficult to work with and very expensive. In the fourteenth century, Italian artisans rediscovered the art of making paper or learned of it from China, where it had been made since the second century. Before long this cheaper and more adaptable material replaced parchment in all but the most richly decorated books. Gutenberg's invention of movable type, combined with the Italians' development of a cheap material on which to print, created an explosion in publishing.

In 1469, less than two decades after Gutenberg's first printing success, German printers set up shop in Venice. By the close of the fifteenth century, as many as 150 presses were operating in the city. Of the two million books produced in Europe during the first fifty years of printing, about one quarter came from Venice. Printed books were generally inexpensive, but many of them were also beautiful. The most celebrated Venetian printer was Aldo Manuzio (Aldus Manutius), an émigré from the countryside surrounding Rome, where new technologies and access to information were less appreciated than they were in Venice. He set up shop in 1489 and before his death in 1515 had printed some thirty small-format editions of Greek and Latin classics still valued by scholars as well as collectors. His shop reprinted Italian classics as well, including *The Divine Comedy.* Manuzio was also the printer of the beautiful and enigmatic *Hypnerotomachia Poliphili,* the focus of continued scholarly debate as well as a recent best-selling mystery. Many scholars consider it the most beautiful book ever printed. The Library represented antiquity and the preservation of the classical heritage, but it also represented Venetian productivity. Conceived as an Athenaeum, it played its part as an industry pavilion.

Sansovino's Library is an extended two-story loggia or portico with an astonishing twenty-one bays. (84) Its first story is elevated above the level of the Piazzetta on three steps. Like his Scuola Grande della Misericordia, which is raised on a plinth, and his nearby Loggetta, with its base a few feet above the level of the Piazza, the Library seems reluctant to get its feet wet. The ground-floor loggia is open, like the Gothic portico on the Palazzo Ducale opposite. Its Doric columns carry an entablature decorated with triglyphs and metopes.

The Ionic columns of the second story support a heavy entablature decorated with swags held by putti at the top of its frieze. Smaller

85

columns frame arched windows with masks at their summits and reclining nudes at their sides. Sansovino intended these to be river deities, a nod from within the restricted classical vocabulary toward the dominant role of water in Venetian life. Balustrades guard the window openings, and a balustrade broken by pedestals and crowned with life-size sculptures of Roman deities hides the roof. (85) Even today, when the rest of the Piazza has been brought to a level of formality that matches this building, the prospect is still impressive. To the generation who remembered the seedy inns, butchers' stalls, and wooden shops it replaced, it must have seemed an almost magical transformation of the Piazzetta.

Sansovino's tenure as state architect took a sudden swerve in December of 1545, when high winds and heavy snowfall bore down on the vaulted roof of the incomplete Library, causing it to collapse. Sansovino was jailed, and only the joint efforts of the revered Titian and the sharp-tongued polemicist Pietro Aretino succeeded in reversing his sentence. The architect was reinstated, but when he died twenty-five years later the building was still incomplete. His collaborator, Vicenzo Scamozzi, remained faithful to the original design and completed the building in 1588.

Sansovino's only surviving incursion into Piazza San Marco is the odd little structure called the Loggetta at the base of the enormous Campanile of San Marco. (86) The Loggetta stands directly across the Piazzetta from the Porta della Carta (the entrance to the Palazzo Ducale) and serves as a Neoclassical counterweight to that Gothic building.

Despite the thoroughgoing classicism of Sansovino's design, this small free-standing loggia is rooted in Gothic rather than classical traditions, and a medieval loggia stood on this site until its destruction in the early sixteenth century. With its detached columns, triple openings, and attic story decorated with sculptural bas-reliefs, the loggia resembles a variant form of the triumphal arch. It also looks something like an aqua castellum, which Vitruvius describes in *De Architectura*—a public fountain placed at the endpoint of an aqueduct. It brings water, which in post-Augustan Rome was always a gift of the emperor and was commemorated in an inscription or frieze. The Trevi Fountain in Rome is the most celebrated embellishment of this tradition. The much earlier terminal fountain of the Acqua Felice is a closer approximation of the Vitruvian ideal.

Of course there is no water flowing from the campanile, but the idea of water and the notion of an imperial gift are both important to the Loggetta. Again, Sansovino has made an ingenious if unlikely use of the classical formal repertoire to represent the importance of water to the Venetians. For each of the niches of the base story, Sansovino cast bronze statues representing Minerva, Apollo, Mercury, and Peace, all suitable tutelary deities for a great empire. Mercury, the messenger god associated with commerce (and thieves), might have been a nod to the Republic's mercantile heritage, but in keeping with a classical tradi-

86

tion that despised the merchant class, Sansovino suppressed any reference to trade. He intended his Mercury to represent eloquence.

The attic scenes include symbols of two of the city's most important colonies, the Greek islands of Cyprus and Candia. They flank an image of Venice as the goddess of Justice. As Francesco Sansovino described his father's creation: "The three panels in bas-relief above represent the Republic and her sovereignty over land and sea. In the central panel Venice is represented in the form of Justice, beneath whom are reclining figures representing rivers which pour out water, and these are the cities of the mainland. In the other panels of the attic are pictured Venus, whose birthplace was Cyprus, and Jove, who was ruler of Candia" (*Venezia, Città Nobilissima,* p. 308). Today, the Loggetta serves as the busy ticket office for the lift that takes visitors to the Campanile's bell chamber and observation platform.

Though it incorporated the foundations of a Roman watchtower, the Campanile does not correspond to any classical building type. In Venice, however, the Campanile came to represent another legendary monument—one of the seven wonders of the ancient world—the Pharos or Lighthouse of Alexandria. That fabled monument still stood when the Campanile of San Marco was begun in the ninth century. In the early fourteenth century, perhaps as the result of an earthquake, the last remaining stones of the great lighthouse tumbled into the sea (to be rediscovered by underwater archaeologists only at the end of the twentieth century). From the mid-fourteenth century onward, Venetians considered their Campanile the successor to the Pharos of Alexandria.

Some portion of the ninth-century Campanile of San Marco withstood the many remodelings that transformed a relatively restrained bell tower into the soaring monolith we see today. Though it was the first landmark that a ship bound for Venice could make out, the tower was invisible from many parts of the labyrinthine city. But its bells could be heard almost everywhere. There were five bells altogether, each with a different pitch, a personal name, and a particular job. The biggest bell, called the Marangona, signaled the beginning and end of the workday, as well as the curfew that restricted the movements of Turks, Germans, and Jews. It rang on Sunday afternoons to announce meetings of the Grand Council. A smaller bell, called the Trottiera, gave the warning that councilors were running late. There was a noon bell, called La Nona, and another, called the Mezza Terza, that announced meetings of the Senate.

The bell least often heard was the Renghiera or Maleficio, which gave the signal for public executions. Like other bell towers in Venice, the Campanile was a place of public humiliation and painful, lingering death. Until the practice was ended in the sixteenth century, priests convicted of blasphemy were imprisoned in a small iron or wooden cage suspended from a beam that projected from the south side of the tower. Exposed to the relentless sunshine and the jeering of the crowd, prisoners faced a month or two of exposure and a diet of bread and water. Few survived.

When the Campanile collapsed at ten o'clock in the morning on July 14, 1902, the four lesser bells of the Republic were destroyed. Sansovino's Loggetta and its sculptures were smashed into fragments. Meeting that same evening, the City Council decided that the tower would be replaced exactly as it was and where it was. The ruined bells were recast from the original metal, the Loggetta was reassembled, and a re-erected Campanile was opened to the public in 1912.

Viewed from the restored bell chamber, modern Venice is a tightly clustered mass of tile-roofed blocks. Streets and secondary canals are buried so deeply within the urban tissue that they are discernible only as shadowy breaks between discordant rooflines. The widest campi stand out, and so do the many bell towers. The prodigious red volumes of the great mendicant churches, with their Gothic finials and ornamental filigrees in sugary Istrian stone, are the most conspicuous landmarks of all. In the Lagoon to the north, just beyond the spire of San Zanipolo, lies the cemetery island of San Michele, with its brick battlements inset with Gothic Revival aedicules. The glass-making island of Murano is a few hundred yards beyond. Much of the Lagoon surface is marked off with long files of pilings. Set in place to define and protect the paths of ferry lines, the pilings give a sense that the urban grid continues into the water, that the clear distinction visitors feel between the city and its watery surround is illusory.

Throughout history the Lagoon was the Republic's frontier—not its opposite nor its limit but the expression of its potential. Land covered by the waters of the Lagoon was parceled and sold, given away and reclaimed. The marshy Lago Badoer, property of the Tiepolo family, became the site of the Frari. Equally unimproved Tiepolo property on the north end of town became the site of Santi Giovanni e Paolo. Not far beyond that church, however, sometime in the sixteenth century, Venice created its long, straight northern margin called the Fondamenta Nuova. It was certainly not intended to mark the city's limit; more likely it was thought of as an extension or adaptation of the development pattern pioneered in Cannaregio. But as time passed, no new land on the northern end of the city was reclaimed. No parallel island beyond the Fondamenta Nuova ever came into being, and eventually it was clear that the city would not grow any further in that direction, or in any other. By the late sixteenth century, the Republic of Venice had reached its height of population and the limits of its physical expansion.

Medieval Venice had relied on the bells of the Campanile to set the rhythm of social and political life. Sometime in the fourteenth century, a public clock was placed on the façade of San Marco. In the late fifteenth century, that clock was replaced by a complex contrivance designed by Giampaolo Ranieri. This new multifunctional clock was installed in a tower whose design is attributed to Codussi. The clock tower serves as the visual endpoint to a long vista that begins at the Bacino's edge and is framed by the columns of St. Mark and St. Theodore. The city's major commercial street, the Merceria, enters Piazza San Marco through its base. (87)

The clock's composite mechanism expresses the passage of time in the quotidian, the celestial, and the liturgical realm. Two Moors with sledgehammers strike the hours on a great bell. Beneath them, against a blue and gilt image of the starry sky, the lion of St. Mark declares the clock a representative of the Republic. Immediately below him, the Virgin and Child sit in a chapel-like enclosure sur-

87

rounded by large windows that display the hour and minute. During Ascension week—the Republic's most significant festival—representations of the Three Magi circle the pair each hour. A gilt and blue twenty-four-hour clock tells the time as well as the phases of the moon and the reigning sign of the zodiac.

88

People in the Renaissance saw time as a remote branch of the natural world that was in many ways analogous to space. The invention of mechanical timepieces represented an incursion into that realm and a degree of mastery over it—a kind of colonization. If the Campanile marked the city's place in space, this clock was its landmark in the ocean of time. Before the clock, the bells of the Campanile rang at intervals based on the hours of the sundial, which shrank or expanded with the seasons. The mechanical clock supplanted the seasonal variations of the solar day with a mathematical standard based on twenty-four invariant hours. With the building of the clock, the control of time ceased to be a matter of observation and became vested in a mechanism that was crowned with the symbol of the state. This newly asserted power over time was most dramatically expressed at the moment of public executions. The city clock was the last thing a condemned prisoner saw as he stood between the twin columns of the Piazzetta awaiting death, and a popular Venetian saying summed up his fate: "Now he knows what time it is!"

Outside the Piazza, but highly visible from the water and subtly linked to the Palazzo Ducale, stands the New Prison (Prigione Nuove). The architect Da Ponte, who designed the Rialto Bridge, planned the prison, which is visited as part of the standard tour of the Palazzo Ducale. It was intended to replace the notoriously cramped and dripping ground-level cells there called the pozzi—the wells or pits. The New Prison was designed around a central courtyard; its wooden-walled cells, though hardly luxurious, are not notably inhumane. Urged by the Council of Ten, Da Ponte consulted a lifer named Zaccaria Briani. The collaborative design provided light, ventilation, space for exercise, even primitive plumbing.

The façade of the New Prison, which was completed in 1614, echoes the design of Sansovino's Mint on the opposite end of the Piazzetta. The ground floor is made up of seven tall, heavily rusticated arcades with masks at the summit of each arch and a projecting entablature supported on corbels. Rustication continues in the walls of the second story; half columns frame large windows with alternating peaked and rounded lintels. A second entablature with brackets supporting its cornice tops the structure. (88) The area behind these large, unbarred openings held administrative offices rather than cells. While the building is considerably more benign than modern prisons, with their chain-link fences and razor-wire coils, and more suited to its urban setting, it is still an unmistakable expression of the power of the state. In the nineteenth century, when that power was just a memory, the state's sinister history was attached not to the New Prison—which continued to house common criminals rather than romantic victims of political injustice—but to the enclosed bridge that spans the Rio di Palazzo, called the Bridge of Sighs. (89)

Three other prominent symbols of the state, the

great flagstaffs in front of St. Mark's Basilica from which the red and gold lion banners of the Republic flew for centuries, were cast in 1505 by Alessandro Leopardi. Until 1576 the flagpoles also marked the site of the Venetian slave market. International traffic in luxury goods included Christians—many of them Slavic, hence the modern word slave—bought from Muslim or Turkish traders. African slaves came with the gold and spices of East Africa. Both were employed in affluent households, where they served more as marks of social distinction than as a large-scale labor force.

Had Sansovino been allowed to continue his program for St. Mark's square, it is very likely that he would have completed in the sixteenth century a very recognizable version of the final result achieved by a series of architects over the next three centuries. In redesigning the Piazza, Sansovino had a classical precedent in mind that many architectural historians have identified as the Roman Forum. Certainly the Forum as a center of political power is an important classical symbol for Sansovino, as it was for architects working in Rome throughout the sixteenth century. To assume that it stands as the direct model for Piazza San Marco, however, overlooks both topographical and symbolic differences between the two.

The Roman Forum is an open space with a clutter of distinct and individually significant monuments at its limits. San Marco is an open space ruthlessly cleared of its clutter, with a regular perimeter that is strictly confined by circumambient multistory loggias. (90) Symbolically, the Roman Forum represented Republican government vested in the Senate. While these would seem to be an unimpeachable political model for

Venetian government, Sansovino—in company with the architects of
Rome throughout the sixteenth century, including Michelangelo in his
design for the Campidoglio—appears to have rejected it in favor of an
autocratic, Imperial ideal.

What Sansovino projected is loosely related to the evolved design of
the Roman Forum but closely related to the uniform plan of the several
Imperial forums that Roman emperors from the time of Julius Caesar
constructed. Each of the Imperial forums was similar in form. A rectilinear open area was enclosed and surrounded by a colonnade. The architectural model that guided the Imperial forum was not a political but a
religious one, the Hellenistic temple precinct. Julius Caesar dedicated
the temple in his forum to Venus Genetrix, his divine ancestor; Augustus
dedicated his temple to Mars the Avenger, who aided him in defeating
Caesar's assassins. The focal point of Piazza San Marco is, of course, St.
Mark's Basilica. In the autocratic world of sixteenth-century Europe, the
ideals represented by an Imperial forum had broad appeal. Sansovino evidently felt that attraction, as did his successors in the Piazza.

The Piazza San Marco took shape gradually over many centuries.
There was always an open
area in front of the ducal
chapel. In early Venice this
area was a small island
completely surrounded by
canals. Two small canals,
one of which transected
the Piazza a little beyond

90

the Campanile and another which paralleled it at the far end of the
Piazza, were both filled in. Landfill encroaching on the originally much
wider Basin of San Marco created a site for the Palazzo Ducale, the
Piazzetta, and Sansovino's Library and Mint. A portion of this expanded
site, property of the Benedictine nuns of San Zaccaria, was purchased by
the state.

A very early church dedicated to San Gimignano stood not far from
the Campanile, limiting the newly available space. It was torn down in
the thirteenth century, rebuilt in the late sixteenth century directly opposite San Marco, only to be demolished again in the nineteenth. A hostel
for pilgrims waiting for passage to the Holy Land was razed in the late
sixteenth century. The Piazza was paved in brick in the thirteenth century, and marble bands were added in 1392 to divide the surface into
large squares. The location of booths for the Saturday market was
inscribed on some of them. The warm rose color of the brick and the
white marble grid, visible in Gentile Bellini's meticulous *Procession of
the Relic of the True Cross on the Piazza San Marco* (1496), now in the
Accademia, must have harmonized with the pattern and color of the
Palazzo Ducale's upper story much more effectively than the gray stone
pavers that replaced them in the eighteenth century. (91) Like all open
spaces in Venice, the Piazza once had its cisterns and wellhead.

The inland side of the Piazza was the first to be systematized. In the
thirteenth century the procurators of San Marco—the highly prestigious
trustees of the enormous patrimony of the state church—were housed in
a long two-story arcaded structure. In 1517 this structure was demolished, and a new one in early Renaissance style by Bartolomeo Bon was

built in its place. Even though it replaced a much older building, this new structure became known as the Procuratie Vecchie. The Procuratie Nuove on the opposite side of the Piazza was begun by Vincenzo Scamozzi in 1586 and completed in the seventeenth century by Baldassare Longhena. During the Napoleonic occupation, the bays of the Procuratie Vecchie farthest from the basilica served as the royal residence. In order to create a palace ballroom, buildings at the far end of the Piazza were demolished and replaced with a compatible double-colonnaded structure called the Ala Napoleonica, which today provides a grand entrance to the Piazza and houses the Museo Correr.

91

Those who labored throughout Venetian history to expand the Piazza, to clear it of encroaching buildings, and to frame it appropriately were driven by a variety of motives. They would have described their aims as ceremonial and religious; we would describe them as political. At some remote time in the Venetian past, there may have been a rough-and-ready political assembly that met and deliberated in the Piazza, as Romans once met in their Forum. What went on in the Piazza throughout most of the Republic's history, however, had nothing to do with political deliberation. Piazza San Marco gained its importance from its setting near the church and near the palace. It was a theater where those two interlocked institutions of Venetian power and legitimacy displayed their virtues. Its size reflected both the city's large population and the extravagant ceremonials carried out in a very dense and inflexible annual cycle.

Venice for many is still the city of Carnevale. Costume shops dot the city; mask-makers are as common as pizza chefs. This annual celebration preceding Lent spurred the development of theater, music, and gambling, but it was a festival of the body and the imagination, with little structure or political meaning. Other, much more solemn, festivals of the Venetian Republic followed it in a fixed order of march. Both the secular government and the clergy of San Marco had officials whose primary role was the regulation and organization of these public processions. Venetian processionals were completely orchestrated, thoroughly rehearsed, and subtly significant. Just as Western analysts of the former Soviet Union or Mao's China carefully watched the annual May Day parades to see which old comrades were absent, which new ones were present, and what slight differences in precedence might signal major shifts in policy, Venetians studied processionals to understand the ins and outs of their own government.

Though the ceremonies differed in form, itinerary, and personnel, their underlying message was always the same: a stable hierarchy characterized by magnificence and piety governs the Republic. Today, a visitor to Venice learns about the Republic's convoluted system of government by touring the Palazzo Ducale. In this palace of memory, the fossilized organs of a vanished government are on display in the apartments of the Doge, the vast meeting room of the Grand Council, and the Kafkaesque antechamber of the criminal judges. Such unrestricted access to the palace, however, reflects its political impotence and its reconfiguration as a museum of art. Venetians did not learn the form of their government by visiting the center of power. They learned about it in the Piazza, through well-orchestrated public processions.

The Corer Museum offers a vantage point on the life of Venice in the sixteenth and seventeenth centuries, including a number of objects that illuminate the ceremonies of the Piazza. The core of the collection is an assemblage gathered by the patrician Teodoro Correr that was originally displayed in his family's palazzo on the Grand Canal. Enriched by donations from many sources, the collection soon outgrew its original home and in 1887 was reinstalled in the reclaimed Fondaco dei Turchi. In 1922 the expanding collection was moved to its present location, which is accessible from Piazza San Marco through the stairway to the Napoleonic Palace. The collection now occupies the Neoclassical rooms of the palace and the upper floors of the Procuratie Nuove.

The collection documenting the life of the Venetian Republic begins in room 6, which is devoted to the Doge. Room 7 includes a woodcut by Matteo Pagano of a procession in San Marco. In the background, men stand between the arcades of the Procuratie Vecchie, while women and foreign dignitaries throng the windows of the second story. The careful labels of the foreground figures identify the state officers and the ceremonial objects in their order of appearance. The procession begins on the right with a group of eight flag bearers followed by minor judicial officers and a squad of trumpeters whose long horns are held up by little boys. Officials of foreign embassies follow, then more horn players and the Doge's chamberlain and squires. San Marco is represented by its richly vested canons and the patriarch. Behind the patriarch, the ducal suite and officers displaying the ducal symbols follow. The first official symbol is a single white candle, followed by the oversized coronation crown, a portable throne, and cushion. The Doge is distinguished by his cap, the corno, and by his ermine mantle. An umbrella similar to those used by Byzantine emperors is carried behind him. Foreign dignitaries are followed by a sword-bearer—often the captain of the fleet or a military commander—and top members of the government, including procurators of St. Mark, the head civil and criminal judges, representatives of the Council of Ten, and administrators of the main bureaucracies.

Room 14 is dedicated to historic maps. The most remarkable object is the huge multipanel bird's-eye view of Venice created in 1500 by Jacopo de Barbari. (The hand-engraved pearwood blocks from which De Barbari's

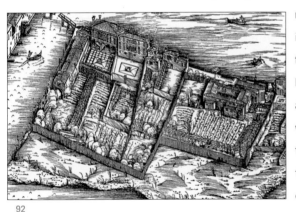

92

map was printed are displayed in room 32 of the museum on the second floor.) The map blends a convincing and appealing overview with a wealth of fascinating detail that Venetian historians continue to mine. De Barbari chose his viewpoint to highlight San Marco. To do this, he was forced to foreground the Giudecca, Venice's orphaned quarter, as remote today from the center of affairs as it evidently was in the sixteenth century. Land there was comparatively cheap, development at a minimum. The large institutions that began to proliferate on that island in the late sixteenth century had as yet made no mark. Instead, the island is covered with patches of waste ground, walled orchards, and elaborate gardens with vine-covered pergolas and crops in neat rows. (92) This was the original pattern of settlement throughout Venice, long squeezed out of the town center by close-fitting houses broken only here and there by cramped courtyards and campi.

Behind a harbor filled with dozens of oceangoing merchant ships at anchor, above a figure of Neptune, god of the seas, the Piazza begins at the water's edge. Brick pavers outlined with marble strips divide the space into a skewed checkerboard. San Marco and the Palazzo Ducale look the same as ever, but the Campanile lacks its pyramidal top. The old Procuratie closes the Piazza on the far side. Anonymous buildings stand in the place where Sansovino's Library will be built. The long multistory building to the left of its site houses the Granai di Terranova—granaries where the government, like Joseph in the San Marco mosaics, stored wheat to provide against need. The granaries were razed in the eighteenth century, and a small park was created to serve the royal palace. Directly above the sea god's head, the twin columns of Mark and Theodore—framing the underpinnings of the gibbet—lead the eye to the gateway in the Torre dell'Orologio (clock tower) and beyond to the first section of the Merceria. (93)

While the realized map is wonderful, the work that it represents is even more extraordinary. We tend to believe that a novel view of any subject must be the result of some new technology. Aerial photography changed mapping and the modern sense of landscape; satellite photography pushed that process even further. De Barbari studied and sketched the city from the Campanile of San Marco and from other bell towers; he may even have drawn the northern edge of the city from campaniles

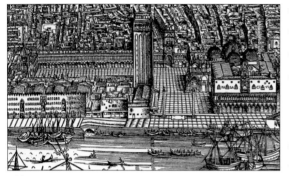

93

along the southern edge. None of those vantage points was high enough or properly placed, however, to offer his overall viewpoint. There was no balloon or kite to lift him into the sky above the Lagoon. His bird's-eye view is a work of imagination, an abstraction from reality that he presented as if it were a real observation. What we see in De Barbari's map existed only in his mind's eye, yet we readily accept it as real and true to life.

The things that distinguish Renaissance painting and drawing from the work of the Middle Ages and also from most Modern painting are realism and perspective. These characteristics can give the unseen and unseeable an uncanny substantiality. Here is the infant Jesus lying in a manger; here we see the Roman workers straining to raise the Cross. Pictorial realism also represents realities for other forms of appreciation besides the spiritual or aesthetic. The dissection of cadavers and the detailed study of anatomy by painters in the early fifteenth century is well documented. Michelangelo's study of corpses made it possible for him to represent human musculature in motion with striking effect. The same skills of accurate three-dimensional representation that give life to the Adam of the Sistine ceiling also made the first illustrated anatomy books possible. The representational skills cultivated by Renaissance artists and peculiar to their art were useful as well as beautiful. Coupled with the mechanical reproduction of images through etching and engraving, detailed observations could be communicated to large groups of people.

The visual presentation of information that the Internet depends on is a Renaissance invention, and De Barbari's map is one of its finest examples. In a certain sense, this map is a spatial analogue of the city clock. It is a declaration of mastery over a natural realm—the realm of space— that consists not in the imposition of power but in the exposition of knowledge and understanding. Such information has a variety of uses. It can contribute to the development of abstract thinking, which was cultivated in Renaissance Venice by a leisure class eager to do significant things with its time and money. The map can equally well serve the spirit of vigilance—of information-collecting and spying that increasingly preoccupied the Republic. For many contemporary historians, the foundations of the modern state are the techniques and structures of surveillance on which social control depends. De Barbari was aware of this potential. His image of the Arsenal lacks the details that enemy agents would have been eager to learn. (94)

The second floor of the Museo Correr houses a large collection of pictures that emphasizes work of the fifteenth and very early sixteenth centuries. The earliest paintings, dating from the late twelfth and early thirteenth centuries, reflect the impersonal and remote style of painting based on Byzantine models that was then common throughout

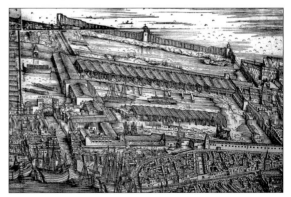

94

Italy. By the fourteenth century, painters like Paolo and Lorenzo Veneziano, following the example of Cimabue, Giotto, and Cavallini, created a style that was more volumetric, more psychologically attuned, and more clearly grounded in three-dimensional space.

Antonello da Messina's enigmatic *Dead Christ Supported by Three Angels* (room 34) is the only one of his works that remains in Venice. The luminous torso of Christ and the deeply receding landscape behind him are its most compelling features. Christ's head and the flesh of the angels are indistinct—either because the painting was never completed or because these areas have deteriorated. Antonello, who was born in Sicily, trained in Naples in the mid-fifteenth century. When he came to Venice in 1475, he brought with him a style that combined Flemish and Italian strengths. He had mastered both the clarity of detail cultivated in the North and the smooth plasticity and spatial coherence characteristic of Italian Quattrocento painting. Vasari credited the Sicilian with introducing this representational technique and the medium it depended on—painting in oil—to the Venetians. Antonello created a magnificent and very influential altarpiece for the church of San Cassiano near the Rialto that was imitated by Giovanni Bellini, Giorgione, and Vivarini. That painting disappeared from the church in the seventeenth century. It was divided into separate parts which were reassembled in the twentieth century. It is now displayed in the Kunsthistorische Museum in Vienna.

The first family of Venetian painting was the Bellini, a dynasty founded by Jacopo, who was born about 1400 and lived to be nearly seventy. Jacopo was apprenticed to the Florentine painter Gentile da Fabbriano. Although he painted throughout most of his long life in Venice and

won many important commissions, almost none of his work survives. The
small *Crucifixion* displayed in room 36 is one of the narrative panels from
the base of an altarpiece. One of Jacopo's daughters married the Florentine master Andrea Mantegna. Two of Jacopo's sons, Gentile and Giovanni, were trained by their father and by their brother-in-law. Gentile,
the older of the two, is best known for his large paintings of the Miracles
of the True Cross, now hanging in the Accademia. His portrait of the
Doge Giovanni Mocenigo can be seen here. The younger Giovanni is represented by three early paintings which show the effects of his training
more than his own abilities.

Vittore Carpaccio, who worked with Gentile on the narrative cycle for
the Scuola Grande di San Giovanni Evangelista, is represented in room
38 by a celebrated fragment of a larger scene. His *Two Venetian Women*
was separated at some unknown time from its male counterpart, a hunt-
ing scene now in the Getty Museum in Malibu, Califor-
nia. Two richly dressed women of the patrician class—
they may be members of the Priuli family—sit on a
sunny balcony surrounded by their pets. (95) A pair of
impressively high platform shoes sit on the terrace
near the feet of a little boy. The sleeves of the women's
velvet and brocade dresses are gored to allow their
linen shifts to show through; they wear their good
pearls. Their blonde hair—Venetian women sunned
themselves in crownless hats to bleach their hair—is
artfully frizzed. They have silly hats on their heads.
And though patrician women must have been used to

95

waiting, these two are clearly bored to the point of exanimation. To his credit, Carpaccio shows the women's alienation, their melancholy, and something of what a life segregated from the political, ceremonial, and cultural pulse of the Republic must have felt like in the fifteenth century.

The Reading Room of the Libreria Marciana is now reached from the Museo Correr, and the architectural narrative Sansovino built so patiently unfolds in reverse order. While Sansovino was ruthless in his exclusion of Venetian models in the exteriors of his buildings, the interior of the Library is clearly related to the decorative patterns of the scuole grandi. An impressive stairway like the Scala d'Oro in the Palazzo Ducale leads from the ground-level entryway to the second-floor Reading Room. The first landing on the stair is crowned with a false dome decorated with remarkable stucco work. Alternating fictive frames enclose small paintings and stucco reliefs. The standing putti above the frames are most unusual; the artist has employed foreshortening and other illusionistic techniques of Venetian ceiling painting to make them appear to be within the space of the wall rather than on its surface. The long barrel vault over the upper staircase uses more familiar patterns of coffering to create frames for inset paintings and shallow-relief sculptures.

The decoration of the stairway makes clear that the Library is not just a repository for books but an Athenaeum where all the arts and sciences known to the classical world are celebrated. The classicizing architecture of the building, the stucco work derived from Roman examples, the paintings and bas-reliefs all contribute to the preservation and cultivation of the classical example. Shortly after Sansovino's death, Scamozzi arranged the sculpture collection of Cardinal Grimani in the Library vestibule. Though the collection was later dismantled and incorporated into the archaeological museum, its form was preserved in a series of etchings by Antonio Maria Zanetti. In recent decades the sculptures have been recovered and replaced in their original position. The room once again presents the typical appearance of a premodern gallery, which can be disconcerting to a contemporary visitor.

A museum curator looking at this room today would see it as overloaded; too many pieces compete for attention. The lighting is too low and too unfocused to suit modern practice, and many of the objects are placed well above eye level, where they are difficult if not impossible to see properly. Evidently, Scamozzi's theory of presentation was different from this twentieth- and twenty-first-century ideal. The collection was first of all an installation, a harmonious blending of architectural background and sculptural objects. The viewer's overall impression was as important as the impact of individual works. Objects were meant to be seen together, in groups and pairings, and the visitor was more or less on her own, free to look at anything that caught her fancy, or that happened to catch the sun on some particular afternoon, or glow in the light of a torch or candle on a winter evening. Of course the collection was intended not just for enjoyment but also for study. Sculptors and painters were expected to draw the objects on display and learn classical proportion and the canons for representing the human face and body.

Beyond the vestibule is the Reading Room itself. Once filled with tables where scholars studied Bessarion's manuscripts, this beautiful room is now a space for temporary exhibits. (The courtyard of the Zecca has been glassed over, and that area is now used by readers.) In the pattern familiar from the upper rooms of the scuole grandi, the coffered ceiling is decorated with inset paintings by a variety of artists. After a nominal competition, all the entrants, including Salviati, Tintoretto, and Veronese, were declared winners, and each was assigned a row of three ceiling compartments to decorate. The subjects are unsurprising for the most part. Some represent general areas of knowledge: nature and the seasons, art with Pallas and Jupiter, agriculture and various deities. Others represent virtues: vigilance and patience, glory and beatitude. There are personifications of the arts and sciences: mathematics, sculpture, astrology, geometry, song, music, and honor. The ideal state is represented by personifications more suited to a mainland autocracy than an island republic: the prince, the army, and the Church. A painting of the River Nile is the lone recollection of Alexandria and its legendary library.

The walls of the room are decorated with a series of full-length portraits that once decorated the Room of the Philosophers in the Doge's suite of the Palazzo Ducale. Veronese's figures of Plato and Aristotle are especially fine. Each stands in a deeply shadowed fictive niche that recalls the arches of Sansovino's façade. Near the door, Plato, in scarlet robes, looks upward and points skyward with the index finger of his right hand; his left hand points toward his chest. At the far end of the room, Aristotle bends forward as he reads a tablet balanced on his knee; a pile of thick books supports his foot. Though Veronese's figures reflect the coloring and the subtle play of light and shadow that marks Venetian painting, the posture of the two figures recalls Raphael's side-by-side representations in the *School of Athens* in the Vatican Palace. Like the figure of the Nile in the ceiling, these philosophers, whose theories Cardinal Bessarion hoped to reconcile, provide another faint echo of the original purpose of the Library. In their isolation and contrasting postures,

Veronese's figures suggest that the work of harmonizing the idealistic and pragmatic strains in philosophy still had a long way to go.

When Sansovino was designing his Mint and Library, the Piazzetta was a one-way street, a ceremonial avenue that led from the water's edge past the palace and basilica through the base of the clock and into the city. In making plans for the monumental church of San Giorgio Maggiore, Andrea Palladio extended this axis and made it bi-directional. The view of the Piazzetta from the city side was amplified beyond the columns of Mark and Theodore and extended into the water. This wonderful effect restored the Piazzetta to a prominence that was diluted when the Piazza was deepened.

The Benedictine monastery on the island of San Giorgio was founded in the eighth or ninth century, when the Lagoon was still a scattering of small, discrete settlements. As Venice consolidated and the first dux chose San Marco as his point of control over the traffic of the Lagoon channels, the offshore island directly across became increasingly important to its defense. Fortifications may have existed there in the earliest period, but as the Republic grew stronger and its abhorrence for visible defenses increased, its ties to the island were expressed symbolically. In the early thirteenth century, the Benedictines acquired a relic of very great prominence, the body of St. Stephen the protomartyr, whose feast is celebrated on the day after Christ's birth. On December 26 every year, the Doge visited the monastery, accompanied by high officials of the Republic, crowds of the curious, and the choir of San Marco. The Benedictines and the choir of the ducal chapel together sang a solemn High Mass. On many of these ceremonial visits, the combined choirs performed new compositions written for the occasion. The earliest surviving

piece, a motet on the verse *Ave corpus sanctum,* was sung in 1329 for

the visit of Doge Francesco Dandolo. His name, along with that of the

96

Benedictine abbot of the time, can be heard distinctly in performances of the motet.

When the project of renewing the church was first proposed in the mid-1560s, the Council of Trent had just completed its deliberations. The Council was convened in the face of the Protestant challenge, the deepest and most disturbing blow to the Catholic Church's prestige and pre-eminence in a thousand years. Like a sixteenth-century Vatican II, the Council recommended sweeping and radical changes that were meant to strengthen orthodoxy, reinvigorate the clergy, and increase lay spirituality. In pursuit of this latter goal, the Council decreed that the screen separating the congregation from the altar of churches be removed. Choirs that had generally stood in front of the altar and blocked the congregation's view (like the one that still stands in the Frari) were to be removed. The dismantled choir of San Francesco della Vigne provided raw material for the Capella Badoer-Giustiniani. The Council also favored a return to the most antique and most authoritative church design, the Roman basilica.

Palladio's plan for San Giorgio Maggiore responded to all the demands imposed by the site, the ceremonial use of the church, and the new orthodoxy. His design—completed in 1611—called for a façade that would be massive enough to seem proportional when viewed from the Piazzetta. (96) He accommodated the unusually large crowd thronging the church on its most important ceremonial day. He created an environment where the music that was the centerpiece of the celebration could be heard and appreciated. At the same time, and in contrast to his own preferences, he embraced the liturgical reforms and structural guidelines of the Council of Trent.

A champion of centrally planned structures such as his Villa Rotunda near Vicenza, Palladio nevertheless created a basilica in San Giorgio Maggiore, though one with unusual proportions. The three aisles of its nave are intersected by a transept, the endpoints of which are exedra that bulge from the side walls. The presbytery, raised on a platform, begins one bay beyond the crossing; an extended apse holds the choir. For most of the year, the choir, with its high wooden stalls, served as the chapel of the monastery, and the rest of the basil-

ica must have stood nearly empty, as it does today. (97) During the great ceremony, however, the hidden choir singing antiphonally with others placed throughout the church became an extraordinary instrument.

Palladio's great church was enriched by the works of other prominent Venetian artists. Iintoretto contributed a painting like that in San Rocco of the *Fall of the Manna in the Desert*, which hangs in the presbytery. At the very end of his life, he painted an enormous *Last Supper,*

97

which hangs opposite. The scene, common in the refectories of monasteries, assumes a different meaning when it is placed near the altar and
paired with the *Fall of the Manna*. The disciples' communal meal
becomes a representation of the Eucharist, the focus of renewed attention in the Catholic Church after Trent.

Early Renaissance representations of Christ's meal with the disciples,
like Da Vinci's, placed the long banquet table parallel to the picture
plane and set it in a shallow alcove that appeared to be just outside the
monks' refectory. Veronese's great banqueting scenes are similar. Tintoretto's table, by contrast, stretches back into the gloom of a richly ornamented upper room, whose inlaid floor, columned walls, and coffered
ceiling recall a principal room in a private palace or, more likely, the
upper room of Tintoretto's beloved San Rocco. The strong diagonal thrust
of the table is counterbalanced by the gestures of the disciples and
transformed into a restless circular composition by the two groups of servants who pass between it and a serving table on the opposite side of the
room. The generally very dark scene is lit by a flaming lamp but also by
the phosphorescent glow from the heads of the disciples. Judas, who has
no halo and sits on the floor at the wrong side of the table, is apparently
arguing with Christ. Wraithlike angels surround the flaming lamp like
moths; a second clutch of them swoops in from the upper right.

The façade of San Giorgio Maggiore is one of Palladio's most important inventions. The Christian basilica, with its high central nave and
lower flanking aisles, presented Renaissance Neoclassicists with one of
their greatest challenges: how to interpret this broken roofline in the language of a classicism based on the temple front. Palladio's solution,

which he pioneered on the façade of San Francesco della Vigna on the northern edge of the city, was ingenious. He treated the endwall as two separate structures and designed a façade for each. One structure is wide and relatively low, the other is narrow and high. Each is treated as a temple front with columns in its main story and a pediment above. The wider structure embraces the aisles, and the top of its pediment follows their roofline. The taller structure placed in front of the other conceals the roof of the nave behind a narrower pediment, which it supports on massive engaged columns set on high pedestals. Colossal statues at the corners and peak of the roofs complete the design. The dome of the church and the two towers bracketing its apse add further height to the building. A bell tower, built in obvious imitation of the Campanile of San Marco, was added in the early eighteenth century. Views from its top take in the whole city at once.

On the island of Giudecca, Palladio was also involved in the design of the church and refuge of Santa Maria della Presentazione, commonly called Le Zitelle, although the construction was carried out in the decade after his death. This complex, with its central church and long wings of apartments for the residents, became a model for institutional buildings in Venice. The hospice was sponsored by the Jesuits in imitation of one founded in Rome by St. Ignatius Loyola. Its purpose was to shelter and educate impoverished young women from all social classes who might otherwise be forced into prostitution. After some years of preparation they would emerge from the institute "well-exercised in all the duties of the household which women must know" and be prepared to marry or become nuns.

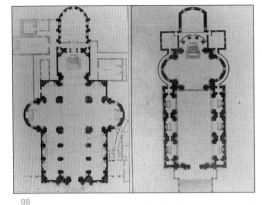

98

In 1576 Venice was struck by an especially virulent outbreak of a plague that may have killed as many as a third of the population. In response to the outbreak, the Venetian Senate voted to build and dedicate a church to Christ the Redeemer. With work well under way at San Giorgio Maggiore, Palladio was commissioned to design the new church on the island of Giudecca. The interior of Il Redentore is similar to the earlier project, but it differs in important ways. In plan it appears to be a basilica with a transept and elevated presbytery. But subtle shifts in the proportions and use of interior spaces transform it into something quite different. The exedra, which bulge out of the sidewalls at San Giorgio, are brought almost into line with them here. (98) The choir is also more restrained. The most significant changes, which also affect the façade, occur in the nave. The side aisles of the earlier church are replaced here by shallow chapels. The nave columns have, in effect, been pushed toward the walls, creating a wide unobstructed central area that is in close contact with the high altar, an important goal of Trent.

The classical proportions of the façade reflect the widening of the nave and subordination of the aisles. Its Corinthian pilasters and fictive pediment are low and broad. The high pediment masking the nave is wider than that at San Giorgio. Palladio created a third implied façade by placing a similar pediment above the central door. Behind this threefold structure he added a fourth in the form of a high flat-topped wall with protruding gables. The idea for this wall probably came from a similar structure behind the pediment of the Pantheon in Rome, which partially masks the dome from view.

Like San Giorgio Maggiore, the façade of Il Redentore can be seen only across a sheet of open water. (99) In the mind's eye, that expanse represents an extension of the piazza or fondamenta on which the viewer stands, but the real effects are quite different. The dense vapor that accumulates above the water of the Giudecca Canal or the Basin of San Marco creates dramatic effects. Palladio was too skillful and too experi-

enced an architect not to understand how that screen of translucent vapor would affect his compositions. He may have relied on it to heighten the illusion created by his foreshortened façades. Seen from a distance and through the mist which obscures shadow, these flattened forms are not so easily read as monodimensional.

The mist that hides and discloses things at will is an appropriate context

99

for buildings which themselves have so little practical purpose. Once a year on December 26, San Giorgio Maggiore prepares to receive visitors; on July 20, Il Redentore throws open its doors. At other times, they recede in public consciousness, just as they fade in the mist. Without ever seeing Venice, Shakespeare understood the uncanny quality of such buildings. Belmont, the magic island in which all the characters of *The*

Merchant of Venice except Shylock find redemption and delight, is apparently near Venice but never quite visible. It advances and recedes without reference to the inexorable calendar of the Rialto. It is one of Shakespeare's fairylands, like the woods outside Athens in *A Midsummer Night's Dream,* in touch with the human world but largely distinct from it. Palladio's remote temples are like that too, always present but never quite tangible. In time, their evanescent beauty will become an image of Venice itself, more and more a city of the imagination, less and less substantial.

Chapter Seven

MERCHANTS AND MARINERS

The island of San Giorgio Maggiore stands opposite San Marco and frames the entrance to the Basin and the Giudecca Canal. Sansovino's Mint and the end of his Library bring the Piazza of San Marco to bear not just on the Bacino but on the Grand Canal. The water gate to the city itself opens between Piazza San Marco and the slim fingertip of Dorsoduro where the Dogana da Mar, or customs house, and the salt warehouses form an opposite pole. (Map 7)

The present Dogana da Mar was built in the late seventeenth century by Giuseppe Benoni. Its apex is a squat tower in rusticated stone surrounded by three porches and surmounted by a kneeling Atlas who lifts a gilded ball on his back. Atop the ball is a bronze figure holding a gilded kitelike sail. She is usually identified as the merchants' goddess Fortuna, though some argue that she is a figure of Justice. Behind this tower the rusticated building continues in a series of uneven arcades with large masks in their apices. Ceremonial crenellations of the kind that marked state buildings from the Gothic period onward top the walls. Warehouses designed for the storage of salt, these buildings are nineteenth-century replacements of the much earlier Magazzini del Sel shown on the De Barbari map of 1500.

The great structure that completes the work of counterpoint begun by the

100

Dogana da Mar is the church of Santa Maria della Salute by Baldassare Longhena. (100) The towering dome of the great church and its smaller spires and statues are a vertical expansion and extension of the golden sphere that guards the harbor. The resulting complex is a massive block sufficient to act as counterweight to the Basilica and Campanile of St. Mark and the Palazzo Ducale.

Longhena's church was born in tragedy. In 1630 a carpenter from the nearby parish of Sant' Agnese returned from a few days' work on the quarantine island of San Clemente. He brought the plague with him, and it soon ravaged the city. In response, the Senate vowed to create a church dedicated to the Virgin Mary as a bringer of health. Longhena, the greatest architect of the Baroque era in Venice and one of the foremost architects of Europe at the time, won the commission. Longhena's pedigree was extraordinary. He was a student of Scamozzi, himself the student and collaborator of both Sansovino and Palladio. The building Longhena designed is a triumphant summation of the most cherished ideals of high classicism that defined Sansovino's generation. These ideals are carried out in a

101

structure that pays full tribute to the virtuosity and love of novelty that distinguish the Baroque.

On the church's complex exterior, Longhena gave greatest emphasis to the main doorway, but he treated each of the other visible faces of the eight-sided building as an independent façade. Above its cascading steps, the entryway takes its form from a triumphal arch. Four applied columns on pedestals divide the front into three uneven zones. The two narrower bays on each side frame elaborate niches with statues in them. A massive single arch fills the center bay. A small pediment above the entablature crowns the façade; balustrades top the entablature.

102

Five statues project above. The lesser façades have four pilasters in their lower stories and an arched window above; a pediment and three statues complete each one.

The most distinctive feature of the building's exterior is defiantly anti-classical and ties the building most directly to the Baroque. Enormous brackets project from each corner of the eight faces of the drum. These end in giant volutes, which are topped by a second row of statues. (101) The bracket is a subordinate element in classical architecture, designed to hold up a console or lintel; it is never independent and never an orna-mental device in its own right, as here.

The interior of Longhena's church is octagonal. Its elongated dome is supported on a high drum pierced by sixteen windows. (102) The drum is carried on piers with antefixed columns crowned by an entablature and balcony. Arches between the piers separate the central domed space from a surrounding aisle that is extended by shallow chapels. The walls are white, and columns, archivolts, and entablatures are of gray stone. The arch opposite the main door opens onto a raised presbytery that fuses a square central space and two semicircular exedra. A second dome flanked by bell towers rises above the presbytery.

The Salute is a giddy compromise between a centrally planned building and a traditional basilica. Its deepest roots are in Hadrian's Pantheon. Later Imperial buildings like Santa Costanza and Santo Stefano Rotondo in Rome, which combined domed central spaces with a surrounding aisle or ambulatory, are its direct ancestors. The Baptistery at San Giovanni in Laterano, built by Constantine, used a similar plan based on an octagon rather than the circle. The church of the Holy Sepulchre in Jerusalem was originally built in this form. In the High Renaissance, Bramante recreated the centrally planned building in his Tempietto, and he intended to apply the pattern in his new St. Peter's.

The conjoining of so many precedents might have produced a muddle, but in fact each contributes to the meaning of the church. Hadrian's Pantheon was dedicated to all the Roman gods, but in 609 the building was rededicated to the Virgin Mary and to the martyrs of Christianity. Santa Costanza, on the outskirts of Rome, was a burial chapel. Santo Stefano Rotonda was a martyrium. The church of the Holy Sepulchre was the burial chapel and martyrium of Christ himself. The Lateran Baptistery combined the forms of the burial chapel—the symbol of death—with the octagon and the waters of baptism to create a building type that con-

notes both death and rebirth. Longhena blended these many precedents
in the Salute in a way that suggests the commemoration of the dead and
the promise of rebirth and renewal through the intercession of the Virgin.
The High Renaissance precedents honor the tradition of sixteenth-century
classicizing Venetian architecture and carry on its theme of transference
of antiquity's heritage from Rome to Venice.

Not far from the Salute in Dorsoduro stands the Hospital for Incurables (Ospedale degli Incurabili), a vast building designed in the early
sixteenth century as a hospice for those suffering from terminal diseases.

(103) Chief among them was
syphilis. This wasting disease—
untreatable until the mid-twentieth
century and extremely debilitating
in its late stages—was unknown in
Europe before the Renaissance.
Many scholars think that it was
brought back from the New World

103

by sailors on Columbus's ships. Marin Sanudo described its symptoms in
a diary entry from 1496.

"Note that through celestial influences in the past two years—that is,
after the French invasion of Italy—a new disease of the human body has
emerged called the French Pox. This disease has spread through Italy,
Greece, Spain, and almost the entire world. It afflicts the hands and feet
with sores, and creates pustules and oozing wounds over the entire face
and body, which are accompanied by fever and joint pain. As with the
measles, the face is covered with lesions, and in women the thighs are

sometimes so infected that the afflicted beg to die. The disease begins in the pubic region and is only spread through sexual contact. They say that even children are infected. The rash continues for a long time, and it is a most repulsive disease, even though few die of it. And even though many say the disease came from the French, they, who have also known it for only two years, call it the Italian Pox" (*Diaries* 1.233–234).

The Incurabili also housed orphans and children who had been abandoned by their parents. After 1640 the hospital, along with three other Venetian charitable institutions (the Derelitti, Mendicanti, and Pietà), became celebrated for its choir. Orphan girls were recruited and trained in singing, playing instruments, and music theory. Top-ranked composers wrote for these choirs, and musicians of great stature—including Antonio Vivaldi, who directed the choir of the Pietà—were hired to lead them. Concerts were typically thronged, and revenues from the sale of tickets and libretti not only paid the high cost of the women's training but sustained the institutions themselves.

The church of San Trovaso, near the center of Dorsoduro, is flanked by two canals. The church's ancient foundation preempts much of the open space at this intersection and creates two campi—a long and shallow one at the side of the church (which was significantly remodeled in the seventeenth century) and a small, nearly square one in front, with a few houses along its sides. This smaller campo has a raised area that corresponds to the outline of the cistern below its central well. What distinguishes this typical array of church, piazza, and domestic buildings from every other campo in Venice is a tiny cluster of buildings at the very intersection of the two canals. From the campo, these are fairly undistin-

guished two-story brick houses. Seen from the opposite side of the canal,
however, the backs of these buildings display a once-prevalent architectural style and a function otherwise extinct in Venice. (104) This area is
the Squero di San Trovaso, the last traditional boatyard in Venice, where

gondolas are repaired and
refurbished.

Medieval and Renaissance
Venice had thousands of
wooden structures like these
houses. On the north side of
the city, logs floating down
the Brenta River on the mainland made their way to the
Sacca della Misericordia,

104

which served as a floating lumberyard through much of the year. On the
south, along the Giudecca Canal, log rafts landed along a waterfront that
is still called Le Zattere, "the rafts." Vestiges of Venice's wooden architecture can be seen today in the heavy ceiling joists in passageways and
the intricately carved wooden lintels above stone pillars. But this boatyard is the only surviving example of battened walls and overhanging
porches, of an entire architecture of wood.

The exposed wood, stained with creosote and blackened with time, is
not only beautiful but self-evidently dangerous. Isolated as these buildings are, they would present no serious threat if they were to catch fire.
Within the densely settled core of medieval Venice, however, fires could
not be contained, and the suppression of wooden architecture was

intended to reduce the danger of fire—an effort that had only limited success.

Sansovino introduced the vocabulary of high classicism not just to public buildings but also to private palaces along the lower part of the Grand Canal. The result was a radical shift in the character of these princely houses and a breakdown of the homogeneity and harmony of the canal itself. Sansovino's palaces are taller than the buildings that surround them, and jut forward from the common line of façades, from which they are separated at either side. While Venetian Gothic palazzi are typically tall and narrow, Sansovino's Neoclassical buildings are square in cross-section. Their massive proportions and isolation accentuate the three-dimensionality of buildings that appear to thrust through a screen of flat façades like a truck driven through a billboard.

Sansovino began work on Palazzo Corner della Ca' Grande (near the

Santa Maria del Giglio vaporetto stop) in 1533. His design reflects Bramante's formula for the Roman private palace, but Sansovino reinterpreted that formula to produce a building of unrivaled grandeur. Like the Library, this building stands on a raised plinth, and the ground-floor entrance is reached by climbing a set of water stairs. (105) With its small central arcade surrounded by two enclosed areas pierced by two orders of massive windows, the rusticated ground floor preserves the traditional three-part division of Venetian palaces. The lower windows

105

are supported on kneeling brackets, flanked by rusticated columns, and topped by an entablature and rounded pediment. Exaggerated brackets frame the square mezzanine windows above.

Roman palaces usually had utilitarian structures at street level, but Sansovino's ground floor serves as an entrance to a great central receiving hall—the andron. Rustication reflects the alien character of the water, not the rough occupations of ground-floor tenants. Sansovino also raised the ground floor of this palazzo well beyond the height typical of its Roman counterpart. He added to the grandeur of the two upper floors by substituting arcades, in the style of his Library, for the more common windows flanked by columns. He used the Tabularium motif—a full-length arcade fronted by attached columns raised on pedestals and supporting a massive entablature—for each upper story. The arcades have masks in their archivolts and sculpted trophies to either side. In the frieze on the second story he added oval windows. Dentals, brackets, and a cornice with small lion masks complete the façade.

Sansovino's palace remained beyond the reach of most Venetian families. Sufficient space was nearly impossible to come by. The cost of the oversized site, demolition, and construction on such a massive scale were too much for all but the richest and the most reckless noblemen. Directly across the Grand Canal from Ca' Corner, the Venier family projected a building on the same scale, but only its rusticated ground floor was completed. The Palazzo Venier dei Leoni remained unoccupied until the twentieth century, when Peggy Guggenheim bought it and had it redesigned as a museum complex that now houses an extensive collection of modern art. Farther up the canal at the Rio del Duca, the Renais-

106

sance architect and theoretician Filarete (Antonio Averlino) planned a sumptuous palace for Francesco Sforza, the duke of Milan, but the building hardly got off the ground before the project was aborted. The plinth, inset corner column, and diamond-point rustication of the first story suggest that this structure would have been as massive and as antagonistic to its neighbors as Ca' Corner.

The Palazzo Moro Lin of the mid-seventeenth century, near the Rio del Duca, is an interesting variation on Sansovino's themes. (106) Its rusticated ground-level arcade stretches across the entire façade and stands right at the edge of the canal, with the bases of its pillars actually submerged in even moderately high water. The two arcaded upper stories with enlarged central openings are decorated with very flat pilasters. A fourth story was added later. The triple arcade and the modest rustication that is discreetly carried into the upper stories suggest a Roman model different from Sansovino's. Romans superimposed arcades on the façades of theaters and arenas, but they piled up arcades more commonly to carry aqueducts

107

across valleys and rivers. Perhaps the anonymous architect of this building thought of the aqueduct as a suitable model for canal-side architecture.

The Grimani family was able to afford a building on the scale that Sansovino introduced. (107) Their palace near the Rio San Luca lacks rustication in its first story but in other ways reflects the style of Palazzo Corner. Fluted pilasters define two narrow side bays in the ground story, which is raised on a modest plinth and reached by water stairs. The central opening combines a large arched doorway with two lower archways topped by small nearly square windows. Fluted antefixed columns define the bays on the upper stories, where wide arches alternate with windows. Masks crown the archivolts, and a heavy cornice completes this towering, blocklike structure.

108

Sansovino designed the Palazzo Dolfin-Manin near the base of the Rialto Bridge in 1538 for Giovanni Dolfin. (108) It now houses offices of the Banco d'Italia. An open arcade with Tuscan pilasters replaces the more typical rusticated lower floor. Smaller and narrower arches arranged to give prominence to the center of the upper floors are irregularly decorated with an applied colonnade. Lion masks jut from the frieze at the top of the building. The structure, while massive, is not on the same scale as the Palazzo Corner, and is actually somewhat smaller than the Gothic Palazzo Bembo next door. It sits almost comfortably among its Rialto neighbors.

As the sestiere of San Marco grew more dense in the eleventh century, the market long established in Campo San Bartolomeo struggled to keep up with the steady expansion of trade. By moving just a few hundred yards across the Grand Canal, the market expanded onto new land that was then being consolidated and developed at the city's frontier. Sometime later, the burgeoning network of streets in San Marco was extended

by means of a pontoon bridge across the Grand Canal. This bridge was built just seaward of the second curve in this generally wide channel. It may be that shoals at the bend were already preventing seagoing vessels from passing farther inland; in any case, the impassable bridge would have

109

ended direct communication between the sea and the mainland via the Grand Canal. The Giudecca Canal, which now provides direct communication between sea and land, was not deepened until the nineteenth century.

In the late fourteenth century the floating bridge was replaced by a wooden one, which collapsed in the mid-fifteenth century. A third wooden bridge was built, this time with steep ramps that carried its middle section high above the waterway. At its center was a drawbridge lifted by great chains anchored in turrets at its summit. Shops lined both sides of the bridge's slopes. Carpaccio's *Healing of the Possessed Man at the Rialto Bridge* of about 1501 shows the bridge in the best possible light. The De Barbari map drawn at about the same time shows jury-rigged reinforcements between its pilings that block the channel. (109)

The bridge that now crosses the Grand Canal at this spot was designed by Antonio da Ponte and built in the last decades of the sixteenth century. (110) Its single span springs from piers that encroach deeply on the canal. Its straight balustrades rise to a small platform above the center of the waterway. This play of line and curved archway is carried on in the superstructure of the bridge, which, like its wooden predecessor, holds a double row of shops. Each shop front is surmounted by an arch, and the linked arches form a pair of rising arcades that merge in two central pediments like great gateways opened to the current of the river.

The market at the river bend first began to take shape sometime in the tenth century. The first record of its existence is a sinister one. Describing the assassination of Doge Pietro Candiano IV, Johannes Diaconus recorded that in a gesture of hatred and contempt his killers threw his dead body and that of his young son on the pile of butchers' offal behind the meat market in Rialto. In the late twelfth century, the group of merchants who had until that time owned the market donated their holdings to the Republic, which was deeply indebted after a prolonged war with Hungary. After 1164 the state leased market property to individual vendors.

110

A host of officials oversaw and regulated the market: customs police, tax collectors, price regulators, quality-control officers, commercial magistrates. Regulations fixed the size of vendors' tables, the size and quality of their products, waste disposal, street cleaning, the purity of gold, the dilution of wine, the width of streets, and the distance that second stories could project into them. Nevertheless, the marketplace took on a life of its own. Construction materials were unregulated, and the market buildings—the majority of them made of wood like the houses at San Trovaso—and the endlessly proliferating inns, bars, and restaurants that served the market crowds clumped together as thickly as possible. Vendors, who rented a marble slab of fixed dimensions, ignored regulations prohibiting them from enclosing their sites with temporary shelters.

According to Marin Sanudo's diary, on January 10, 1514, while the Republic was again involved in a mainland war, "a fire was discovered in a weaver's shed sparked by a burning coal that escaped from a brazier and ignited the cloth. The guardians of the Rialto did not act quickly enough to prevent this shop and the surrounding ones from catching fire. It started around seven in the evening as one by one the weavers' and cordwainers' shops burst into flame. Soon there was an enormous fire driven on by high winds out of the east during a period of intolerable cold. The bells were rung in the Rialto and everyone who had a shop or an office came running.

"I ran myself to the Osteria della Campana, from which I draw all my income. The fire continued to burn with no one to fight it because everyone was intent on emptying their shops of merchandise and retrieving their account books. Crowds of foreigners came to see the fire in the Rialto, which is the richest part of Venice, and others came to steal. The

crowds became so thick that it was impossible to get through. Some people carried off the goods from their shops, while others looted. Boats of
all shapes and sizes brought to the fondamenta to carry off the merchandise were themselves at risk of catching fire, but still no one fought the
flames. People started heading for the banks of the Pisani and the
Augustini, which were open, and especially from the Pisani bank they
took both the cash and the account books that were there, and did the
same at the other banks, the Vendramin, Priuli, and Lipomani.

"Meanwhile the high winds were spreading the fire through the whole
of the Rialto and nothing was being done about it. The commissioners of
the night watch plus Hieronimo Tiepolo and Stefano Contarini from the
Council of Ten were there, but they could not accomplish anything
because no one would follow their orders. Everyone was intent on retrieving his own merchandise or looting someone else's, and hordes of people
were standing around watching. Gentlemen of reputation and importance
were there, but they were intent on retrieving the records from the
offices, especially the tax records. The priests of the nearby churches,
San Giacomo, San Giovanni Evangelista, and San Matteo, came with the
Body of Christ, which they carried around the perimeter of the fire, but it
did no good. The bells of San Giacomo and the neighboring parishes
sounded continually and hordes of people came, but no one helped; they
were too intent on stealing what they could get their hands on. Even
women came to steal, and the streets were full of merchandise . . .

"All night long the winds kept the fire going, and people stood in the
streets to watch; they came running like they do for a processional. Large
numbers of foreigners, including rebels from Padua and Treviso, came to

look, and in my heart I believe that they were glad to see our ruin, even though they didn't dare to try any mischief. Early in the morning, top members of the government were sent by the Doge to prevent the fire from spreading and destroying the rest of Venice. The wind had quieted and there was a fair amount of ice in the Grand Canal. The three Commanders of the Arsenal and all the magistrates were sent, the Arsenal was closed so that the workers could fight the fire . . .

"A magistrate was said to have found a ball of pitch in one of the shops which was thought to contain gunpowder. It was brought to the Doge, but it turned out not to be dangerous. The fire was not set by men from the rebellious cities or by other enemies. Still, they say that during the same night the Lazaretto Nuovo burned down, that there were fires at the Carmine, at San Nicolo, and in various other parts of the city far from the Rialto, but these were quickly put out. Fires started spontaneously in chimneys throughout the city because it was very cold and because the wind was high.

"That morning there were no officials in the Palazzo Ducale except for a few judges; the rest had gone to see the fire, and having seen it, they were shocked and disheartened. To ensure order during the night to come it was decided that the night watch, the officials of the sestiere, and all the rest of the government were to be armed and positioned around the perimeter of the fire so that no one could enter the area. Parish officials throughout the city were ordered to patrol all night to see that no fires were lit in any house. Members of the scuole grandi were to arm themselves and to gather, so that they could be posted wherever they were needed. Sailors were to guard the Palace and Piazza San Marco; the

Arsenal was put under special guard. The governors of the mainland
towns were ordered to put their soldiers in boats and station them around
the city. The boats of the Council of Ten and the other offices of the city
were also to be on patrol. Armed foreigners from Padua, Treviso, and
Vicenza who were discovered during the night were to have their weapons
seized. No boat was to leave the city and no bell was to sound.

"God willed that at eight o'clock the fire diminished and there was no
longer any fear that it would spread. And God be praised, but it was late
in coming. During the night there were terrible winds, and the fire flared
up again in a few houses, without the risk, however, that it would spread
further. Boat traffic picked up a little, and men began clearing the ice
from the canals. Two gibbets were erected, one at the fish market and
the other near the base of the Rialto Bridge" (1.458–463).

The Venetian Senate recognized that it was essential to rebuild this
center of trade—and tax revenue—as quickly as possible. Four plans
were presented, including one by the designer of the flagpoles in front of
San Marco, and a very interesting proposal by one Friar Giocondo, an
amateur hydraulic and military engineer and an enthusiast of classical
architecture. According to the art historian Vasari, Fra Giocondo proposed
a complete reorganization of the site that would take the shape of a
Greek forum. There would be an open piazza with a church in its center,
surrounded by a double portico where shops and offices would be
located. Giocondo's plan, which seems like a premonition of Sansovino's
project for Piazza San Marco, was rejected. In typically cautious Venetian
fashion, the Senate preferred a less complicated and less expensive
scheme proposed by Scarpagnino.

111

It was not simply a matter of classical idealism versus pragmatics. As Sanudo observed, Scarpagnino's plan, unlike that of Fra Giocondo, respected the history of the marketplace and the legal rights of leaseholders. The distinction may have been a bit of rhetorical misdirection on Scarpagnino's part. In reality, his plan, which still governs the marketplace today, was not all that different from Gio-condo's. Scarpagnino's structural vocabulary was classical, and his final design included an open piazza with a church flanked by porticoes. He succeeded in part because he presented his work as a response to tradition, not a repudiation of it, as Fra Giocondo evidently did.

Scarpagnino's work is confined to the area of the marketplace nearest the Rialto Bridge. At the base of the bridge on the left stands the Palazzo dei Dieci Savi. (111) Rebuilt by Scarpagnino, this structure, which faces the Grand Canal, is arcaded on the ground floor, and its two upper floors are lit by modest rectangular windows set directly on thin cornices. An emblem of the lion of the Republic hanging from a lion mask marks the center of the piano nobile; a statue of Justice guards its corner. The savi, or experts, housed in this building were the chief financial officers of the Republic.

On the other side of the bridge stands the much larger and grander Palazzo dei Camerlenghi. (112) Historians disagree about the identity of the Renaissance architect who worked on the building—though they know it was not Scarpagnino—and also about the fate of the previous palazzo on the site. The camerlenghi were financial officers charged with tax assessment and the supervision of debt. For many years the debtor's prison occupied the ground floor of their building. Located on the inner curve of the bend in the Grand Canal, the building has an irregular ground plan. Its prominence more or less demanded that it be decorated more richly than its equally utilitarian neighbors. The Palazzo dei Camerlenghi looks like the home of a wealthy Venetian family sumptuously decorated in the style of the early Renaissance.

Each of its three façades is characterized by a three-part division, arched windows flanked by pilasters, and a heavy cornice with a frieze of swags. Groups of square windows mark the two larger façades; only the smallest is symmetrical. The prominent symbols of the Republic that mark the Palace of the Ten Savi are replaced here by more subtle representations. Polychrome pateras, many of porphyry, link the building to the decorative system of San Marco and the Palazzo Ducale.

112

Inland from the bridge, along the Ruga degli Orefici, Scarpagnino designed a street-level portico with shop fronts along its back wall and office or storage space in its two upper stories. The Istrian stone of the porticoes gives way to austere stucco walls above, with thin cornices and unadorned rectangular windows. This building was occupied for the most

113

part by drapers and jewelers. Beyond the church of San Giacomo di Rialto, the street opens into a small campo. (113) Scarpagnino designed a similar portico opposite, to enclose the far end of the campo, and continued it along the other side of Ruga degli Orefici. The buildings on this side were occupied by the private international bank called the Bancogiro—which became state-owned in the late sixteenth century—and by state offices. On the nearby Calle della Sicurtà—street of the insurers—from 1300 on stood the offices of groups that assessed and underwrote the multiple risks of sea-faring merchants. As development continued in the area, these structures became known as the Fabbriche Vecchie.

At the end of the campo opposite San Giacometto is a stub of a porphyry column, called the Colonna del Bando. Porphyry, which was a traditional symbol of the Byzantine imperial family, is displayed on the Basilica of San Marco and the Doges' Palace as a symbol of power and authority. This miniature column stands as an expression of state power in the marketplace, and its top was used as a platform from which official notices, decrees, and judgments were read. The three stone steps leading up to the column top are supported on the back of a bent figure, a porter of the marketplace probably, who soon

114

became known as the Hunchback of Rialto. (114) This popular figure eventually acquired a fictional life, and his sarcastic comments and anti-authoritarian sentiments were expressed in anonymous poems and epigrams. The Hunchback also played a conspicuous part in the state's prosecution of thieves. Punishment for theft started at San Marco. The thief ran as best he could from there to the Rialto while being whipped. Once he reached the Hunchback, the whipping stopped.

In the mid-1550s Sansovino was commissioned to design the Fabbriche Nuove di Rialto to meet an increasing demand for market space. His multibayed building running along the Grand Canal carries on both the work and something of the utilitarian style of Scarpagnino's buildings. Derived from Bramante's House of Raphael, the structure is a more pragmatic version of his Library. Its adoption in the market suggests that high classicism was becoming the official architectural style of the Republic by the mid-sixteenth century.

Scarpagnino's building had stepped back from the canal to leave room for the vegetable market at its verge. (115) Sansovino sited

115

his building near the edge of the canal; its ground-level arcade served both as water access and shelter for shops and warehouse space. Sansovino's arcade on the canal side is rusticated, and the two upper stories are separated by cornices and marked off in bays by pilasters. The windows—one to each bay—are crowned by pediments. While the long succession

116

of bays is nearly unbroken, there are subtle differences. (116) The center bay and each end bay have wider openings in the arcade and double pilasters on each of the upper levels. Scarpagnino's structures had segregated government offices, banks, and high-end mercantile enterprises from the messier, busier, and far less lucrative markets on which Venice depended for its nourishment. Sansovino's new building with its extensive portico created an enclave for the Wall Street and Rodeo Drive level of commerce and a barrier that effectively divided these enterprises and their clientele from the shoppers in the daily markets.

Like so many traditional structures in Venice, this division of the market complex into two segregated zones has been turned on its head in the modern city. The division still exists, but the crowds have shifted. The produce markets near the Fabbriche Nuove now serve the relatively small resident population of Venice, while the shops along the Ruga degli Orefici and on the Rialto Bridge are thronged with the far more numerous tourists. This inversion of the traffic flow makes any passage through the Rialto a trial, but it insulates and protects the fresh food market.

For most of its history the Rialto was the main market where the necessities of daily life were sold, though not the only one. A Saturday market was held in Piazza San Marco for many centuries, and small daily markets continue to appear in campi throughout Venice. The biggest change in the Rialto market came about in the twentieth century, when the retail and wholesale markets—originally combined on this site—were split. The wholesale produce, meat, and fish markets are now located on the Tronchetto at the end of the roadway from the mainland. Restaurant and hotel chefs shop there, leaving the Rialto market to serve the needs of individual families. The old produce and cheese markets are for the most part unoccupied—empty squares less than a hundred feet from the press of human traffic to and from the Rialto Bridge.

The daily market now takes place in the open-air campo between Sansovino's Fabbriche Nuove and the Neo-Gothic fish market. Every morning the space is crowded with stands shaded by awnings. (117) A wide variety of seasonal fruits and vegetables is carefully laid out in ordered mounds and piles. By early afternoon the unsold produce has been stored in boxes and rolled away on

117

market carts, and the file of iron-wheeled dumpsters along the edge of the quay overflows with trash. Crews of men in orange suits sweep the ground. Their loaded carts are lifted from the water's edge by boats with little cranes. Once suspended over the boat, the bottom of the cart springs open and the trash cascades into covered bunkers. The boat takes it back to the Tronchetto, where it is loaded onto trucks and driven to mainland dumps.

The old fish market at the end of the island closes off the complex. It was built in 1907 to imitate a Gothic loggia, with open arcades on the first story and an enclosed second story with multiple windows framed with stilted arches and an open porch. The building not only reflects the style of the Gothic period, but it is also said to contain remains of a medieval casa fondaco that once stood on the site. Property of the Querini family, the house was confiscated and torn down in the wake of the abortive 1310 uprising that gave birth to the Council of Ten. The activities of the fish market were closely regulated, as all commerce in Venice was. Plaques that fixed the minimum lengths of common types of fish were prominently posted. The fishermen and fish vendors were organized in a guild, which was also regulated by the state. Fishing was a hard and sometimes dangerous business; productive life was short, and the risk of disability was great. Under state supervision, the guild established a two-tiered system. Young men fished; men over fifty with a minimum of twenty years' experience were qualified to sell fish in the market. This simple distribution of labor provided an incentive for younger fishermen and a guaranteed income for older men. It was typical of the multiple strategies that enabled Venice to provide for the welfare of its citizens.

Some of the fish sold in the Rialto came from the Adriatic, but in the days before refrigeration the bulk of it came from the Lagoon. Fish, shellfish, and aquatic birds, which were also sold in the Pescheria, were the Republic's main local product. Nearly everything else the Venetians ate or drank was imported. There are many varieties of fresh fish on sale in the Rialto market today, but none comes from the Lagoon. The Adriatic provides some fish, the Mediterranean a bit more, but the bulk of what is displayed day by day comes from commercial fisheries in the Atlantic, Pacific, and Indian Oceans. Seafood is everywhere in Venice, but none of it is local. The environmental threat posed by the acqua alta gains international attention, but the pollution of the Lagoon and the disappearance of its fisheries is in some ways a deeper and more intimate wound.

For about a century beginning in the 1350s, Venice controlled prostitution by confining it to a small area in the Rialto. The state appointed six overseers who reported to the committee responsible for nighttime security. The overseers in turn appointed resident superintendents for the area, which became known as the Castelletto. Segregation was a common approach to the problem of prostitution throughout Europe during the Middle Ages, but in Venice these provisions created, in effect, a state-run brothel governed by an elaborate code of conduct. These rules restricted where prostitutes could solicit, limited the hours when they could enter hotels, regulated the sale of alcohol to patrons, established Saturday as the only day when prostitutes could leave the Rialto, and required them to wear a yellow scarf when they did so.

These regulations were later supplemented by others designed to protect the women from economic exploitation by pimps and madams. But no law protected prostitutes against violence; and no sexually active person was safe from syphilis. For once, the controlling hand of the Venetian state was ineffective. In the mid-fifteenth century, prostitutes simply walked away from the Castelletto and established themselves in small enclaves throughout the city. Powerless to control the traffic, the authorities eventually gave in.

Prostitutes were not the only group segregated by law in Venice. In 1516, just two years after the Rialto fire, the Republic enacted the first of a series of regulations that confined the Jewish community to a small island in Cannaregio called the Ghetto Nuovo. The island had been industrial land at one time. Ghetto means foundry in Venetian dialect, and a nearby foundry in Cannaregio had extended onto the island. The motives for confining the Jewish community to this spot were a poisonous blend of prejudice and benign, if not positively good, intentions. The Renaissance Venetians were certainly bigots, but they were not proto-Nazis committed to the extermination of Jews. The Ghetto was an invidious form of segregation, but it was an end in itself, not a stepping-stone to further disenfranchisement or a prelude to annihilation. Because they wanted and needed to have Jewish bankers in their community, the Venetians tried to find a way to accommodate a religious minority they found threatening.

The experience of the last century intrudes to suggest that the Ghetto must have been formed by rounding up the Jews of Venice and forcibly relocating them. Many historians point to the island called Giudecca and identify it as the historical home of the Venetian Jews. Giudecca probably comes from the word for justice, however, and reflects the use of the island in the earliest years of the Republic as a place of exile or execution for those who had undergone judgment. There is no evidence of a Jewish community in Venice before the late fourteenth century, and in the following century the Jews were ordered out of Venice and required to settle in the mainland community of Mestre. Their access to the Rialto and to Venice was limited to a handful of days per year. All Jewish men were required to wear a yellow beret—the same color that identified prostitutes—when in the city to sharply distinguish them from Christian Venetians, who commonly wore black hats.

With the establishment of the Ghetto in 1516, Jews could again live in Venice. Many members of the Jewish community welcomed its creation as a softening of residential restrictions that had made life unpleasant and business difficult. Jews from Spain and Portugal who had been driven out of their homelands or forced to convert to Christianity found refuge in the Venetian Ghetto, where they were free to practice their religion without persecution.

Inviting Jews to settle in Venice was a calculated though controversial policy from which the Republic expected to benefit in three ways. The immediate benefits came from the contract established between the Jewish community and the Venetian state. In order to do business in Venice, the Jewish community agreed to pay a substantial annual fee—in some years as high as ten thousand ducats—which went directly to the state treasury. Jewish merchants were active throughout the Mediterranean, and whatever percentage of their trade Venice could draw to itself also increased tax revenues and customs duties. While these were important sources of supplemental revenue for the state, in themselves they would not have been enough to overcome the widespread hatred and distrust of this community. But Jews brought something else to the table. If their mercantile abilities and successes did not distinguish them from other groups, in one area of commerce they were unique. They had the ability, as Shakespeare's Shylock makes abundantly clear, to lend money at interest.

Medieval Catholicism had its hot button issues. On the sexual front, the medieval and Renaissance Church focused on acts that produced pleasure but not babies. Masturbation, nonreproductive heterosexual activity, and homosexual intercourse—punishable by death—were grouped under the name of sodomy. Usury was the other great demon of medieval and Renaissance theologians. Usury did not mean charging exorbitant interest, which is the modern meaning of the term; usury in the Middle Ages meant charging any interest at all. Medieval theologians—and poets like Dante who understood them—saw usury as a crime against nature and a metaphorical form of sexual deviance. Dante placed usurers in the part of Hell where sodomites suffer an endless rain of fire.

Shakespeare's Shylock in *The Merchant of Venice* links sexuality with usury and bases his defense of the practice on an obscure narrative in Genesis 30. In Jacob's unending struggle to get a fair deal from his father-in-law, Laban, he proposes a division of their flocks. Laban will keep all the solid-colored sheep, and Jacob will keep all those with mixed-colored fleece. When Laban agrees, Jacob divides the sheep, then sets up rods of poplar with their bark partly removed where the sheep can see them when they are copulating. These rods of mixed color seen at the moment of conception cause the ewes to produce a disproportionate number of lambs of mixed color, and Jacob finally becomes rich. Antonio, Shakespeare's spokesman for Christian orthodoxy, objects to Shylock's proof text: "This was a venture, sir, that Jacob served for; / A thing not in his power to bring to pass, / But sway'd and fashion'd by the hand of heaven. / Was this inserted to make interest good? / Or is your gold and silver ewes and rams?" Shylock replies, "I cannot tell; I make it breed as fast" (1.3).

Unlike sheep, money is sterile. To make it produce even metaphorical offspring by requiring interest confuses two realms that God has rigorously separated—a kind of economic sex crime. Usury was also thought of as hostile and anticommunal. Shylock loans Antonio money "as to an enemy." Antonio, "in low simplicity . . . lends out money gratis" to any Christian in need. This was the course of action that medieval Christian doctrine demanded; moneylending was seen as a form of social assistance. Not being members of the Christian community, Jews were not obligated to assist Christians.

Many Italian communities established a loan pool, called a monte di pietà, and the Venetians debated the idea as an alternative to contracting with the Jewish community. In theory the idea made sense. Wealthy individuals donated to a fund that was available interest-free to those in need. When the benefici-

aries of this public charity got back on their feet, they would repay the loans. The reality, of course, was quite different; the funds were quickly emptied of cash, which was only slowly replenished as loans were repaid. *If* they were

118

repaid. This was not a scheme to appeal to Venetians. So they invited the Jewish community back into the city and contracted with them to provide loans at regulated levels of interest.

The Ghetto Nuovo is a tiny island with a now disproportionately large campo ringed on three sides by unusually tall buildings. (118) Similar buildings that had hedged in the island on its fourth side were torn down in the nineteenth century. In their place is a rest home, which the SS used as its headquarters from 1943 to 1945, and a brick wall topped with barbed wire and inset with monuments commemorating members of the Venetian Jewish community consumed in the Nazi death camps. The Ghetto is linked to neighboring islands by three bridges; before the nineteenth century there were only two. Each was staffed by a Christian guard whose salary was paid by the Jewish community and whose duty was to close the entries to the Ghetto at night. Water entrances to all the buildings were blocked up, and watchmen patrolled the surrounding canals until dawn.

The towering apartment blocks of the Ghetto were linked by passageways so that almost every household communicated with every other. The doorway of the Red Bank, which made loans secured by pawn, is still visible under a portico near the Ponte di Ghetto Nuovo; two similar banks were located elsewhere in the campo. Today, the Museum of the Hebrew Community occupies many of these buildings, which can be visited only by guided tour, and oversees three of the synagogues built into the melded structures.

The residents of the Ghetto Nuovo were Jews from northern inland areas with which Venice had long traded. They were followers of the Ashkenazi rite. Their remarkably small synagogues, which the Venetians thought of as scuole rather than churches, are located on the top floors of the Ghetto buildings. With the exception of the protruding end of the Scuola Canton, all are invisible from outside. The interiors are dominated by two structures: the Aron ha Kodesh or Torah ark where scriptures are kept, and the Tevah or pulpit from which the Torah is read. The ark must face toward Jerusalem, and its position determines the layout of each synagogue.

The Scuola Tedesca, built in 1535, was remodeled in the eighteenth century. Because of weakness in the floor, the Tevah, originally located in the center of the room, was moved toward one corner at the same time. In addition to the required structures, the elongated room has benches for the male congregation around its sides and an elliptical gallery on its second level for women. The Scuola Canton, built in 1531, was remodeled in the seventeenth century, and its opulent interior reflects the taste of the Baroque era. The Aron is a Neoclassical aediculum flanked with Corinthian columns and crowned with a broken pediment. Benches line the long walls, and small windows on the right conceal the women's gallery. This synagogue's most unusual, indeed unique, feature is a series of carved wooden panels on both side walls depicting eight scenes from the book of Exodus. These scenes include the battle of Jericho, the crossing of the Red Sea, the fall of the manna, and Moses striking the rock.

The Ponte di Ghetto Vecchio leads from the Ashkenazi Ghetto Nuovo to its paradoxically named extension, the Ghetto Vecchio. The "old foundry" was added to the territory of the new foundry in the 1530s to accommodate the many Jews from the Mediterranean region who were drawn to Venice in the wake of Spanish, Portuguese, and Turkish oppression. These Jews were for the most part Sephardim. The Ghetto Vecchio was not surrounded by water; its enclosure was ensured by bricking up windows and doors on its outer edges and creating a single guarded doorway that opened onto the fondamenta of the Cannaregio Canal, the most carefully watched water route in Venice. (119) The Ghetto's one main street began at this gate, jogged left through a small campo, and continued on to the Ashkenazi sector.

Two synagogues overlooked the central campo. Founded in 1538, the

119

Scuola Levantina was extensively remodeled in the seventeenth century by an architect familiar with the style of Longhena. Indeed, many have argued that the synagogue is the work of Longhena himself. Built at the intersection of the Ghetto's main street with its only campo, the building has two façades. The more important overlooks the square. A few courses of rusticated stone form a basement; the upper surfaces of the wall are stuccoed and decorated with raised panels. The central arched doorway is framed by a square lintel; arched windows on the piano nobile are similarly treated. Mezzanine windows under the modest cornice are lozenge-shaped.

Across the square from the Scuola Levantina stands the Scuola Spagnola. Founded in the second half of the sixteenth century and remodeled in the early seventeenth, this is the largest of the Ghetto synagogues. The building has a plain stucco façade with square windows on the ground floor and a side entrance. Large arched windows light the sanctuary on the piano nobile. From a modest ground-floor room a double stairway, typical of Venetian scuole, leads to the sumptuous place of worship on the second floor. In this magnificent room, the scuola as conceptual model has been replaced by the theater, an effect that is especially marked in the women's balcony. Light streams in through high gilt-framed windows on three sides. Venetian chandeliers hang from the ceiling. The men of the congregation sit in benches on either side of the long room, with its red damask accents.

The foundry that gave its name to the Ghetto may have been one of the many industries that were folded into the expanding state Arsenal. Established in 1104 on two parallel islands inland of both the Basin of San Marco and the Lagoon to the north, the Arsenal communicated with each through narrow, easily defended canals. In the early fourteenth century it quadrupled in size, and at the end of the fifteenth century when the Arsenale Nuovissimo was built, the limits of the complex extended into the Lagoon at the north. As the Arsenal increased in importance, its workforce, the arsenalotti, grew to extraordinary proportions. In 1423 an estimated sixteen thousand workers were employed there.

Medieval industries were generally small and loosely coordinated. Even enterprises that required the cooperation of many specialists, like silk manufacture or the weaving and finishing of brocades, were performed in shops that were distant from one another. In defiance of this tradition, the Arsenal consolidated every aspect of boat building into a single location. It created an industrial organization in an era when there were no examples to follow. It standardized and systematized not only its product but its workflow. Teams of workers specialized in particular operations; parts and tools were interchangeable. A committee of three overseers chosen from the Senate and three patrons chosen from the Grand Council supervised the work. Each overseer was responsible for the integrity of the Arsenal for a fifteen-day period. He stayed in the Arsenal, held the keys, and was obliged to tour the buildings at night. The engineering and technical supervisor was called the magnificent admiral. He supervised the protomagistri, the top workers in each of the principal skills—frame and hull carpenters, mast and oar makers, smiths and metalworkers, sawyers and gunsmiths.

The state bakery is the only Arsenal structure that fronts on the Basin of San Marco. Now enlarged by the addition of a second story, its original roofline is marked by the ceremonial crenellations that distinguish state buildings. The bakery produced ship's biscuit or hardtack, the virtually incorruptible and easily transportable unleavened bread that sailors in the Republic's galleys were fed. A store of biscuit produced here in 1668 and uncovered three centuries later was reported to be still edible. The narrow Rio dell'Arsenale leads inland past the bakery, one end of the foundry, and the oarmaker's shop to the entrance gates of the state navy yard. At the break in the long crenellated walls that surround the complex, two square brick towers rise from sloping rusticated foundations. Each has a crenellated balcony supported on stone brackets at its summit and an observation post with windows that command all four directions. Crenellations outlined with Istrian stone complete these structures. The towers, which mark the water entrance to the complex, were built in the late seventeenth century when the canal was widened to allow the passage of square-rigged ships. Directly behind these gates is the Old Arsenal (Darsena Vecchia), the twelfth-century core of the complex.

The ceremonial land entrance to the Arsenal is immediately to the left. (120) The entryway, which was designed in 1460, resembles a triumphal arch. The lion of St. Mark, attributed to Bartolomeo Bon, was added a few years later. After the improbable and short-lived Venetian victory over the Turks in the battle of Lepanto in 1571, winged victories and an inscription were placed above the door. The sculptures in front of the gate are also commemorative. Added in the late seventeenth century when the original entrance ramp was transformed into an enclosed porch, they represent Roman gods. Along with two unidentified deities, there are images of Neptune (god of the sea), Mars and Bellona (the god and goddess of warfare), along with personifications of Vigilance, Abundance, and Justice. The far more engaging lions set on rough plinths to either side of the porch are spoils of war. The standing lion comes from Piraeus, the port of Athens. The crouching lion was found along the road between Athens and the sacred city of Eleusis. Both were captured by Admiral Francesco Morosini during his campaigns on the Greek mainland in the late seventeenth

120

century. While he was bombarding the Athenian acropolis in 1687, one of Morosini's shells ignited a Turkish powder store in the largely intact Parthenon, destroying the roof and one of the building's long sides.

In the nineteenth century a bronze bust of Dante was set into the wall to the right of the gateway. Like the statues of Garibaldi and the nationalistic street names that proliferated in the same century, it is part of a national effort to Italianize Venice. In this case the transformation was not an easy one. Like most Florentines of his era, Dante had nothing but contempt for Venetians. The incessant, fervid industry of the Arsenal struck him as demonic, and he used it as a metaphor for a particularly nasty corner of Hell. Because he was Italy's national poet, however, his mere mention of the Arsenal was worthy of celebration.

The interior of the Arsenal is a military zone off-limits to visitors. The Venice Biennale—the international exhibit of contemporary art from around the world that Venice hosts every second year—makes use of some of its structures. The nearby Naval Museum, which is housed in a former state granary, offers the best overview of the complex, the ships produced there, and Venetian boat-making in general. It provides a naval history of Venice from the beginning to long after the fall of the Republic to Napoleon. After conquering the Adriatic, the Venetians extended their stato da mar, or sea empire, throughout the Eastern Mediterranean, and many of their island colonies and outposts endured for centuries; room 5 on the first floor contains three-dimensional models of these Mediterranean island fortresses. The second floor of the museum displays an enormous collection of ship models, the most authentic of which come from the Arsenal itself, where in the late seventeenth century a building was set aside to preserve scale models of the ships in production. During the French invasion and the uprising that followed, many of these models were damaged or destroyed. Those that survived were repaired and installed in this building in the early twentieth century.

Among the most precious objects in the collection is a large model of the Doge's ceremonial ship, the Bucintoro, in room 17. The first Bucintoro was built in the fourteenth century. A second was created in 1526, which was replaced by a close copy in 1606, then again in 1729. The origin of the vessel's curious name is uncertain. Francesco Sansovino believed that it was a corruption of the Latin word for two hundred—the number of sailors aboard—but more imaginative derivations include a nod to Virgil and acknowledgment of its golden surface.

The ship had two decks, with space for 168 rowers and 42 additional hands below. Rowing the boat was a privilege granted to the most prized of the arsenalotti. The richly decorated upper deck was reserved for the Doge's suite and special guests of the Republic. The boat seldom left the Arsenal; when it did, it welcomed important visitors or carried the new Doge to his coronation in San Marco. Once a year, on Ascension Day, the ship led a great marine procession to the site of the annual wedding with the sea. Emerging from beneath a gilded image of Justice, the Doge dropped a ring into the water and proclaimed, "We wed thee, sea, in sign of true and perpetual dominion."

While the Naval Museum celebrates the triumphs of Venetian naval history, it fails to record the most significant transformation of the galley fleet. Oarsmen were originally free men who voluntarily took on this most difficult and dangerous task. By the middle of the sixteenth century, however, the labor pool had diminished. Turkish invasions of Greece and the Near East reduced the supply of foreigners who had served in great numbers in the Venetian galleys. The cost of labor rose steadily in Venice during the sixteenth century, and wages for rowers could not keep pace. At mid-century a galley captain named Cristoforo da Canal wrote a treatise urging that convicts from Venice and its colonies be sentenced to the fleet. Expediency was not his only rationale. After noting that the Genoese and Papal States used boats powered by prisoners, he went on to argue that condemnation to the rowing benches was more humane than mutilation—the common punishment for many crimes. Rather than retribution, he declared, rowing was a form of rehabilitation: it was healthy, open-air work, and it taught a marketable skill. However disin-

121

genuous his argument, Canal prevailed. The Venetian fleet came to include more and more galleys rowed by prisoners. Canal himself served as commander of the condemned for a few years in the late 1540s.

Just east of the Arsenal complex an archway on the Basin esplanade opens onto a Renaissance housing project. The arch, which was built in 1645, was designed more as a signpost than an entryway, a form of wordless advertising for the houses. Built around 1500, apartments in these four blocks were offered rent-free to the families of sailors in the Republic's galleys who had distinguished themselves in her service. The archway advertised the reward they could expect. Its three-story row houses have multiple arched windows on the second floor. (121) The beautiful complex, called the Marinarezza, is still fully occupied today. A modern shrine, of the kind that was once common throughout Italy, decorated with a large cursive $\mathcal{M}$ honoring the Virgin Mary, stands at the front of the central row. The remarkable assemblage of photographs inside—most in black and white—shows a cohesive community with deep roots in the Venetian past.

Chapter Eight

THE STREETS OF VENICE

From the end of the sixteenth century until the spring of 1797, Venice lived in a golden twilight. Venetian commerce suffered ups and downs from which the luckier members of the nobility were increasingly insulated, as they invested more and more of their wealth in mainland properties and state securities. Many of the old merchant nobility sank into a desperate poverty that was relieved only by charity and government jobs. Having reached the peak of their ambition, the Turks stopped attacking and settled into a morbid decline that left Turkey the "sick man of Europe." Venice, known for its power, audacity, and industry, weathered in the European imagination. Antiquity, nobility, and beauty became the chief attractions of a city rich in painting and architecture and famous for its colorful public ceremonies. The calendar of festivals and processions that once expressed the city's majesty and discipline became exotic curiosities, thronged with foreign visitors. The launching of the Bucintoro and the Doge's wedding to the sea on Ascension Day became the holy grail of Venetian tourist attractions.

Venice had more to charm a visitor than processions and monuments, however. Music of the highest quality was performed throughout the year in convents, churches, and hospices. Despite early opposition from the government and Church, by the end of the sixteenth century every parish in the city had a theater, housed in the palazzi of noble families. At first the theater season ran from Christmas to Carnival. Later it expanded to include early fall and the two weeks after Ascension Day. No matter what the time of year, nobles attending public theaters were required to wear masks that both guarded their identities and proclaimed their social rank; infractions were punishable by law. Theatrical fare was mixed, and the crowd of men and women, which was never in full darkness, was often more intent on flirting or acting up than watching the stage. By law, theater boxes had to have their doors partly open, and prostitutes attending performances were required to dress "decently." Dramas were punctuated by music and dance. Musicians sat at floor level and sometimes blocked the audience's view.

The improvisational commedia dell'arte of pratfalls and stock characters was still alive. Developed in the Renaissance as popular, often scandalous, outdoor entertainment in which women as well as men performed, the commedia was more like a chain of vaudeville acts than a coherent drama. The standard characters included the ingénue Colombina, the impertinent servant Pulcinella, the braggart soldier Captain Spavento, the more or less insane servants called zanni—from which we get the word "zany"—and Pantalone, the stingy, goat-bearded character dressed in red and black from whom Shakespeare developed his merchant of Venice. Songs, dances, tight-rope walking, feats of strength, juggling, scatological clowning, and a certain amount of female nudity punctuated the unfolding storyline.

By the eighteenth century this once vital form had more or less run its course. Working within its conventions, the Venetian playwright Carlo Goldoni produced the wonderful *A Servant of Two Masters,* but after the success of his play he rejected the form altogether and led a critical attack against it. His great rival, Carlo Gozzi, produced texts for a commedia dell'arte troupe that yielded the operas *Turandot* and *A Love for Three Oranges.* Despite the decline in quality and popularity of the commedia dell'arte players, the traditional costumes of its characters Harlequin and Pulcinella remained the most popular Carnival disguises for men.

Noble families entertained in their palazzi and hosted intimate parties in their private retreats. These were small apartments, the most prized of which overlooked Piazza San Marco. Actors, opera stars, and singers might be met and heard in any of these settings. Games, amateur theatricals, and gambling were also common entertainments. Spending time in Venice was comfortable, if expensive. Long used to accommodating traveling merchants, the city had always been well supplied with inns, restaurants, and taverns. Wealthy travelers rented apartments in the palazzi of Venetian nobles.

Venice was unusual in its tolerance of gambling. The first public gaming room was opened in 1638 in a palazzo of the Dandolo family on the Calle Valaresso not far from San Marco. (Map 8) The elegant Ridotto, now part of the Hotel Monaco and Grand Canal, was open to noble and non-noble patrons during a portion of the year that expanded from Carnival and eventually matched the long theater season. Masks were obligatory, and a variety of entertainments were available, including conversation, gaming, and, if Casanova is to be trusted, seduction. (122)

122

Sexual liaisons were chic in eighteenth-century Europe, and Venice was at least up to date if not ahead of the curve. From the Renaissance onward, the Venetian sex industry—once it escaped from state control—was mythologized by locals and travelers alike. Wide-eyed foreigners reported that thousands of women and girls displayed themselves, rouged and topless, in every part of the city; that seeming princesses lured young noblemen to their doom; that eight-year-old girls were sold in the streets. The paradoxical blend of titillation and outrage that marks these accounts makes it hard to tell just how widespread and assertive prostitution might have been. In the popular imagination, Venice could be a libertine's paradise or a sex-crazed hell.

Malvasia, a fortified wine like sherry or Madeira, was a popular Venetian drink throughout the Middle Ages and Renaissance. Trade with the Near East brought coffee to the city in the late sixteenth century. Once available only at high cost in apothecary shops, by 1640 the beans were being roasted and brewed in the first Venetian cafe. By the end of the eighteenth century, Venice had more than two hundred coffee houses, where nobles, intellectuals, and artists gathered and conversation was lively. Caffè Florian in Piazza San Marco was founded in the seventeenth century and remodeled in the eighteenth.

The fatally named Teatro La Fenice (The Phoenix) is one of four theaters that survived the fall of the Republic at the end of the eighteenth century. Located in the sestiere of San Marco, the theater was underwritten by a group of financiers—former box-holders at the theater of San Benedetto—who had been evicted by its owners. The society organized a competition to design a new theater in which more than two dozen architects participated. The winning design was passed over, and the commission was assigned to Gian Antonio Selva. The theater's name refers to the mythical bird that combusts at the end of its life and is born again from its own ashes. The Teatro San Benedetto had burned in 1774, and the organizers of the new theater thought of La Fenice as its new incarnation. The name was more appropriate than they would ever know. Burned to the ground in 1836, the theater was rebuilt a year later. (123) Then, during the night of January 29, 1996, La Fenice was deliberately set on fire and again burned to the ground.

Rebuilt "as it was and where it was" at a cost of millions of euros, the theater reopened in 2003. The reconstructed interior reflects the eighteenth-century design and the stucco and gilt work of the original theater. A deep horseshoe-shaped space fitted with rows of seats in the orchestra is surrounded by tiers of boxes. There is a royal box of expanded dimensions above the main entry. The orchestra is hidden by a raised screen; the new stage curtain is a reconstruction of an eighteenth-century view of the Column of St. Mark, the Palazzo Ducale, and the Bacino.

123

Despite abandonment by its principal patrons, the nearby theater of San Benedetto was also rebuilt. Mozart attended a performance there before the fire. After Rossini's death in 1868, the theater was renamed in his honor. In the twentieth century the Rossini was converted to a movie theater. Even more frequently redesigned and reconstructed than La Fenice or San Benedetto, the modern Teatro Goldoni, near the Rialto vaporetto stop, is heir to a tradition that began in 1622. The first theater on the site was built by the Vendramin family and named for the nearby churches of San Luca and San Salvador. When that theater burned a few decades later, it was rebuilt at the same spot. Musical theater, sometimes with elaborate sets, was its most common offering until the 1750s, when Goldoni became involved in its productions. Several of his plays, though not the most enduring, had their premieres there. The theater was completely rebuilt in 1776. In 1833 it was renamed the Apollo, and twenty years later it was remodeled yet again, this time, paradoxically, in the Neo-Gothic style. It was renamed the Goldoni shortly after that. Condemned in the aftermath of World War II, the theater was abandoned until a reconstruction faithful to the Neo-Gothic Apollo began in 1969.

The idea of the theater spread to other types of buildings. In the Ghetto, the followers of Longhena who designed the Scuola Spagnola and the anonymous builders who remodeled the Scuola Canton introduced theater-style seating and theatrical opulence to these places of worship. The burgeoning façade of the church of San Moisé creates an astonishing theatrical backdrop visible from a distance down the long axis of the Calle Larga XXII Marzo, near the west end of the Piazza San Marco. Even in the compacted city of the seventeenth century, this church was unusu-

ally easy to see from its ample piazza. Designed by Alessandro Tremignon, Longhena's pupil, the complicated façade is ornamented in every
conceivable way and infested with sculptural groups.

Four belted columns on high pedestals with protruding entablatures
above them divide the lower zone of the façade into three areas. The central area frames an arched doorway, with an inner framing of smaller
columns that support a garlanded sarcophagus crowned with sculptural
work and a soaring plinth with a bust at its top. Pediments above the
side doors support groups of seated and standing figures. Shelves projecting from the wall above each of them support smaller sarcophagi,
seated putti, and busts. An enormous garland runs across the façade
beneath the entablatures at the height of the Corinthian capitals. The
second zone, subdivided into three parts by two layers of pilasters, is
pierced at its center bay by an arched window with great lolling figures
draped along its sides. A standing figure breaks through the entablature
and leads upward to a huge heraldic stemma in a square attic story.
Oversized dentals in this upper area outline the roof. Standing figures
project beyond its corners and peak. The tombs and busts are those of
diverse members of the Fini family who commissioned Tremignon's
remodeling of the ancient church and the transformation of its façade
into a virtual billboard vaunting the status and achievements of family
members.

The main altar of the church was designed by Tremignon and sculpted
by Heinrich Meyring. The sculpture that is displayed in an architectural
setting on the façade is grouped more naturalistically to create a tableau
vivant that represents Moses receiving the tables of the law on Mount

Sinai. A pyramidal backdrop of stones represents the pinnacle of the mountain. A sculpted Moses kneels and points to the tablets which God, surrounded by trumpeting angels, reveals to him. The installation serves much the same purpose as a painting, but it is more closely linked to the groups of wax figures that were used in such popular devotional centers as Loreto. The aim in both cases was to heighten the emotional impact of scenes commonly represented in painting by making them three-dimensional.

The nearby church of Santa Maria del Giglio (Santa Maria Zobenigo) was redesigned at almost the same time by Giuseppe Sardi. Sardi's

124

façade is dedicated to Antonio Barbaro, the governor of Dalmatia. The more successful and more harmonious structure includes statues of the dedicatee and interesting maps of the cities under his command. The campo that the building overlooks is hopelessly shallow, however, and the façade in its entirety can be seen only from an oblique angle.

Ca' Rezzonico, one of the largest and most commanding palazzi on the Grand Canal, is now a city-owned museum focused on the life and art of the eighteenth century. (124) The massive marble structure, which gives its name to the nearby vaporetto stop, replaced two decrepit palazzi belonging to the Bon family and a number of lesser buildings that were torn down in the middle of the seventeenth century. Longhena, architect of the Salute and the most prominent designer in Venice at the time, was commissioned to build the palace. He died when only the first two stories of the structure were complete. Financial difficulties prevented the Bon family from continuing the project, and the half-built structure topped by an improvised third story was sold to the Rezzonico family. Originally from Lombardy, the Rezzonico were ennobled in the seventeenth century after contributing enormous sums to the Republic to finance the endless wars with Turkey. Giorgio Massari, the most sought-after architect of the eighteenth century, completed the building in a style that was compatible with Longhena's design.

Though the building faces directly on the Grand Canal, it is elevated on a plinth above water level, and a flight of steps leads up from the canal to its central entryway. The ground floor is divided into three parts, typical of Venetian palazzi. Two bays with double columns at the corner and paired rectangular windows stand at either side of an open central bay with two free-standing columns. This story is completely rusticated, in the style that Sansovino introduced to Venice in the Mint. While rustication served to fortify that public building, here it defines the water level of the structure as something rough, foreign, and nonurban.

Longhena's second story is based on the Tabularium motif. Columns at the corners are doubled, and balconies run across the façade at the height of the pedestals. Massari's third story is also an open arcade with attached columns and a balcony. He has placed oval windows above each open bay in an attic story above. Massari also designed the grand staircase that leads from the ground floor to the piano nobile. At its top he created a two-story ballroom or reception hall of regal proportions.

The last Rezzonico died in 1810, and the property quickly passed

through the hands of a number of heirs, who rented the palazzo to distinguished foreigners. In the 1880s Robert Barrett Browning, a painter and
son of the distinguished poet, bought the building. His father died there
at the end of the decade. John Singer Sargent rented a studio on the
third floor. Browning sold the property to a nobleman, who quickly fell
into financial difficulties. In 1935 the palazzo was bought by the city.

Many of the ceilings of the palace were painted with frescoes by
Giambattista Tiepolo and lesser-known artists of the eighteenth century.
Giovan Battista Crosato painted the *Chariot of Apollo* on the ceiling of the
ballroom. In the room of the *Marriage Allegory* next to it, Tiepolo, working
with his son and an assistant, painted a ceiling fresco that honored the
marriage of Ludovico Rezzonico and Faustina Savorgnan. The wedding
procession is transformed into a classical triumph, with the couple carried across a milky sky on the chariot of Apollo. A blindfolded Cupid
holds the marriage torch, while allegorical figures representing the virtues
hover around them; the lion of St. Mark sits on a cloud bank. The allegorical classicism that represented the Venetian state in official art
adapted easily to the glorification of individual families.

Pastel portraits of eighteenth-century men, women, and children are
displayed in the next room. While the ceilings of the palace were decorated with images that depersonalized and mythologized the nobility,
these intimate portraits show individuals of very differing qualities and
character. Quicker to produce and less studied than formal portraits in
oil, these pictures convey more immediacy and directness, though the
sitters still look slightly unfocused.

Tiepolo's ceiling fresco in the throne room of the palazzo definitely belongs in the category of hyperbolic praise; it was based on a celebra-

tory poem composed to honor the Rezzonico-Savorgnan wedding. The

Allegory of Merit commemorates the moment in which the Rezzonico

family achieved noble rank in Venice, an act that is recognized in the fig-

ure of a winged putto holding a large leather-bound volume of the *Libro*

d'Oro, in which all Venetian nobles are inscribed. Aside from the open

register in the putto's hands, the only genuinely Venetian element in the

painting is the atmosphere. The thick ground-hugging fog, the distant

temple lost in a luminous white mist, the white sky with here and there a

trace of cloud but no hint of blue, represent both the atmosphere of

Venice and the steady retreat of its substance into myth.

The rooms on the second piano nobile display Venetian paintings from

the eighteenth century in all genres by some of the most significant

painters of the era. This wonderful collection includes two early and very

significant works in the portego by Antonio Canale, called Canaletto. The

great painters of the fifteenth century, the Bellinis and Carpaccio, often

set their religious paintings against backgrounds that represented the

Venice of their day. Occasional painters in the sixteenth and seventeenth

centuries did the same, but during those centuries Venetian landscape

painters, for the most part, followed the example of other Italian masters

in preferring images of the pastoral landscape to images of the city. Rep-

resentations of architecture, where they existed, were classical or classi-

cizing. Canaletto was among the first painters to rediscover the city as a

subject for landscape. His early work as a painter of theatrical scenery

equipped him to reconfigure the city in a conventional style that his audi-

ence knew and understood. On a visit to Rome in 1719, the young

125

painter encountered another former scenery painter, Giovanni Paolo Pannini, whose views of that city were extremely popular.

In Canaletto's *Veduta del Rio dei Mendicanti,* the canal at the northern rim of the city and its buildings are bathed in a widely diffused pearly light like that in the Tiepolo *Allegory of Merit.* (125) The composition is dominated by the central portico and one long wing of the great hospice of San Lazzaro that sheltered lepers. Across the canal, a series of tenements, their rooflines crowded with multiple chimneys, recede along a stuttering diagonal into the far distance. Laundry hangs from ropes and poles; rows of dark rectangular windows look out onto the few boats in the water and small groups of men on the fondamenta.

As early as the Renaissance, theater backdrops represented a single urban street. That stable scene, drawn from the repertoire of Roman comedy, could be represented by permanent façades built into the theater structure. But more commonly the backdrop was created by illusionistic painting. Canaletto's scene replaces the conventional street with an actual Venetian canal and substitutes real buildings for fictive ones. In keeping with stage conventions, he darkens the right foreground to create a second diagonal across the picture frame, unifying a subject that might otherwise disintegrate into two separate blocks on either side of the canal. He also illuminates the façades along both sides of the canal simultaneously, a trick of theater lighting that the sun would be hard pressed to equal.

The more striking and more harmonious *Canal Grande da Ca' Balbi* replaces artificial light with post-storm sunlight reflected from the under-surface of heavy clouds. Both sides of the Grand Canal are shown natura-listically, with the left side bathed in light and the right side in shadow. The light, which picks out every detail of outline and structure, gives the multicolored façades of the palazzo along the canal a chromatic harmony that they certainly lacked and helps to organize them into a homogenous mass that recedes deep into the picture space. Convention has not lost all its power. The foreground darkness that submerges Palazzo Balbi and stretches across the canal is impossible but useful, guiding the eye diag-onally into the composition.

While Venetians were eager patrons of Canaletto's views, he found an even wealthier and more enthusiastic audience among tourists, especially English noblemen on the Grand Tour of the continent. A Canaletto repre-senting a favorite Venetian scene became as essential a part of the increasingly packaged experience as seeing the Doge wed the sea or gam-bling in a mask at the Ridotto. As Canaletto's prices rose, the expatriate British consul Joseph Smith became his agent—with such success that Canaletto moved to Britain in 1744. He returned to Venice eleven years later and continued until the end of his life to produce canvases that were often formulaic and repetitious.

Other Venetian painters, including Luca Carlevarijs, Bernardo Bellotto, Michele Marieschi, and Francesco Guardi, created views of the city as well. With Smith's sponsorship, the engraver Antonio Visentini reproduced forty of the most popular views of Canaletto in his *Urbis Vene-tiarum Prospectus Celebriores* printed in 1735. Like Piranesi's images of Rome, these engravings made selected Venetian prospects available to an even wider audience. Marieschi produced a series of twenty-one views entitled *Magnificentiores Selectioresque Urbis Venetiarum Prospectus* in 1741.

While scenic painters memorialized the buildings and canals of Venice, the tradition of imaginative painting flourished as well. Among the treasures of Ca' Rezzonico is a collection of frescoes removed from the Tiepolo villa in the mainland town of Zianigo. These remarkable scenes by Giandomenico Tiepolo, son of Giambattista, were painted in the family retreat over a period stretching from the mid-eighteenth century to its end. Removed from the walls of the villa in 1906 for sale in France, the frescoes were bought by the city after their exportation was blocked by the Ministry of Instruction. Part of the Rezzonico collection since 1936, they were restored and reinstalled in 2000. The frescoes, which have no formal program, represent allegorical scenes, episodes from Italian poetry, scenes of patrician country life, and the antics of Pulcinella.

The magnificent fresco called *The New World* is filled with figures who

turn their backs on the viewer. (126) The New World of the title is evidently an optical effect that can be seen through an opening in a domed

126

tentlike structure near the center of the picture but almost completely hidden by the crowd. A man in a red frock coat and tricorn hat lifts a boy dressed all in yellow who peers into this opening. A mountebank dressed in black, standing on a stool, gestures with a long black rod toward this group. The rest of the frame is filled with the backs of the many different sorts of people who patiently wait their turns. These include a man in the white clothes and conical hat of Pulcinella, a masked man, unmasked noblemen and women, dandies and commoners. As viewers, we share the curiosity of the crowd; like the patient men and women in this diverse and well-behaved group, we are waiting for something we cannot quite imagine. Since the painting was completed in 1791, a mere six years before the fall of the Republic, it has been almost irresistible to see it as an image of Venice on the brink of the unknown. While the picture may reflect a fin-de-siècle uncertainty mixed with nostalgia, it does not evidently anticipate anything very dire or very different from the way things were.

In the following room the focus shifts to the commedia dell'arte and the figure of Pulcinella. Like all the stock figures of the comedy, Pulcinella is not a person but a mask. By the eighteenth century the mask was so popular as a Carnival costume that the appearance of multiple Pulcinella figures in the same place caused no comment or confusion. In *Pulcinella and the Acrobats,* a crowd stands within the stalls of a theater and looks on as two men perform handstands. *Pulcinella in Love* shows a Bacchic snake dance led by a masked woman in white, whom Pulcinella presses from behind as he reaches around to cup her breast. Two more Pulcinellas follow with beakers of wine and a tambourine.

The *Departure of Pulcinella* is more complex. In a colorless dawn, a gray-clothed Pulcinella takes his leave, as one of a group of companions clustered together at the top of a hill points the way. Another Pulcinella sleeps on the ground with a wine jug beside him. A racquet and shuttlecock lie at his feet. This is not the triumphant dismissal of a despised symbol of vice but the exile of a seasonal mood of lighthearted playfulness. The same playful spirit is represented in the oval ceiling fresco called *The Swing*. The swing is a bare rope loosely hung between two trees on a pinnacle of rock. A youthful Pulcinella kicks his legs as a companion swings the rope; two others sit below in conversation. The end of a ladder used to tie up the rope and two curious urns sit beside them. With rare exceptions a ceiling fresco opens a window on some superterrestrial realm. God, the Virgin Mary, the Risen Christ, or less exalted angels and allegories hover there in midspace, free of the ties of earthly gravity. Pulcinella's transcendence requires some obvious technological aids like the ladder and the rope, but with their help he kicks up his heels and dances in the sky above the earthbound viewer.

The French army that occupied Venice on May 12, 1797—the first enemy army ever to enter the city—was fired by revolutionary zeal. The Soviet Army that overwhelmed Hungary in 1956 may have been moved by similar ideals, but both the French and the Soviets were as eager to protect their borders from potential invaders as they were to spread their revolutionary ideologies. The French had no fear of a still-disunited Italy; they invaded the peninsula in order to push back the Austrians. Like Russia and England, autocratic Austria opposed the Revolution. Driving the Austrians from their Italian strongholds in Lombardy served the cause of French national security, but the campaign was framed as a liberation movement, an expansion of the ideals of the Revolution beyond the confines of France.

The French army was led by Napoleon Bonaparte, at age twenty-eight already a general and commander of some fifty thousand troops. His army entered Italy in the east and swept through the Kingdom of Savoy and the duchies of Milan and Mantua, driving the Austrians ahead of it. Austrian leadership was timid, and the campaigns speedy. Behind them, Napoleon's army left puppet republicans who proclaimed liberté, egalité, and fraternité for Italians while they prepared to join the French sphere of influence as a Cisalpine Republic. Beyond the limits of Lombardy, the French chased the Austrians into the mainland territories Venice had controlled since the fifteenth century.

Despite an official policy of armed neutrality, the Venetians made no effort to defend their client cities; still, Napoleon began to characterize Venice as a threat. Unless he neutralized the Republic before swinging northeast toward Vienna, Napoleon would leave an unconquered power on his right flank. During a lull in the fighting, while he was feeling out the Austrians, Napoleon wrote to the Directorate governing France, "If hostilities resume, it will be necessary above all to take measures against the Venetians, otherwise it will require an army to contain them. I know that the only course of action one can take is to destroy their atrocious and blood-thirsty government. In this way we will deprive of all security a place which, in the absence of such action we would have to guard more closely than the enemy himself" (*Correspondence* 3.11).

Bonaparte overrated Venetian power and resolve, either because he was taken in by the city's centuries-old reputation for political astuteness or because he needed to justify his own plans. He had already negotiated an armistice with the Austrians that would in effect trade the Benelux countries (then known as the Austrian Netherlands) for Venice and her territories. Handing over Venice to the Austrians, however, required him to occupy the city, which he quickly set about doing. On May 8 he reported to the Directorate from Mestre, "I am at the moment located only a short distance from Venice and I am making preparations to enter it by force if necessary. I have chased all the Venetians from the mainland, and we are at this time the sole masters of the region. The people manifest great joy at their deliverance from the Venetian aristocracy. The Lion of St. Mark exists no longer. Soon after my arrival here, three envoys from the Grand Council arrived with full power to negotiate an end to our differences . . . I have just received a second deputation which informs me that . . . the entire government has been dissolved by the Grand Council and that body has declared that it will abdicate its sovereignty and establish whatever form of government seems most appropriate to me. I plan, after their abdication, to establish a democracy and to send three or four thousand troops into the city" (3.31).

Bonaparte continued to present himself as the liberator driven to democratize Venice and free her citizens from their millennial oppression by the nobility. But what he actually did was send in five thousand French troops—necessary, Napoleon wrote a few days later, to protect property in the face of the liberated people's "exuberance." The property most in need of protection, from the French point of view, was the enormous booty extorted from the Venetians as the price of occupation. Five secret articles that were added to the treaty of peace signed on May 16, 1797, spelled out these supplemental costs: payment over three months of three million French pounds to Napoleon's Army of Italy; three million pounds' worth of materials from the Arsenal; three ships of the line and two frigates fully armed and equipped. The final article is the most shocking: "The Republic of Venice will turn over to the commissioners responsible for these matters twenty paintings and five hundred manuscripts to be chosen by the commander-in-chief" (3.51).

While pillage was the traditional privilege of invading armies, Napoleon rationalized the process through careful note-taking and an obsessive legalism. His was the first army to be served by art experts whose job was the identification and collection of suitable works to be sent back to France, where they soon formed the core collection of the Louvre. The number of objects he required from the Venetians was relatively modest compared with his demands in Rome. From the papal collections he obtained six colossal statues, several hundred individual sculptures and sculptural groups, as well as bas-reliefs, mosaics, medals, manuscripts, paintings, miscellaneous small objects, and large marble columns. He wrote to the Directorate two days after the fall of Venice to inform them that "the objects from Rome will soon be arriving in Livorno. It is urgent that the naval minister send three or four frigates to collect them in order that they be protected against all dangers" (3.46). Since they had already fallen into the hands of the French, it is unclear what further dangers they faced.

If the Venetians expected value for their money, they were sadly disappointed. Their government was dissolved and their empire dismembered.

Rents and profits from landholdings on the mainland, which had sustained the roughly twenty percent of the nobility who were not already impoverished, dried up. The Mint and the Bank were drained, and their depositors made suddenly destitute. The Arsenal was stripped of everything the French could use on their own ships; and anything the Venetians might conceivably use against them, including historic Renaissance cannon, was carried off. What the French could not use, like ship models or the Bucintoro, they smashed. The thousands of arsenalotti were suddenly unemployed and quickly became destitute. As for art, Venice lost far more than the twenty pictures Bonaparte originally demanded. St. Theodore was removed from his column and sent to France; the four bronze horses looted from Byzantium in 1204 were packed up and sent to the Louvre. But there was more to come.

The treaty of Campo Formio formalized the exchange of territories that had driven Napoleon to occupy Venice in the first place. By the terms of this cynical pact between a self-styled liberator and his autocratic enemies, control of Venice passed to the Hapsburg Empire of Austria. Destructive as it was of Venetian autonomy, the treaty was a rare bargain for the signatories. Deprived of Milan and Mantua, Austria was amply compensated by the Venetian territories in northeast Italy plus those in Dalmatia. Having been almost entirely land-locked—only the city of Trieste offered access to the Adriatic—the Austrians suddenly had a highway to the sea. Venice promised Austria a navy—a tool that would become increasingly important in the global politics of the Napoleonic era and beyond—and a territorial integrity that the scattered Hapsburg holdings had clearly lacked. The French Revolution and the Napoleonic wars had the general effect of consolidating territories around national and ethnic themes.

France made out just as well. It turned over the continental territories of the Venetians' sea empire to the Austrians but kept the colonies in Greece for itself. Most important, the hated Austrians were pushed well away from the French border. Through the creation of a client state, the Cisalpine Republic, France established a buffer between its enemies and itself, much as the Soviets would do in the aftermath of World War II.

The Austrians had hardly settled in to the job of governing a much-reduced and much-saddened Venice before Napoleon began once again to redesign Europe. In 1799 he invaded Italy a second time. He incorporated the Cisalpine Republic into a larger Italian Republic with himself as president. This dignity seemed insufficient after he proclaimed himself emperor of the French in 1804, and so he renamed himself king of Italy. After defeating the Austrians at Austerlitz, Napoleon imposed conditions on the defeated Hapsburgs that cancelled their 1797 agreement. Austria lost all her territories in Italy, and the French returned with renewed energy to the task of looting Venice.

French troops entered the city for a second time in January 1806. On this occasion they planned to stay, and to make lasting changes in government and social institutions. The most powerful tool in their carpetbag was a newly instituted code of laws imported wholesale from France. Within a few months of his arrival, the French viceroy announced that all monasteries in the Lagoon would be consolidated to reduce duplication. All the Benedictines, for example, were to be grouped in one foundation, and those abbeys emptied of monks would become state property. When

this proved impractical, in 1810 the monasteries were suppressed out-
right, their goods confiscated and their members dispersed. The only
exception was made for houses that served such social purposes as caring for the sick or teaching. More than seventy foundations were closed;
more than two thousand monks and nuns were secularized and at the
same time deprived of the means to live. The monastic churches that
were closed included some of the most important monuments in the city:
the Frari, San Zanzipolo, San Francesco della Vigne, San Zaccaria, the
Scalzi, Il Redentore, San Giorgio Maggiore.

On St. Mark's Day in 1806 the French viceroy delivered an even more
vicious and debilitating blow to Venetian tradition and welfare. He
ordered the closing of the vast majority of the scuole, confraternities, and
parish lay associations and the confiscation of their patrimonies. Five of
the six scuole grandi were closed—San Rocco was the only exception—
along with more than three hundred other lay organizations. As much as
five million ducats in assets passed through the city treasury on their way
to France. The many impoverished or invalid Venetians who depended on
the charity of the scuole were suddenly deprived of their sole means of
support. The French must have anticipated this result, but their greed
and the fear that lay organizations might become centers of resistance
overcame their humanitarian misgivings.

The third step in Napoleon's project to rationalize religion in Venice
was a reduction in the number of parishes and a consolidation of parish
churches wherever possible. The plan was to reduce the historic seventy
parishes by nearly half. This reorganization became more complicated
and more impractical when suppressed monastic churches were

included. Churches on the scale of the Frari and San Zaccaria were saved from demolition by their conversion to parish churches, but they became white elephants to the neighborhoods they served. The tiny congregations that cluster in the sacristies of Venice's monumental churches today are continual testimony to the Hobson's choice that Napoleon's policies imposed. The final blow to the artistic patrimony housed in the suppressed convents and churches came with state-sponsored auctions of their treasures. No one knows how much art left Venice during the French occupation.

While Napoleon's reforms played hell with the churches, the emperor revamped religious instruction. In the new catechism introduced throughout Italy by decree on March 14, 1807, Napoleon was described as "the anointed of the Lord, minister of His power and His image on earth whom He has guided through difficult circumstances so that he might establish public worship of the true religion and serve as its protector." Even death could not put Venetians beyond the emperor's reach. In 1807, in a reform measure that was repeated throughout the occupied territories in Italy, the French, for reasons of sanitation, closed all the cemeteries in the city. From that date, the dead were to be buried in the newly created cemetery on the island of San Cristoforo della Pace, halfway between Venice and Murano. The policy would continue even after the unification of Italy.

In 1837 the cemetery expanded onto the nearby island of San Michele. Not only were all future burials to take place on this remote spot, but those Venetians buried throughout the city would be disinterred and removed to the same site. Like other traditional Christians in premodern Europe, Venetians had buried their dead either within churches or in graveyards next to them. This practice created strong ties between the communities of the living and the dead, who in effect shared a common space in the center of communal worship. Napoleon's reforms disrupted this practice. By the removal of the graveyards from the areas of the churches, the French also restructured many of the city's open spaces. The typical Venetian campo, which today may spread along the side and around the back of a church, was historically divided into a public area and an enclosed campo santo, a holy ground devoted to the dead.

Having impoverished the nobility, the clergy, the citizen employees of the government, the arsenalotti, and the indigent in the care of the scuole, Napoleon then threatened to destroy the last vestiges of Venetian economic life. Unable to invade England, he tried to ruin her commerce through a continental ban on English goods. In response, England blockaded French ports, including Venice, crippling one of the last viable commercial activities in the city and adding the merchant class to the growing list of impecunious and increasingly desperate Venetians.

Napoleon's influence in Italy came to a sudden end in 1814, when he was forced to abdicate as emperor and king. After his final defeat at Waterloo, the Congress of Vienna redistributed his conquests. The former Venetian empire, combined with the province of Lombardy, passed into the hands of the Austrian crown.

Anti-republicanism and assertive orthodoxy prompted the Austrians to undo the Napoleonic reforms, but it was too late. Under Austrian rule, the parishes were again reorganized, but few significant changes were made. The monastic clergy were free to return, though most were unable to do so. The suppressed scuole were allowed to reopen, and some of them did, but the majority, stripped of their endowments, their precious relics, and their art, could not reorganize. Those that did come back to life took on entirely new forms. These once semi-official arms of the state, which distributed private charity under public supervision, became simple religious confraternities under the supervision of the patriarch. With their wealth already dispersed, they were in no position to serve the needs of the sick and poor. The crowded calendar of public ceremonies, in which the scuole were prominent participants, had vanished with the Doge.

Fortunately, in one area where the Austrians might have been able to turn back the clock and erase the Napoleonic reforms they did not do so. Napoleon's forced democratization of Venice had erased a millennium of social disadvantages, and these were not reinstated. This was especially important for the Jews. They were now citizens entitled to vote and serve in public office. They were no longer required to wear identifying marks, and the Ghetto in Cannaregio, where the majority continued to live, became a Venetian neighborhood like any other. Throughout the nineteenth century, Jewish families achieved a prominence in Venice that finally corresponded with their wealth and international influence.

The ecclesiastical property that had been auctioned off could not be recovered, though the most notorious expropriations of the French, like the horses of San Marco, were returned. The Austrians were more circumspect than the French, but they too expropriated works of art and sent them out of the country. The great altarpiece of the Frari, Titian's

Assumption of the Virgin, found its way to Vienna, not to be returned to the city until 1876. The palazzi of impoverished families began to crumble. Many were still inhabited by ruined counts and countesses, while others were rented to foreigners or transformed into hotels. The city, which at the height of its powers had awed visitors with its majestic buildings and archaic ceremony, now charmed a new sensibility with its romantic decay. Nature, beloved by the Romantics, was credited with the transformation, but neglect, poverty, and political emasculation were the forces behind the city's sudden and precipitous decline. (127)

> Her palaces are crumbling to the shore,
> And music meets not always now the ear:
> Those days are gone—but Beauty still is here.
> States fall, arts fade—but Nature doth not die,
> Nor yet forget how Venice once was dear
> The pleasant place of all festivity,
> The revel of the earth, the masque of Italy.
> But unto us she hath a spell beyond
> Her name in story, and her long array
> Of mighty shadows, whose dim forms
>   despond
> Above the dogeless city's vanish'd sway.
>
> (Byron, *Childe Harold's Pilgrimage,* Canto Four, I–4)

The Austrians did not possess their Italian empire in tranquility. In the 1840s Italy, like many other European nations, was the scene of uprisings led by revolutionary nationalists. For a brief period the Austrian army was forced to withdraw from its colonies and retreat to defensive posi-

tions along the line of the Alps. By 1849 the
Italian revolutions had all been suppressed.
The Austrians reoccupied Venice and held it
for another seventeen years, until Italian
armies led by Giuseppe Garibaldi drove them
out. In the interval, the Austrians governed
with a heavier hand than before, and they
worked more diligently to transform Venice
into an imitation, however imperfect, of a
land-based European city.

127

Their most enduring project was the construction, begun in 1841, of
the railroad viaduct linking Venice with the mainland, the first link in a
projected Venice-to-Milan railway. Their most visible monuments are two
bridges spanning the Grand Canal near its inland and seaward ends. The
Ponte del Accademia was a single-span steeply arched iron bridge
erected in 1854. In 1934 a wooden bridge, intended to be temporary,
was put in its place while a suitable structure was being designed. That
wooden bridge, heavily reinforced with steel, still stands. At the far end
of the Grand Canal, the Austrians built another iron bridge in 1858 that
was also replaced in 1934. The modern Scalzi Bridge, designed in evident imitation of Da Ponte's span at the Rialto, links the train station in
Cannaregio with the sestieri on the opposite side of the canal.

The Italian liberators of Venice, while certainly more welcome than
the French or the Austrians, were just as uneasy about the city's water-
based way of life. They continued building streets in Venice both to simplify movement within the city and to capitalize on the direct link the

Austrians had created with the mainland. That link allowed Italian planners to imagine Venice once again as a seaport, and they set about constructing an entirely new deep-water commercial port at the northeast end of the city. Oceangoing vessels began to enter the Lagoon through the Lido gateway and sail up the Giudecca Canal to the U-shaped port, where goods could be transferred to trains. In the area surrounding this new port, the government encouraged the creation of an industrial zone. A tobacco-processing plant built in the last years of the Republic had already opened the area to industrialization. In the last third of the nineteenth century, a privately owned consortium opened a cotton mill nearby. State warehouses were built near the turn of the nineteenth century. Across the Giudecca Canal, an enormous flour mill called the Mulino Stucky and a nearby brewery were also served by ships bringing wheat from abroad.

State policy and the whims of commercial development are volatile, however, and the industrial zone created in the aftermath of Italian unification endured for what in the Venetian scale of history was a very short productive life. After World War I, the Italian government sponsored an extension of the commercial port and the industrial zone onto the mainland near Mestre. With room to expand and with greater access both by train and truck, the mainland factories of Marghera quickly outpaced and soon supplanted those in Venice. The displacement of factories spurred workers to relocate. Since the mid-1930s, Mestre has continually grown, while the population of Venice has been simultaneously shrinking and aging. This trend led the Italian government to incorporate Venice and Mestre into a single administrative unit.

By the early 1950s most of the buildings that had housed the Venetian industrial revolution joined the functionless Arsenal at the other end
of the city as structures without purpose. Even though it was a very brief
episode in Venetian history, the Industrial Age transformed an entire
urban precinct and then, just as suddenly, left it an empty shell. Recovery, which still continues, has been very slow, and the old industrial zone
in Santa Croce and the Giudecca is, today, a hodgepodge of public housing, government ministries, prisons, and parking structures. The cotton
plant was scavenged for classroom space; it now houses the very influential architecture school of the University IUAV of Venice. A large free-
standing flat-winged V visible from the ferry marks its entrance. The
Mulino Stucky, which suffered extensive fire damage in 2003, is slated
to become a luxury hotel.

The legacy of Marghera is measured not only in dislocation and abandoned structures in Venice but in the deep and enduring damage that
industrialization has caused to the Lagoon. Pesticides, PCB, dioxin, and
a host of less virulent chemicals have transformed this estuary into one
of the most severely polluted bodies of water in Europe. This heavy dose
of poison has reduced a diverse and complex ecosystem into a habitat
that sustains only the most resistant species, and has turned Venice into
something of a desert city. Added to this natural tragedy is the human
cost, measured in the loss of the millennial interdependency between the
city and the fish and fowl of the Lagoon.

What remains of industrial Venice is monumentalized in its triumphal
ontryway, the Piazzale Roma. Designed as the terminus of the new motorway that in 1930 joined Venice to Mestre, Piazzale Roma shares the fate

of many piazzas in its namesake city to the south. Rimmed with neither shops nor apartments, the sterile piazza is hedged in by travel agencies and multistory garages. The area is like the car and bus lots outside a theme park or sports arena—not a place in itself, hardly worth a glance as the traveler hurries somewhere else. For all Venice's other troubles, its bicephalic link with Mestre has had the most serious and tumultuous consequences for the city. San Marco and its carefully crafted extensions, like Palladio's San Giorgio Maggiore, the Dogana da Mar, and the Salute, were the Republic's continually evolving grand gateway. After the creation of the train station and Piazzale Roma on the land side of the city, everyone now enters Venice through the back door, and Piazza San Marco is marooned at the end of a cul-de-sac on a round-trip that begins and ends on the wrong side of the island.

The first railway station—opened in 1860 in an area cleared by the demolition of two religious foundations—was replaced by the present train station in 1954. The anonymous design of this building, a spin-off of the international Modernist movement, is much more insensitive to the history of Venice than even the high classicism of Sansovino. The façade occupies several hundred feet of the most prestigious, the most historical, and the most finely crafted landscape in Venice. Yet in a city where buildings tend to be tall and narrow, it is low and wide. Where buildings typically crowd the waterway, it steps back; where buildings merge with their neighbors, it stands aloof. In one of the richest architectural environments to be found anywhere in the world, it spurns context.

Near the palazzo of the railroad administration, the Spanish architect and engineer Santiago Calatrava will build a fourth bridge over the Grand

Canal linking Piazzale Roma with the train station and obviating the one-
stop vaporetto trip that is now the most direct connection between them.
Calatrava's bridge, constructed of steel, glass, and Istrian stone, will
forge the final link in a series of wide pedestrian throughways that have,
over the last century and a half, been carved out of the dark warren of
Venetian streets.

Historical Venice was full of tiny streets that led everywhere within an
islanded neighborhood but nowhere beyond it. The names of the streets,
which have been carefully preserved in modern Venice, make this wonderfully clear. Atlanta is notorious for its fourteen Peachtree streets. In
Venice, fifteen streets are named Boatyard and as many are called School
Street. There are ten different Church Streets in four different parts of
town. Ten streets bear the name of Christ; eight are called Street of the
Priests. It is common for the streets surrounding a building—a warehouse, for example—to include one street called Calle del Magazen and
another called Calle drio el Magazen, that is, Warehouse Street and
Behind-the-Warehouse Street. These names never include particulars;
they never specify which warehouse, church, boatyard, or priests they
might be referring to.

Long before the pedestrianization of Venice, these names posed no
problem. Obviously, Street of the Priests meant street of *our* priests,
Boatyard Street referred to *our* boatyard; there is only one neighborhood
warehouse, one parish church. But street names like this are of limited
value to the outsider; even the Post Office finds them useless. Though
the street names are carefully painted on uniform white blocks at nearly
every corner, Venetian postal addresses make no mention of them. Today,

every structure in every sestiere of the city is numbered consecutively.

A city so rigorously insular must have seemed nightmarish to those who thought of canals as barriers between land masses. After the opening of the train station, the Austrians first and then the Italians set about creating a system of throughways that would make it possible to walk from one end of the city to the other. In many cases, access was opened by creating a bridge to link the inner roads of one island to those of the next. Where bridges were insufficient, canals could be narrowed to create walkways alongside, which imitated the wide fondamenta on the city's northern and southern edges. (128) Wider and generally longer passages could be created by simply filling in canals. Calle is the traditional Vene-

tian word for street; a name that begins with Rio Terrà usually means that the street was once a minor canal or rio. In many cases the creation of pedestrian links required ingenuity and the imaginative use of once-private property. The sotto-portego is a sometimes spooky Venetian feature that allows streets to pass under buildings. In some cases the public sottoportego follows the façade of a palazzo and flanks a canal. In others it allows the street to access what was once the ground-floor entry to a building, pass through its inner courtyard, and out the back way.

128

The Baroque church of Santa Maria di Nazareth, commonly called the Scalzi, is the immediate neighbor of the train station. Before the enlargement of the railyards in the 1860s, locomotives and passenger cars were parked directly behind it. Designed by Longhena in the mid-seventeenth century, the church served the Discalced—literally, shoeless—Carmelites, an offshoot of the thirteenth-century order who followed the austere example and mystical teachings of St. John of the Cross.

129

Longhena's façade on the Grand Canal is divided into two stories. (129) Pedestals raised on a high platform support six pairs of columns that frame an arched central door and four subordinate niches with statues. A heavy inflected entablature is surmounted by a second tier of linked pedestals supporting four pairs of columns with statues in niches between them and a pediment at their top. The central bay of the top story is wider, and a curved lintel breaks through the upper entablature, giving the center of the building the prominence characteristic of Roman Baroque buildings. The sculptures along the roofline and at the sides of the upper story, along with the rich decoration, make the façade more sumptuous than its Roman counterparts.

The interior, which is simple in plan, is also richly decorated with polychrome marble. A nave, flanked by shallow chapels with vaulted roofs, looks toward a presbytery where the main altar is embellished by a massive baldacchino raised on serpentine columns that imitates Bernini's high altar in St. Peter's. Stretching out behind it, a deep choir like the one in San Giorgio Maggiore is reserved for members of the order. Giambattista Tiepolo painted the nave ceiling in the early eighteenth century. His fresco, which depicted the miraculous transport of the Virgin's house from Nazareth to Loreto, was destroyed during the Austrian bombardment of the northern edge of the city in 1915. The Carmelites were expelled by the French in 1810, but they returned during the Austrian occupation and resumed responsibility for the church.

The Rio Terrà Lista di Spagna begins just beyond the Scalzi. The wide thoroughfare was created in 1844 when the Rio dei Sabbioni was filled in, and it was intended to be an upscale commercial street. Today it holds a typical Venetian mix of stores and restaurants, plus the inevitable mask and T-shirt shops and Internet boutiques. The Lista di Spagna ends at the Campo San Geremia, a broad open area that has changed little in size and makeup since the sixteenth century. Despite its size, however, like most Venetian campi it stands behind buildings with major façades on the water. Indeed, the prominence of the waterfront here is impossible to overestimate. This is the junction of the Cannaregio and Grand canals, as important and historic an intersection as any to be found in Venice. (130)

Two structures dominate the campo: the Palazzo Labia, remodeled and enlarged in the eighteenth century and now the Venetian headquarters of the state television network RAI, and the church of San Geremia. The palazzo, decorated with frescoes by Tiepolo, has an asymmetrical façade on the campo with a rusticated ground story, two ceremonial floors with arched windows, and small balconies. Its façade on the Cannaregio Canal and the smaller one visible from the Grand Canal are considerably richer, to match their prominence and the importance of these arteries. Built entirely of Istrian stone, these façades begin with a

rusticated lower story topped
by two more strongly unified
main floors. The first piano
nobile has a continual balcony in front of recessed
arched windows. The second
floor balconies are broken.
Strutting eagles stand

130

between lozenge-shaped mezzanine windows; sculpted brackets support
the cornice. Masks project from the archivolt of each window.

The original church on this prominent site was dedicated in the
eleventh century to the prophet Jeremiah. Like the nearby church of Job
or the more distant one dedicated to Moses, this dedication reflects the
prominence of these Old Testament figures in the Greek rite. The building
was extensively remodeled in the thirteenth century, then completely
demolished in the eighteenth. Construction began in mid-century and
continued even after the fall of the Republic. Corbellini, an architect
from Milan, understood that the Grand Canal, the Cannaregio Canal, and
the campo each required a majestic façade. He created a centrally
planned building with a monumental presence on three of its four radiating arms and a soaring dome which collects and centers the building's
dispersed masses. The huge structure with its many prospects success-
fully dominates its site.

The soaring interior is equally impressive, but like so many large
Venetian churches, it has an air of disorder and abandonment. The continued viability of the church depends less on its neighborhood than on

the reputation of its most significant relic. When the train station was enlarged in 1860, the church of Santa Lucia was demolished to make space. By the twelfth century, the relics of the Sicilian saint had been transferred to Constantinople. They were removed by Enrico Dandolo during the thirteenth-century sack and brought to Venice. They were first placed in the Benedictine monastery at San Giorgio Maggiore and then brought to the refurbished church of Santa Lucia later in the century. They remained there until 1860, when they were relocated to the church of San Geremia. A modern inscription on the Grand Canal façade of the church records their presence.

The Ponte delle Guglie, marked by its characteristic obelisks, once required a second bridge across the Rio San Leonardo to complete its work of linking the areas of Cannaregio. That bridge also served as a surveillance point and a choke on traffic between terra firma and the Grand Canal. The Rio San Leonardo recalls the name of a nearby church built in the eleventh century, rebuilt in the fourteenth, and suppressed in 1805. It has never been resanctified. The buried canal that took its name forged the next link in the passage from the train station to the heart of the city. In a reconceived pedestrian Venice, this newly created roadway erased one of the boundaries of the Ghetto Vecchio and increased the physical integration of the old Jewish quarters into the nineteenth-century city. While Rio Terrà San Leonardo has its share of tourist businesses, the wide and pleasant street is also home to the kinds of stores that neighborhoods depend on and is the scene of a daily market.

At Campo dell'Anconetta, the flow of traffic bears right, crosses a bridge, and emerges into a second buried canal, the Maddalena. This waterway took its name from a church built in the thirteenth century and dedicated to St. Mary Magdalene. This structure was demolished in 1760, and the present building in the Neoclassical style was erected in its place. The architect of the Maddalena, Tommaso Temanza, was a historian and critic of the arts, and his study of classical models is evident in this building. The main body of the church is a cylindrical drum dissected into two unequal upper and lower zones by a cornice and into bays by shallow pilasters. A shallow dome and lantern complete the structure. Its main entrance, where pairs of half columns support a pediment and attic, is a variation in the Palladian manner on the porch of the Pantheon. An eye within a linked triangle and square and the inscription "Wisdom has built a house for herself" stands over the door. The inner face of the cylindrical nave is divided into bays by pairs of antefixed columns. This space, a simplified version of the Pantheon interior, also recalls the Salute. A raised presbytery is set in an oval-shaped extension of the building—again recalling the plan of the Salute—at the end opposite the main entry. A secondary entrance faces the canal at its side.

The broad Strada Nuova formed the last and the most disruptive link in the chain of pedestrian throughways that led from the train station to the church of Santi Apostoli. The walkway, some ten meters wide, was created in the immediate aftermath of the incorporation of the city into the Italian Republic. Its official names honoring Victor Emmanuel II and the twenty-eighth of April commemorate this event, but the walkway is never called anything but "the new road." Crowded with pedestrians at all hours, the street blends tourist shops with neighborhood resources, including a supermarket and low-end department store. The street was cut into the neighborhood very much against the grain of its historical structure. Parallel to the Grand Canal, it flows along the back walls of the great palazzi overlooking that waterway in an area where earlier streets had moved away from the waterway toward the center of Cannaregio. Its inland wall was created by demolishing blocks of houses.

The linked streets that culminate in the Strada Nuova lead pedestrians to the church of the Holy Apostles, one of the oldest buildings in Venice. A parish as early as the tenth century, the church was already in need of remodeling in the eleventh century. It was enlarged in the thirteenth century and reconstructed in the form of a three-aisled basilica. The interior was transformed at the end of the sixteenth century by a radical rebuilding that in effect pushed the nave columns toward the sides of the building to create a unified interior space. The campanile and the Corner Chapel, with its arched extension and tall dome built in the early sixteenth century, dominate the Campo Santi Apostoli. (131)

This once out-of-the-way spot was transformed by its many linked walkways into a major pedestrian hub. Streets that begin at the apse end of the campo lead past San Canciano and Santa Maria dei Miracoli to the

131

Municipal Hospital at Santi Giovanni e Paolo. Another sequence of roadways across the Rialto Bridge leads through San Polo and Santa Croce to join the pathways from the Piazzale Roma. From the bridge near the Corner Chapel, yet another pathway

leads past Palazzo Falier into the Salizada di San Giovanni Crisostomo and from there, in a few hundred
yards, to Campo San Bartolomeo near the Rialto
Bridge. Venice's oldest landway, the interlaced traces
of the Merceria, lead from Campo San Bartolomeo
toward Piazza San Marco.

Pedestrians who persevere in their strolling beyond
San Marco gradually leave the zone of intense tourism
and pass into the backstreets of Castello. Near the
Arsenal, the crowd thins dramatically and its composition suddenly shifts from a few Venetians suspended
in a wash of outsiders to a smaller volume with a heavy concentration of

132

natives. (132)

Past the Rio dell'Arsenale, the Via Garibaldi cuts inland from the
Bacino toward the Lagoon and the northern rim of the city. Though still a
pedestrian passage, this grand avenue is long and straight, like a canal in
Cannaregio. In this new quarter of the city, developed in the nineteenth
century, a continental and entirely non-Venetian sense of space and scale
commands. A few hundred yards from its beginning, the roadway opens
on the right to a park. With the exception of the much-degraded Pap-
padopoli Gardens near Piazzale Roma, central Venice has no room for
public parks. Just inside the gates, a monument to Garibaldi stands in a
shallow basin. A complacent Venetian lion reclines among mosses peren-
nially moistened by an oozing water source in the city's only public fountain. Where water is so abundant and so material to the city's way of life,
only a foreign sensibility could imagine the need for a fountain. Deeper

in the extensive park are the national pavilions where the exhibitions of the Venice Biennale are held. The park walkways lead back to the fondamenta, which offers the stroller an excellent view of the historical entryway to the city. (133)

For a thousand years Venice flourished yet stayed within the bounds set by its environment. It preserved and sustained its unique culture, and

133

maintained the health and welfare of its citizens, without destroying or even seriously compromising the Lagoon habitat. A brutal invasion in the last decade of the eighteenth century redirected the city's history and came close to ending it altogether. Since then, Venice has struggled to reinvent itself, always under the watchful eye of some dominating outside power.

Historic Venice was amphibious and autonomous. Modern Venice is neither. The Adriatic, which Venice embraced early in its history, has lost all connection with the city. Surges of high water back up each winter from the sea, flooding the lowest-lying parts of the city. (134) In November a meter of water in Piazza San Marco is not unusual. Motorboats are everywhere in Venice, and their powerful wakes—the moto ondoso—which set the ferry landings rocking boisterously and the gondoliers cursing vociferously, are a serious and constant problem. In the right sort of spy or caper movie, Venice becomes the scene of a high-speed motorboat

chase, a refreshing variant on the choreog-
raphy of narrow escapes and multiple car
crashes in more mundane films. But the
water surge from high-powered motor boats
loosens the stones that flank the canals and
invades the foundations of buildings.
Water—once the city's domain, the region
of its frontier and its possibility—is now its
antagonist.

134

Divorced from its element and dependent on outsiders for commercial
and political viability, modern Venice has been transformed into a new
kind of political entity. Declared a World Heritage Site by UNESCO, the
city is increasingly under the surveillance and supervision of national and
international organizations. A host of authorities at every level watch over
it. Civic, provincial, and national laws control development, commerce,
the environment. Surveillance, maintenance, and restoration of the city's
infrastructure and waterways by public and private institutions is thor-
ough and ongoing. Associations of concerned citizens monitor the Lagoon
and the urban fabric. The United Nations maintains an office in the city.
International groups of every stripe, from those concerned with ecology to
those dedicated to the preservation of the city's antiquities, are generous
with their time and money; they are vigilant and active in maintaining
and restoring the city's patrimony. The newest environmental initiative,
backed by the Italian government, calls for a set of movable gates at the
Lido ports to counter the acqua alta.

When the Campanile fell in 1902, the City Council resolved to rebuild it "as it was and where it was." The same promise was made when La Fenice burned in 1996. But "as it was and where it was" cannot serve as the criteria for preservation in substantial areas of Venice. For structures that have lost their purpose, the past offers no useful guideline. The hospices and scuole grandi, the palaces and churches lost their way two centuries ago and have either crafted new identities in the interval or disappeared. No one wants to bring the industrial district of Santa Margherita back to life. The Arsenal has a similar problem. Its vast central area, remarkable buildings, inland channels, and basins require an innovative plan of redevelopment and reuse.

Planners at every level of government will decide what becomes of those urban structures that cannot readily be restored to their original function. Their efforts will be disinterested; they will work on behalf of a city that threatens to become an abstraction or, possibly worse, an attraction. Not Venice for Venetians—of whom there are too few—but Venice for the world. The danger is that the world may not need the same things from the city that its own citizens would require. An idealized, abstracted historical theme park would perhaps suit the world just fine. But this theme park will have no autonomous way of life or unique interdependence with its environment; its historic infrastructure will vanish. These will be sacrificed—have already been sacrificed, for the most part. Only the built fabric of Venice will persist, and in that fabric the memory of the city's vitality, energy, and beauty will survive like an insect in amber. Since the French occupation, the idea of Venice has strayed very far from its origins in the mixed salt and fresh water of the Lagoon. Like a fish sprouting legs, the Republic has slithered from the waters and mutated into a land-based creature of uncertain species.

Modern city planners have not been successful at grasping the city's
historical aquatic character. For contemporary planners, Venice is a paradise not because it is built on the waters but because it is a city without
cars. That does not mean that modern planners see it as a city of boats;
rather, they see it as a pedestrian city, just as the occupying powers
before them did. In the modern planners' view, the vaporetti—which were
originally French-built steamboats, introduced in 1882 and replaced in
the mid-twentieth century by diesel-powered motorboats—are the city's
quirky mass transit system; it happens to be aquatic, but it could just as
well be a monorail or tramline. The intricate system of inland waterways
that traditionally served every structure in the city is treated as alleyways
for work boats and water taxis. Only the occasional pleasure boat or
tourist-filled gondola making its way around tight corners, under low
bridges, and along silent fondamenta defies, however briefly and ineffec-
tually, the systematic degradation of these waterways.

Venice is covered with active work sites, many of which bear the
insignia of Insula, the private-public consortium that sees to the rehabilitation of structures and, perhaps more importantly, looks out for the welfare of canals. Damming and draining waterways in sections, workers
clean silt and garbage from the canal floor and repair and repoint the
stone linings of their fondamenta. (135) But there are also eternal projects, work zones without workers that persist for decades, producing
nothing but shoals of neighborhood trash. The church of San Lorenzo is
the most notorious; the Scuola Grande della Misericordia is nearly as bad.

The resources of the city are strained to the limit at the height of the
tourist season. Trash clean-up lasts all through the day, only to start up
again at the next sunrise. But if the infrastructure that supports mass

135

incursions of strangers to the city has disfigured Venice, these visitors have some right to intrude, having been in the nineteenth century the city's rescuer and remaining today its primary economic resource. Without the swell of tourism, Venice—devastated by the French two centuries ago—might very well have vanished. The buildings along the Grand Canal that survived that cataclysm did so in large part because they were readily convertible to hotels and vacation rentals. Non-Venetians have a stake in the city: they continue to work to secure its welfare, look after its monuments, and preserve its history and heritage.

Though modern planners tried to remake Venice in the image of a terrestrial town, there is no terrestrial town quite like it. The vaporetto is more exciting and its route more beautiful than that of any city bus or monorail in the world. The competition for the front or back seats is intense. The crowd milling in the midsection of the boat, refusing to budge to let off passengers or allow new ones on, is obstreperous but civil. There is no shouting or cursing and very little shoving. A general holiday sense is palpable, even early in the morning, when the boat is nearly empty and the few souls aboard are all Venetians.

No one swims in the canals as they did before the war, but on any decent Sunday the smaller waterways are apt to see a crew of amateur rowers—both men and women—standing at their oars and pushing their craft along at a steady clip. A single boatman, standing at the stern like a gondolier, a mast and sail carefully stowed beneath the seats, does his best to keep up. The industrious rower powers his boat out into the Lagoon with his sweep, not his auxiliary motor, then sets sail. (136) When the herring are running in the Bacino, middle-aged men spaced twenty feet apart line the seawall and cast their baits into the water. Zigzag lines of nets, visible from buses on the causeway or from the air just after takeoff, still snake across the polluted Lagoon. Since it is officially off-limits to commercial fishing, what these fishermen capture and where the catch ends up remains a mystery.

There is a paradoxical Italian expression that bears repeating. Fully aware of the disaster that always threatens, people observe with more than a shrug, "Sempre crolla ma non cade"—it's always collapsing but it never falls down. As much as one realizes intellectually that Venice is increasingly overburdened with tourists and undermined by surg-ing water, the slant of the after-noon sun—especially after an overcast November morning—awakens entirely different thoughts of Venice as eternal, Venice as the ethereal Belmont miraculously brought into being

136

over centuries and miraculously preserved today. Without question the city is falling down. Any survey of its campanili will reveal a number of truncated bell towers like the one next to Santa Margherita, or a handful leaning outrageously to left or right, like those at Santo Stefano or San

Giorgio dei Greci. Bell towers do fall, but they do so very rarely, with no regularity or predictability. Meanwhile, the work of shoring them up, of reburying and replacing the pilings on which they rest, of protecting their foundations from erosion continues at a steady pace.

The waters of Venice have been pushed into the background, but they have by no means disappeared. Their presence is in the atmosphere. Across the Bacino, light still strikes the glistening façade of San Giorgio Maggiore and drives the church to rise golden at evening like the moon between the columns of Mark and Theodore. Under those circumstances, no one can be blamed for believing that what merely totters may never fall.

INFORMATION

Each chapter in this book presents a slice of Venetian history focused on a discrete section of the city, as shown in Maps 1 through 8. Buildings, monuments, bridges, campi, and other geographical locations are described in an order that is easy for visitors to follow on the ground. Street markings in Venice are ubiquitous, but they generally point to only the most obvious locations—the train station, the car park at Piazzale Roma, the Rialto Bridge, Piazza San Marco, and the Municipal Hospital at Santi Giovanni e Paolo. Sadly, the bulk of tourist traffic is almost entirely absorbed by this handful of landmarks. Walking beyond the crowded herd paths that connect them requires more care and preparation, but the reward is access to a city of extraordinary beauty and surprising tranquility.

Chapter 1 of *Venice from the Ground Up* describes two magnificent churches on small islands outside the city, one on Torcello in the far northern Lagoon and a nearer one on the island of Murano. Both churches can be reached by ferry on a round-trip that takes up most of a day. For visitors whose time in Venice is limited, little is lost by beginning the itinerary at the church of San Giovanni Decollato (in Venetian dialect, San Zan Degolà) in the sestiere of Santa Croce. The simplest way to reach this church is to take the #1 vaporetto, which travels up and down the Grand Canal, to the San

Marcuola stop. From there a traghetto—a two-man gondola ferry—crosses the canal. The Salizada del Fondaco dei Turchi heads inland, and either of two right turns from it leads to the church. The other two early medieval Venetian churches discussed in this chapter are within easy walking distance of San Zan Degolà.

Chapter 2 describes the Basilica of San Marco and the working out of a distinctly Venetian legend for its patron. San Marco, which is one of the most absorbing buildings in the world, is tremendously crowded both because of the press of visitors and because of the increasing restriction on accessible areas of the church. The basilica is open for Mass and illuminated morning and evening. It is least crowded within the first hour of opening, but the mosaics are best seen when the electric lights are turned on, which generally happens between 11:30 a.m. and 12:30 p.m. The separate tickets required to visit the presbytery and the balconies are well worth the price, primarily because they give access to mosaics and views of the basilica that cannot be seen otherwise. The narthex or porch of the church, which most visitors seem to overlook as they wait in line to enter the main building, has a mosaic program of incomparable charm and richness that is relatively easy to see in the low-roofed structure.

Venetians learned their civics from watching public parades in the Piazza San Marco, but modern visitors get a taste of the history of Venetian institutions, both the democratic and the sinister ones, from touring the Palazzo Ducale, which is described in the first part of Chapter 3. This building too is likely to be mobbed, but its vastness makes the crowd easier to manage. The second half of the chapter describes private palaces of the Venetian nobility, most of them located on the Grand

Canal. The itinerary begins in Campo San Bartolomeo, a short, pleasant trek up the twisting street called the Merceria from Piazza San Marco, or an even shorter walk from the Rialto vaporetto stop. The best general view of the most representative Gothic palaces of Venice is from the open-air front or back seats of the #1 and #82 vaporetti.

Chapter 4 begins with the Franciscan church of Santa Maria Gloriosa dei Frari in the sestiere of San Polo and moves through the churches and religious foundations (scuole) on the Rialto side of the Grand Canal. It includes Tintoretto's overwhelming program of paintings in the Scuola Grande di San Rocco and ends with a set of magnificent fifteenth-century paintings by Carpaccio, Gentile Bellini, Giorgione, and Titian housed in the Accademia Gallery. Chapter 5 continues through the parallel religious institutions on the north side of the city, including the exquisite church of Santa Maria dei Miracoli, before concluding with a consideration of the façade of San Zaccaria near San Marco.

The itinerary for Chapter 6 begins with the Zecca, or Mint, which faces the Basin of San Marco, and looks at a number of buildings around the Piazza, including the Library, Clock Tower, New Prison, Campanile, and Logetta. Across the Basin from the Piazzetta, Palladio's magisterial churches on the islands of San Giorgio and the Giudecca are among the many examples of Venetian High Renaissance architecture covered in the itinerary.

Chapter 7 begins with the tragic origins of the Baroque church of Santa Maria della Salute, across the Grand Canal from Piazza San Marco, and guides visitors to Venice's most famous boatyard in nearby Dorso-duro. After a consideration of sixteenth-century palaces on the lower

Grand Canal, the itinerary explores two Venetian institutional complexes that were significantly redesigned in the Renaissance: the Rialto market and the Ghetto. A vaporetto ride back down the canal and a short walk to the Arsenal—another Renaissance institution—concludes the day's exploration.

The two faces of eighteenth-century Venice are the subjects that open the final chapter. The first is the mythical Venice of the Grand Tour, splendid in art, music, theater, and Carnival, seductive and dangerous at once. This part of the itinerary begins near San Marco in the first Venetian casino and explores the great Venetian opera house La Fenice, along with other theaters and theatrical church façades in the area. The Baroque palace Ca' Rezzonico on the Grand Canal—now the home of a museum devoted to the eighteenth century—displays fine works by Tiepolo, Canaletto, Guardi, and others. The opposite face of Venice is revealed in the cataclysmic aftermath of the French occupation in 1797. In the nineteenth and twentieth centuries, the city turned away from the sea and evolved into an essentially land-based pedestrian city dependent on the mainland for its sustenance. The itinerary for this phase of Venetian history begins near the train station and explores the chain of major pedestrian thoroughfares that lead from this nineteenth-century point of embarkation through the city to the Rialto, then past San Marco and on to Venice's only green space at the eastern end of the city, site of the Biennale di Venezia.

FURTHER READING

Calimani, Riccardo. *The Ghetto of Venice.* Trans. Katherine Silberblatt
 Wolfthal. New York: Evans, 1987.
———— *Venice: Guide to the Synagogues, Museum and Cemetery.* Venice:
 Marsilio, 2001.
Calli, Campielli e Canali: A Guide of Venice and Its Islands. Ed. G. Paolo
 Nadali and Renzo Vianello. Venice: Edizioni Helvetia, 2003.
Churches of Venice: The Museum in the City. Venice: Chorus (Associazione
 Chiese di Venezia) / Marsilio, 2002.
Concina, Ennio. *A History of Venetian Architecture.* Trans. Judith Landry. New
 York: Cambridge University Press, 1998.
Demus, Otto. *The Church of San Marco in Venice: History, Architecture,
 Sculpture.* Washington, DC: Dumbarton Oaks, 1960.
———— *The Mosaics of San Marco in Venice.* 4 vols. Chicago: University of
 Chicago Press, 1984.
Franzoi, Umberto. *The Grand Canal.* New York: Vendome Press, 1994.
Howard, Deborah. *The Architectural History of Venice,* rev. ed. New Haven:
 Yale University Press, 2002.
James, Henry. *Italian Hours.* New York: Ecco Press, 1987.
McGregor, James, H. S. *Rome from the Ground Up.* Cambridge: Harvard
 University Press, 2005.
Muir, Edward. *Civic Ritual in Renaissance Venice.* Princeton: Princeton
 University Press, 1981.

Pullan, Brian. *Rich and Poor in Renaissance Venice: The Social Institutions of a Catholic State, to 1620.* London: Blackwell, l971.

Redford, Bruce. *Venice and the Grand Tour.* New Haven: Yale University Press, 1996.

Ruskin, John. *The Stones of Venice.* Ed. Jan Morris. Boston: Little, Brown, 1981.

Sansovino, Francesco. *Venetia, città nobilissima, et singolare.* Venice, 1663.

Schulz, Juergen. *The New Palaces of Medieval Venice.* University Park: Pennsylvania State University Press, 2004.

ACKNOWLEDGMENTS

I want to thank my wife, Sallie, and our son, Ned, for sharing Venice with me; their company made the fabled city even more wonderful. My son Raphael cheered us on from the sidelines. Sadly, it is too late to thank Robert P. Bergman, director of the Cleveland Museum at the time of his death in 1999. Bob was a dear friend, a wonderful traveling companion, and a champion best man. He loved and understood Byzantine art and was gracious enough to show me San Marco for the first time more than thirty years ago. At Harvard University Press, Lindsay Waters has been the book's advocate; Susan Wallace Boehmer took the manuscript in hand and expertly reshaped and enriched it; Jill Breitbarth created the design; and David Foss coordinated production. I am also grateful to Wendy Strothman and her staff for their help and support.

ILLUSTRATION CREDITS

The Aldine (January 1872): 89; p. 289

Allan Macintyre / Fogg Art Museum, Harvard University Art Museums: 99
(Canaletto, *The Church of the Redentore,* Bequest of Charles A.
Loeser, 1932.325)

Antonio Visentini, *Urbis Venetiarum prospectus celebriores, ex Antonii Canal
tabulis xxxviii* (1742): 61, 105, 106, 107, 108, 130, 131

Bildarchiv Monheim GmbH / Alamy: 49

Cameraphoto Arte, Venice / Art Resource, NY: 19, 37, 57, 62, 65, 68, 82,
122, 126

Clifford Boehmer / Harvard University Press: 2, 3, 4, 5, 6, 7, 8, 9, 10, 11,
12, 13, 14, 15, 16, 17, 18, 20, 21, 22, 23, 24, 26, 27, 28, 29, 30,
31, 32, 33, 38, 40, 42, 43, 44, 45, 46, 47, 48, 50, 52, 53, 55, 59,
60, 66, 67, 69, 70, 71, 72, 73, 74, 77, 78, 79, 80, 83, 85, 86, 90,
96, 97, 100, 101, 102, 104, 110, 111, 112, 114, 115, 116, 117,
118, 119, 124, 128, 129, 132, 133, 134; pp. iii, 1, 335

Dionisio Moretti, *Il Canale Grande e La Piazza San Marco* (1831), 84, 87

Erich Lessing / Art Resource, NY: 35, 63, 95, 125

Gallerie dell'Accademia, 91

Houghton Library, Harvard College Library, Department of Printing and
Graphic Arts: Typ 725.41.559 PF (Michele Marieschi,
Magnificentiores selectioresque urbis Venetiarum prospectus . . .
[Venice, 1741]), 51 ("Templum et plate F. F. Ord. . . . "), 56 ("Aedis

Divi Rocchi facies rudis adhuc ex cocto latere . . . "), 76 ("Templum

cum Platea Sanctae Mariae Formosae . . . "), 120 ("Magni

Armamentarii Veneziarum portae duae . . . "); Typ 725.63.260 PF

(Canaletto, *Prospectuum aedium, viarumque insigniorum urbis vene-*

tiarum nautico certamine, ac nundinis adiectis . . ., Giovanni Battista

Brustolon, engraver [Venice, 1763]), 113 ("Prospectus plateae et

ecclesiae Sancti Jacobi . . . ")

Il gran teatro di Venezia (1720): 34, 39

Isabelle Lewis: Maps 1, 2, 3, 4, 5, 6, 7, 8

James H. S. McGregor: 41, 121, 135, 136

Katya Kallsen / Fogg Art Museum, Harvard University Art Museums: 25

(Canaletto, *Piazza San Marco, Venice,* Bequest of Grenville L.

Winthrop, 1943.106), 88 (Canaletto, *The Prison in Venice,* Bequest of

Grenville L. Winthrop, M10332)

Leopoldo Cicognara, Antonio Diedo, and Giovanni Antonio Selva, *Le fabbriche*

e i monumenti cospicue di Venezia (1815—1820), 98

Library of Congress: 127 (Calle dell'Angelo a San Martino, photochrom print,

1890—1900); front endpaper, 92, 93, 94, 109, pp. 33, 79, 131,

173, 207, 251 (Jacopo de Barbari, *Perspective Plan of Venice,* 1500);

back endpaper (Ludovico Ughi, *Iconografica rappresentatione della*

inclita citta di Venezia, 1729)

Luca Carlevarijs, *Le fabriche, e vedute di Venetia . . .* (1703), 75, 103

Musei Civici Veneziani: 36, 123

Paolino da Venezia, drawn after Tommaso Temanza from the parchment codex

Chronologia magna of 1376: p. 7

Scala / Art Resource, NY: 54, 64, 81

Scuola Grande di San Rocco: 58

Spaceimaging.com: 1

INDEX

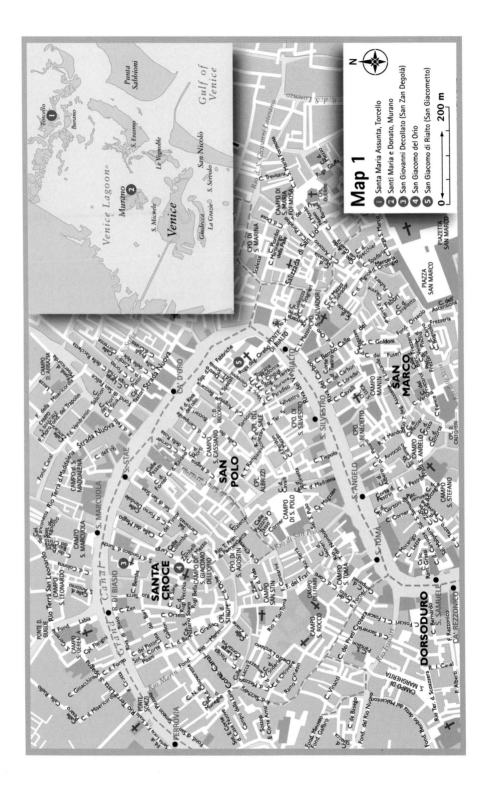

Map 1

1 Santa Maria Assunta, Torcello
2 Santi Maria e Donato, Murano
3 San Giovanni Decollato (San Zan Degolà)
4 San Giacomo del Orio
5 San Giacomo di Rialto (San Giacometto)

0   200 m

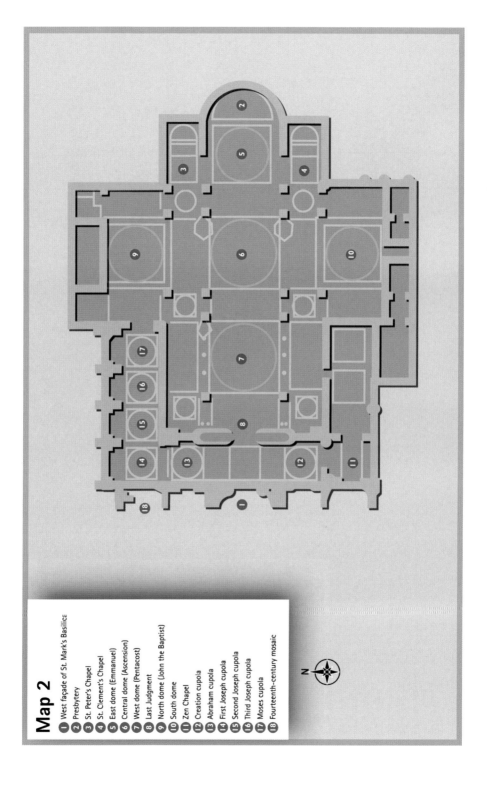

Map 2

1. West façade of St. Mark's Basilica
2. Presbytery
3. St. Peter's Chapel
4. St. Clement's Chapel
5. East dome (Emmanuel)
6. Central dome (Ascension)
7. West dome (Pentacost)
8. Last Judgment
9. North dome (John the Baptist)
10. South dome
11. Zen Chapel
12. Creation cupola
13. Abraham cupola
14. First Joseph cupola
15. Second Joseph cupola
16. Third Joseph cupola
17. Moses cupola
18. Fourteenth-century mosaic

N

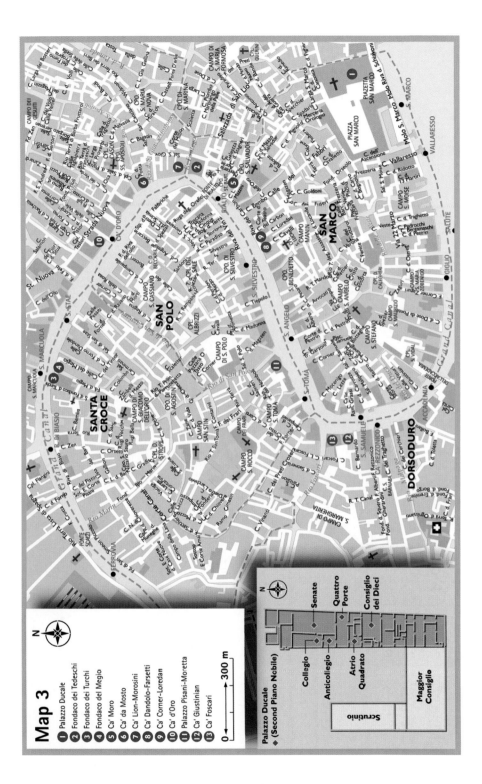

Map 3

1. Palazzo Ducale
2. Fondaco dei Tedeschi
3. Fondaco dei Turchi
4. Fondaco del Megio
5. Ca' Moro
6. Ca' da Mosto
7. Ca' Lion-Morosini
8. Ca' Dandolo-Farsetti
9. Ca' Corner-Loredan
10. Ca' d'Oro
11. Palazzo Pisani-Moretta
12. Ca' Giustinian
13. Ca' Foscari

0 ——— 300 m

N

Palazzo Ducale
◆ (Second Piano Nobile)

Scrutinio

Collegio
Anticollegio
Atrio Quadrato
Senate
Quattro Porte
Consiglio dei Dieci

Maggior Consiglio

N

SANTA CROCE

SAN POLO

SAN MARCO

DORSODURO

PIAZZA SAN MARCO

PIAZZETTA SAN MARCO

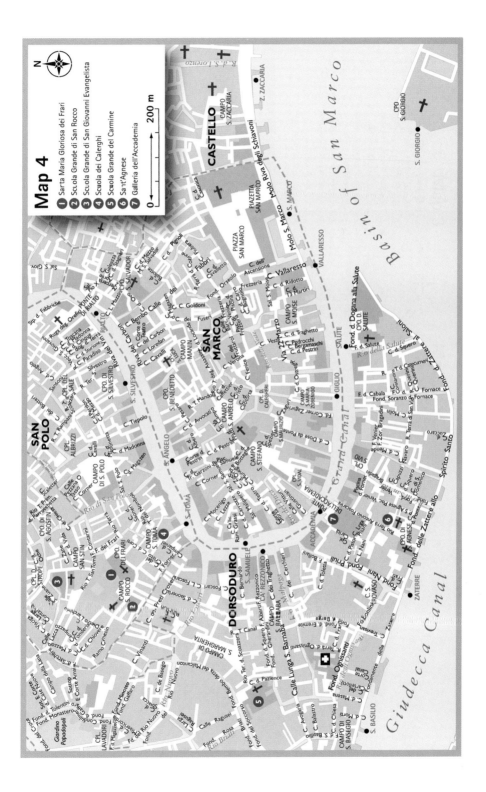

Map 4

N

1 Sarta Maria Gloriosa dei Frari
2 Scuola Grande di San Rocco
3 Scuola Grande di San Giovanni Evangelista
4 Scuola dei Calerghi
5 Scuola Grande del Carmine
6 Sant'Agnese
7 Galleria dell'Accademia

0 ——————▷ 200 m

Map 5

1. Madonna dell'Orto
2. Tintoretto's house
3. Scuola Vecchia della Misericordia
4. Santa Maria dei Miracoli
5. Santi Giovanni e Paolo
6. Scuola Grande di San Marco
7. Santa Maria Formosa
8. San Francisco della Vigna
9. Scuola de San Giorgio degli Schiavoni
10. San Zaccaria

0 —————— 200 m

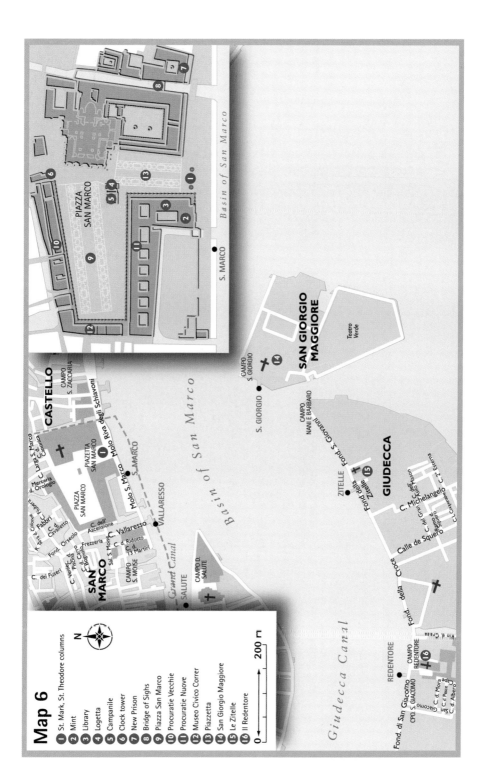

Map 6

- ① St. Mark, St. Theodore columns
- ② Mint
- ③ Library
- ④ Logetta
- ⑤ Campanile
- ⑥ Clock tower
- ⑦ New Prison
- ⑧ Bridge of Sighs
- ⑨ Piazza San Marco
- ⑩ Procuratie Vecchie
- ⑪ Procuratie Nuove
- ⑫ Museo Civico Correr
- ⑬ Piazzetta
- ⑭ San Giorgio Maggiore
- ⑮ Le Zitelle
- ⑯ Il Redentore

0   200 ⊓

N

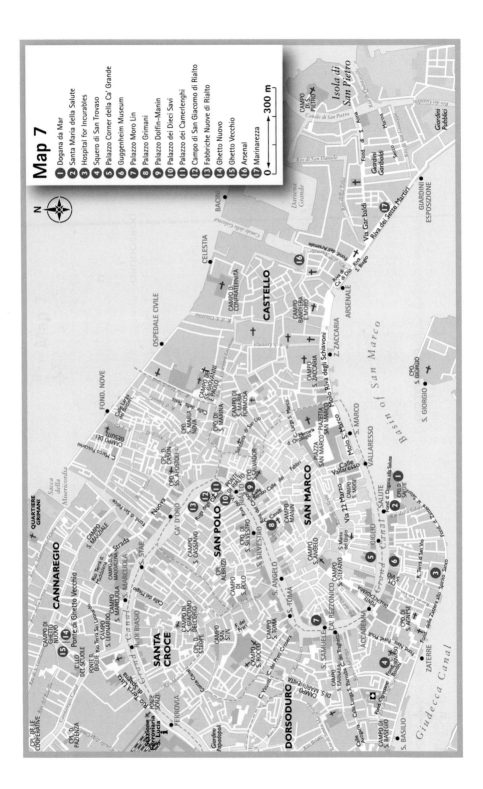

Map 7

1. Dogana da Mar
2. Santa Maria della Salute
3. Hospital for Incurables
4. Squero di San Trovaso
5. Palazzo Corner della Ca' Grande
6. Guggenheim Museum
7. Palazzo Moro Lin
8. Palazzo Grimani
9. Palazzo Dolfin-Manin
10. Palazzo dei Dieci Savi
11. Palazzo dei Camerlenghi
12. Campo di San Giacomo di Rialto
13. Fabbriche Nuove di Rialto
14. Ghetto Nuovo
15. Ghetto Vecchio
16. Arsenal
17. Marinarezza

0 ——— 300 m

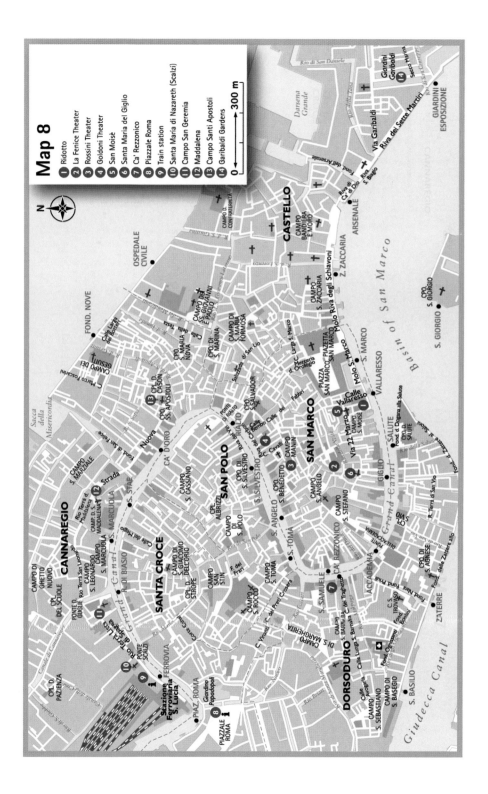

Map 8

1. Ridotto
2. La Fenice Theater
3. Rossini Theater
4. Goldoni Theater
5. San Moisè
6. Santa Maria del Giglio
7. Ca' Rezzonico
8. Piazzale Roma
9. Train station
10. Santa Maria di Nazareth (Scalzi)
11. Campo San Geremia
12. Maddalena
13. Campo Santi Apostoli
14. Garibaldi Gardens

0 ———→ 300 m